THE ART OF DECISION-MAKING

THE
ART
OF
DECISION-MAKING

BY JOSEPH D. COOPER

Doubleday & Company, Inc., Garden City, N.Y.

Library of Congress Catalog Card Number 61-9498
Copyright © 1961 by Joseph D. Cooper
All Rights Reserved. Printed in the United States of America

To
DEAN CATHERYN SECKLER-HUDSON
The American University
Washington, D.C.

Table of Contents

PREFACE

The actual writing of this book — the putting of words on paper after many months of preparation — was begun at a mountain retreat. Seeing me surrounded by a mass of papers, a fellow retreater noted this incongruity in that environment and asked the nature of my task. I told him I was writing a book on decision-making.

"A whole book!" he exclaimed. "How can anyone write more than a chapter or two? Now, really, there are only a few rules: define the problem, get the facts, weigh and decide. What more can you say?"

I started to tell him: decision-making is the definition of problems in relation to goals . . . the analysis of facts which usually are incomplete . . . the identification and valuation of alternatives . . . the anticipation and analysis of behavior . . . the settling of differences of opinion . . . and so on. And as I did so he began to reflect. He said, "Now that you mention these things . . ." Then he asked when he might read the book.

Of course my task was not one of finding topics. I had to limit myself to *one* book which would provide helpful suggestions:

1. To individuals who wish to improve their own abilities to find facts and solve problems, to predict behavior, to plan and to conduct themselves well in decision-making conferences.

2. To organizations which would like to improve their internal arrangements and procedures in order to have a better environment for decision-making, to assure that decisions are

brought to a head promptly and to minimize risks due to individual failings.

As you may sense, the origins of this book go back over many years. My first direct involvement with the formal processes of decision-making began about 1948, when, in the U. S. Department of State, I served as executive secretary of a task force concerned with decision-making and action processes and related matters. The chairman was the Hon. W. K. Scott, later Assistant Secretary of State, whose influence I must acknowledge with gratitude. This experience led to my doctoral dissertation on "Decision-Making and the Action Process in the Department of State," under the guidance of Dr. Catheryn Seckler-Hudson, now Dean of the School of Government and Public Administration, the American University, Washington, D.C.

The present approach was laid out, in summary, in a paper I prepared in 1953 for the use of the American Telephone & Telegraph Corporation, at the request of Elwood C. Allen, and again in 1957 for the use of the American Management Association, at the request of Andrews M. Lang.

Dr. Jack Moshman, Director of the Technical Services Department of C-E-I-R, Inc., read certain chapters and made helpful suggestions. I am indebted to my former secretary, Miss Irene E. Jacobs, for the insistence, persistence and assistance which eventually brought me to writing this book.

Harold Kuebler, my editor, deserves a note of appreciation for his patience and constructive suggestions.

JOSEPH D. COOPER

Chevy Chase, Md.

THE ART OF DECISION-MAKING

Chapter I

DECISION-MAKING: MAGIC OR METHOD

Among executives the subject of decision-making stirs a variety of personal feelings:

1. *The right to make decisions is sought eagerly* because it is associated with relative rank, authority, prestige and pay level.

2. *The actual making of a decision is usually accompanied by inner doubts and anxieties,* apart from any brave exteriors. Like great actors on the stage, who approach each new performance a little fearfully, the most highly regarded decision-makers endure their own private ordeals of doubt and anxiety.

3. *Decision-makers are reluctant to admit any need for improvement in their own techniques of decision-making.* This stems from the executive's desire to maintain his image in the eyes of others as an able decision-maker. He fears that to seek help openly might be construed as a denial of his own competence.

In the privacy of his own musings, then, the executive may well ponder such questions as these: What are the ingredients of personal success as a decision-maker? Is success dependent upon some magical formula or some intuitive powers possessed by a lucky few? Is there some private methodology, known to very few, which leads to consistently good decision-making? How can I acquire this capability?

The reply to these questions is this: success in decision-making depends less upon "magical" powers than upon the mastery of a systematic approach. Herein lies the aim of this book: to

1

present the techniques through which individuals and organizations are most likely to produce consistently good decisions.

I do not deny the importance of certain personal attributes. In a later chapter we'll review these, along with suggestions for improving one's personal skills of analysis and creativity. I place much greater importance, however, upon the mastery of these two areas of understanding:

1. *A knowledge of the various forces of decision* — the pressures and restraints of the past and the present, the interplay of forces in the environment, and the behavior of people in the face of decision.

2. *A knowledge of the processes of reaching decisions* and taking action; especially the techniques of blending and coordinating the inputs of many people.

Now the idea of a methodology which governs decision-making may not be in accord with the popular image of executive action created by books and movies.

In the popular mind the dynamic decision-maker may be the captain of industry who receives a telephone call or memorandum and then barks commands into a squawk box to move the machinery of enterprise into action. Or he may be the executive who listens to his advisers and then dramatically makes a decision contrary to their judgment — a decision which turns out to be the right one. And, of course, there is the executive who acts only after all of his "yes-men" share the responsibility by agreeing with him.

Interviews with prominent executives have actually lent some *apparent* credence to these popular views. Presumably the executives themselves should be the ones to say how they make decisions. When you ask them for their methods, however, they say they use common sense or they get the facts and then decide — or some other oversimplification. Whether they are striking modest poses or whether they really believe what they say is a matter for conjecture.

A few years ago *Fortune* magazine put such a question to a number of eminent decision-makers. This is what several of them said:

Charles Cox, president of Kennecott Copper: "I don't think businessmen know how they make decisions. I know I don't."

Charles Dickey, chairman of the executive committee of J. P. Morgan & Co.: "There are no rules."

Benjamin Fairless, former chairman of U. S. Steel: "You don't know how you do it; you just do it."

John McCaffrey, president of International Harvester: "It is like asking a pro baseball player to define the swing that has always come natural to him."

Dwight Joyce, president of Glidden Co.: "If a vice president asks me how I was able to choose the right course I have to say, 'I'm damned if I know.' "

The New York real-estate and theater wizard Roger Stevens, reversing Thomas J. Watson's famous maxim, said, "Whenever I think, I make a mistake."

In spite of these disclaimers there *must* be a method which shapes their judgments. *No corporation, especially any of those listed, can afford to commit resources on the basis of personal judgment alone.* Now and then — yes! In the long run — no! There are two more plausible probabilities:

1. The individual may have shaped his methodology through training and through trial and error, without having ever consciously laid out the principles which do guide him.

2. The organization itself may have developed its decision-making processes. All within the enterprise — including those at the head of it — are channeled by the established work ways.

These two capabilities usually go hand in hand. The skilled decision-maker needs the support of the organization and its specialized resources. On the other hand, the ineffective decision-maker can be carried by a good organization, in spite of his deficiencies, for a surprisingly long time.

To sum up, thus far, I said that:

1. The popular view of executive decision-making presents an oversimplified picture.

2. Executives themselves are really insecure about their effectiveness in decision-making, in spite of their outward expressions.

3. Instead of reliance upon a "hunch" or intuitive approach to decision-making, good executives acquire a knowledge, in depth, of the *forces* that influence decisions and of the *processes* through which decisions are reached.

To make one other point: what may seem to be a quick and casual decision-making judgment is really the exercise of a high order of skill. The top-notch decision-maker is able to see the problem in its total context very quickly. He does not have to labor his way through the problem, point by point. Having made his quick analysis, he then senses, just as quickly, how to use the machinery of organization to bring the situation to a head and to carry out the action. He acquires these skills through observation, training and long practice.

In subsequent chapters we shall examine, in detail, the methods which lead to successful decision-making. Before doing so, however, I would like to make certain points about the *forces* and *processes* of decision-making, for these will be involved in most of the chapters of this book.

THE FORCES OF DECISION

For convenience I have grouped the forces of decision under three headings:
1. The dynamics of the individual
2. The dynamics of the group
3. The dynamics of the environment

In each case the word "dynamics" has been included as a reminder that nothing remains the same. Moreover I must warn that while we may put things, events and people into neat categories, doing so is a dangerous oversimplification. Rules and generalizations are to be regarded only as central tendencies. In each case you must ask: "How does this conform with the general rule? How does it differ?"

Throughout the book you will find analytical check lists for anticipating the behavior of individuals and groups and for predicting the probable march of events. The comments which now follow are intended as guidelines, *in general,* to predicting human action.

The Dynamics of the Individual

If you know the history of a man you can usually foretell, with remarkable accuracy, how he is likely to act in new circumstances. This is not to say that people don't change. Indeed they do, but changes in behavior patterns come about gradually unless powerful experiences or motivations are introduced.

A stable person is more predictable than one who seems to be unstable. Here we enter into a rather frothy area in which the psychologists themselves seem not to be in agreement. Nevertheless the businessman *must* take a chance at predicting reactions. He is risking his resources. He cannot proceed on hope alone. Nor can he put all of his colleagues and competitors on a psychiatric couch (one at a time, of course!) in order to ferret out their unfavorable childhood experiences. Besides, he is not concerned with causes and cures, for purposes of decision-making. He wants only to be able to predict how people may act under given circumstances. Accordingly, this brings us back to a knowledge of the pattern of previous behavior, whether you regard it as stable or unstable.

An important clue to behavior and reactions may be found in the individual's self-image. This is what he synthesizes from his aspirations, his experiences and the evaluations of those who hold him dear. Many personal decisions are made either to protect the self-image or to enhance it. Therefore, if you can know how a man regards himself, you can make further assumptions as to his motivations and his reactions to future events. Since he is not likely to bring his entire self-image out into the open, you will need to look to the history of his actions and experiences in order to paint it for yourself.

If personal goals are markedly in conflict with official goals, you can expect some straining, at least, of the individual's dependability. This is not easily detected. A man may seem to be traveling a path which leads toward the goals of his employer, but his principal preoccupation may be self-fulfillment. Fortunate are all when both personal and official goals can be served in the same effort.

The Dynamics of the Group

The organization — or a segment of it — develops predictable patterns of behavior not unlike those of the individual. In fact, groups can be thought of as being well adjusted or maladjusted, even to the point of having neuroses!

In predicting group behavior, then, you may proceed, as a starting point, as though you were analyzing the individual. What is its self-image and what are its goals? What has been its pattern of behavior up to now? What have been its powerful successes, failures and other vibrating experiences?

Then you must spot the group on its maturity curve, for this will tell you much more about how it is able to respond to events. Although growth and maturity are continuous, I'll describe three major stages. *You* can fill in the intermediate stages for your own situation and needs.

The period of initial growth is one of enthusiasm and flexibility. A structural or procedural twig bent in one direction can be straightened out without major surgery or without risk of snapping the limb. Goals or purposes are being clarified, key personnel are being selected, and operating policies and practices are being tested. There is an atmosphere of pioneering and experimentation. Decision-making is not hampered by rigid internal precedent nor by fixed alignments of personalities and cliques.

The attainment of a settled maturity is indicated by fixed patterns of organization, policies, procedures, status systems, codes of behavior, etc. The earliest signs of approaching rigidity are noted in the emergence of the infamous "We've always done it this way." No longer does the organization have its early vitality and drive. It has settled into a comfortable and self-deceiving routine. The active decision-maker must expect, then, a preoccupation with "playing it safe" and not "rocking the boat" unless the stakes are worth the risk.

The fully settled organization, of advanced age, may become so rigid that it can no longer respond effectively to the need for change. The original purposes of policies, procedures and operating practices may have long since been forgotten, but they continue almost as ends in themselves, in spite of all the logic offered in support of change. Except for the most routine, nondisturbing actions, decisions having a broader impact are made only after protracted soul-searching. The group convulses its way through each brave new decision.

As it matures, the group acquires a definite and describable personality. The members tend to think and act harmoniously. The behavior of one will typify the behavior of the group as a whole. Thus you can anticipate the position that the representative of a certain group will take in a conference if you know the goals, behavior patterns and attitudes of the group he represents.

The Dynamics of the Environment

All the influences and conditions which surround the decision-making problem constitute its environment. Each problem will have its own environment, different from all others if only in some minor particular.

In an ultimate sense all decisions must bow to the pressures of the environment. Thus, when the horse and buggy began to yield to the horseless carriage, no amount of marketing promotion could, in the long run, sway the public to remain loyal to Old Dobbin. It is true that decisions may be made in the hope that they will actually alter the environment itself. This happens when an entirely new kind of product is launched. Sometimes it meets with public acceptance and sometimes not. The decision-maker must ask: "Is the environment ready for such an innovation?"

The environment serves also as a testing ground for the self-image of the individual (or of the organization). You may want to be regarded in a certain way, usually to have others recognize the legitimacy of your personal goals. When these are made apparent through your actions, they may be received with acceptance, modification, rejection or indifference. From these reactions you will take confirmation of how you believe you stand or you will plan to change either yourself or conditions around you. Similarly, you will take readings from your environment in order to anticipate how a proposed action might be received in the light of the image you have created.

The reading of the signs in the world about you should therefore be a constant preoccupation. The more skillful you become in sensing outside trends, the more fortunate you are in having adequate lead time in which to prepare for decisions. In fact, many decisions are made solely to put one in a more favorable (or less unfavorable) position in the operating environment, as a prerequisite to making subsequent decisions.

The environment of a decision may be external — involving customers, suppliers, competitors, bankers, etc. — or it may be localized within the house, or both. It changes as the problem changes.

For example, a decision on a personnel matter may affect only a few employees, whose interests need to be considered, while a similar personnel problem may affect hundreds or thousands of people in the same organization. The pressures upon the decision, from those affected, will be different in each case.

In another example, the proposed purchase of an item of capital equipment may be a simple budgetary matter under one set of circumstances. Under another, it may have implications for labor relations, if the union should think it would replace labor.

THE PROCESSES OF DECISION

In the active organization there is an endless stream of action. Tens, hundreds and thousands of decisions of lesser or greater importance may be made in a single day. In some way these need to be synthesized so that they are all in harmony. Moreover, because some decisions are more important than others, the processes of the enterprise must bring these forward for priority attention.

Much of this book concerns itself with these processes. They aim to minimize dependence on human initiative as well as to minimize the risks of individual error. The immensity of the effort involved is introduced in the following comments.

The Fragmentation of Decision

The single decision must be woven into a larger complex of activity, to assure continued balance and consistency in the over-all scheme of things. Usually this starts a chain reaction of judgments and decisions on related matters. When broad decisions are made, a pyramiding reaction sets in, for subsidiary decisions of all kinds must then be made.

Here is one of the most challenging of the executive responsibilities: to give leadership to the blending of all these fragmentary decisions into one smoothly interacting complex. From a mechanical standpoint alone, the task is not easy. It is made ever more difficult by the need to coalesce many human viewpoints representing varying degrees of objectivity, ability, understanding and communicability.

The Endless Stream of Decision

A single decision is merely a moment in time. Once it is made and carried into effect, it precipitates changes in the environment of the decision. Then new problems are created for which new solutions are required. Hence, if you think you have settled things and that you can relax for a while, you are deceiving yourself. The ever-present forces of change compel an endless updating of decisions and actions. New conditions, new experiences and new information are always coming up to require the modification of goals, policies, programs or procedures and the creation of new ones.

The Priorities of Decision

Some organizations seem to be in a continuing state of crisis. The smallest matter for decision becomes an urgency and produces an organizational tremor. This is usually a symptom of a lack of delegated authority and the absence of policy and procedural guidelines.

While you will never completely eliminate crisis decisions, assignment to some hierarchy of importance will assure more timely consideration for the truly important matters. Somehow, then, the lesser matters will take care of themselves.

Lesser decisions may take on unique importance when there are many of them of the same kind. They are best handled as categories rather than as separate bits and pieces. You then consider the common problem elements, laying out policies and procedures for the guidance of subordinates in making the individual decisions.

The Recognition of Significance

It is not sufficient to be able to divine the future; you must also be able to understand the significance of trends and indicators.

On the eve of World War II, I made studies of the growth of Washington, D.C. from the time of its founding. I observed how each national crisis brought about new growth which was retained after the crisis had subsided. In 1940 the country was already mobilizing for war, so I drew some projections of growth; then I put them away, and that was all. The war ended; entrepreneurs made fortunes from the sale of what once had been cheap acreage, and I am left with my forecasts of accuracy which I have not cared to look at since.

A familiar story? Not quite! Most tales start with "If I had known . . ." In my case I knew.

Of course this story has a moral. I had made the study for a purpose entirely unrelated to real-estate matters. I had no sensitivity to real estate. Thus, I did not see implications that would — and did — send others to the bank. The moral is that

1

to derive the full benefits of fact-finding and analysis you must have qualified people charged with responsibility for sensing and understanding the significance of facts.

ORGANIZATION OF THIS BOOK

The main body of this book is divided into three parts. The first deals mainly with the *processes* of decision, but it also embraces an understanding of the *forces* of decision. The two are inescapably interrelated. Actually we rely upon procedure as a means of channeling the many forces of decision.

Part two covers the personal techniques which we need to master if we are to become individually effective as executive leaders of decision-making.

Part three is a collection of chapters of a somewhat more advanced nature. Largely these are expansions of ideas that arose in the course of developing the chapters in part one. To me they are among the more interesting ones.

The Basic Procedures of Decision-Making

Chapter II

HOW TO BEGIN TO DECIDE

The usual advice on decision-making is to get the facts, weigh them and then decide. The theory is that you're supposed to keep free of any actions or preliminary judgments that will force the turn of your eventual decision.

In actual practice we all violate this rule — consciously or otherwise. We influence our decisions by the problems we take up for action, by the way we define them, by our selection of facts and by our designation of those who contribute to decision-making.

By the time management brings a major decision to a head it may already have taken the steps that will govern what it is going to decide. This was a finding of Dr. Herbert A. Simon and his colleagues who have been making studies of practical decision-making in industry, at the Carnegie Institute of Technology.

This finding has very serious implications. It says that we make decisions conform to what we'd like them to be, rather than what they should be. In other words, we stack the cards against ourselves, even though we may not be aware that we are doing so. Although many of us tend to do this in our private lives, we just don't accustom ourselves to thinking that an organization may do likewise.

If this should be the prevailing pattern of decision-making in an enterprise, it must inevitably go into a decline, for it will fail to adjust to changing conditions and operating assumptions. Conversely, one of the keys to success in a truly dynamic enterprise is that it sets up safeguards to assure that decisions are made in the light of facts rather than desires or wishful thinking.

The starting point for this is with the way the enterprise is organized. This, however, is itself a subject of some magnitude covered in other chapters.*

The next safeguard against loaded decision-making is procedural. Senior decision-makers usually get into problems only after much work has been done on them. By then the die may already have been cast. The decision-maker may be ratifying a semicommitment or he may be nullifying costly staff work. He needs the protection of well-ordered staff work. This, in turn, depends on having the right people get into the problem at the earliest stages, people who know how to define problems and how to bring facts to bear on their solution.

This chapter, accordingly, will be devoted to those first steps in decision-making which may determine final outcomes.

THE THRESHOLD OF A PROBLEM

The author of a book is obliged to proceed in some kind of fixed sequence. On paper it is easy to say, "This is the starting point of a problem. First, we recognize its existence. Then we examine its implications in order to know who to assign to it and how to deal with it in the light of policies, goals and other situations." And so on. In real life the problems are not so obliging as to permit an easy, logical sequence of attention. They conceal their true nature so that halfway down the path of a decision you may find that you must retrace your steps for a new beginning. Or you may have alternatives for decision presented to you which, in your belief, are not the only or best

* If you would like to review it, briefly, I suggest you refer to Chapter XV, "Organizing for Decision-Making." Certain aspects of organization are covered, also, in Chapter XIII, "The Internal Information System," as well as in Chapters III through VI.

possible courses. This, too, will send you back to the beginning.

Even more vexing is the general "problem of problem-solving." While you are finding and analyzing facts, governing conditions are undergoing change. Therefore, when dealing with important or complex decisions in a dynamic environment you must, from the very first, provide for rechecks to be made of the facts, to make sure there have been no vital changes.

The guidelines which follow are applicable only in the most general sense. The situation with which you are dealing will dictate the particular pattern of analysis you must follow.

RECOGNIZING AND ADMITTING THE PROBLEM

The principle of the Polaroid Land camera resulted from a chance conversation between the inventor, Edwin H. Land, and his daughter, who asked about having some pictures developed which they had just taken. In a flash he saw here an opportunity to revolutionize photography with a process which would yield a finished print within moments after exposure. This set off the train of events which led finally to the picture-in-a-minute camera. Similarly, it was the observation of the glare of automobile headlights that started Dr. Land on the research out of which came polarizing screens.

These are instances of the flash recognition of a problem. Why did Dr. Land respond as he did, while millions before him, confronted daily with the same stimuli, did not respond at all? The difference lay in his background and interests and in his *alertness to recognize a problem crying for a solution*.

In the conduct of a business, however, we cannot afford to wait for the flash insight of a researcher. Rather, we must anticipate the problems which will confront us and organize to deal with them before they become crises.

Thus we rely upon procedural devices which automatically trigger off attention to a problem. A report of a build-up in accounts receivable due to slow payments will tell us to look into selling practices, the economic climate, credit policy and sales forecasts, among others. A report of an increase in accident rates may call for studies of safety and precautions, but if the report correlates with increased absenteeism and increased turnover, you are more likely to turn to an examination of the morale of employees, from there to isolation of the causes and then to a determination of the corrective action to be taken.

Many problems are spontaneously generated. A machine flies apart; a key official dies; a big contract is canceled; a plant is destroyed by fire; a challenging business proposal is received in the mail. With experience, each business anticipates *the kinds* of problems which may arise spontaneously and charges various of its executives with responsibility for preparedness, just in case. Then there are the official monitors, analysts or reviewers who sift through the raw intelligence coming into the house and through that drawn from internal operations, in order to spot trends or forecast events of significance.

This work may be likened to that of police intelligence work. Far from being the thrilling endeavor depicted by mystery novelists, it requires painstaking compilation, assembly, correlation and analysis of data of all kinds: search, sift, search some more and thus, bit by bit, fit the pieces into the jigsaw puzzle.

In a small organization each man is his own information monitor. In a big enterprise special staff members or groups may be charged with watching trends and sifting through reports, in order to recognize the need for action as early as possible. These internal facilities may be supplemented by outside services, such as technical consultants, public-relations advisors, clipping bureaus and other special informational sources. To get an intimate awareness of retail-marketing problems some corporations have even set up retailers' advisory committees. Typically these are small groups of dealers elected from among all the dealerships or distributorships. The Bell & Howell Company and the American Motors Company have done this, to name just a couple.

Whatever the means of recognizing the problem, this must come about as early as possible, for if events are allowed to shape themselves, they may proceed along lines not to the best advantage of the company.

When a problem comes knocking at one's door it may be assigned routinely for staff analysis and attention, but if it has any unique characteristics the problem should be given a preliminary screening to validate and clarify it. The following questions may be asked:

1. *Is the problem clearly understood?* Can it be expressed clearly on paper in your own words? Can you outline the implications and significance of the problem? If you cannot do this you may not really understand or the matter may not have been presented satisfactorily. Perhaps more facts are needed or perhaps the problem should be reinterpreted by the one who brings it in.

2. *Is the stated problem the real one?* Are you treating symptoms or causes? For example, is the problem one of closer supervision over production schedules or is it one of more realistic schedules in the first instance? Are you trying to punish an employee for a lack of initiative when your real problem may be to get after the supervisor who discourages initiative and innovation?

3. *Does the problem "feel" right?* How can one suggest any hard criteria for sensing the impossibility or unlikelihood of a problem on the mere face of a report? It is a faculty which comes with extensive experience in drawing the facts out of many situations. Maurice H. Stans, former Director of the U. S. Bureau of the Budget, taught me that a report of a problem should be challenged out of hand (1) if it lacks a feeling of inner consistency, (2) if the behavior or actions of people seem substantially inconsistent with their previous behavior or (3) if the report upsets known trends and expectations. This kind of tempered skepticism protects you from taking action on the basis of half-truths and unreliable reports.

4. *Are you the right one to consider the problem?* Does your responsibility go to the heart of the problem or a certain aspect of it? One check on this is to identify the specific goal toward which the problem is related. If you do not have action re-

sponsibility for the matter, the problem should be passed on to whoever does.

5. *Do you have an open mind?* Are you inclined to stereotype the problem within some category of past experience without stopping to reflect on new circumstances calling for a new approach? Are you confusing your attitude toward the problem with your attitude toward the key personalities involved? In short, do you have a completely open mind?

PRELIMINARY ACTION ON PROBLEM

If you are making the first decisions on what to do about a problem, your judgments may be the ones to shape the final decision. This is a critical stage of action. Among the questions you must consider, as outlined below, is whether the matter is one appropriate for decision.

1. *What is the situation which triggered off the problem?* Does knowledge of this give you any sense of the urgency, magnitude or personality implications of the problem?

2. *What is the background of this and similar problems?* What action has been taken in the past, by whom, under what reasoning and with what effect?

3. *How does the matter relate itself to currently existing goals, plans, policies and programs?* Is the matter similar to or in conflict with other pending decision matters?

4. *What are the probable consequences of even considering the matter?* What impact would any of the feasible courses of action have upon the organization and its relationships and conditions of operation? What new problems would be created?

5. *Does attention to the problem seem warranted and reasonable within the feasibilities and capabilities of the enterprise* or would any foreseeable action seem to lie outside the reach of reality?

6. *Is this the best time for decision?* Would a decision now be premature? Is it already too late to take action? Would a later timing be better? When is the latest that a decision should

be made? What would be the consequences of a late decision?

7. *Is this a one-time decision or a continuing one?* If it is a one-time matter, is it of such key significance, in relation to other matters, or is it of such magnitude in itself that it deserves any great amount of attention? In fact, regardless of the nature of a decision, how much attention can you afford to devote to it? Should some other problem be taken up before the current one is disposed of?

8. *Should you handle the problem initially or should you merely identify someone else to whom to assign it?* Should you refer it higher on a question of the policy implication in merely taking the matter up? Should you, without further ado, defer consideration of the matter or avoid it entirely for any reason? Should the matter be referred to someone outside of your jurisdiction and not in line of authority over you?

Careful study of the facts in the earliest stages pays off. Many a manufacturer or seller has rued the day when he impulsively let himself be panicked into marketing a new product or service because of the action of a competitor. True, the competitor might have a "hot item," but he might also have a "turkey." There might be only enough market for one of you with a loss to both if you add to the competition. Prudent judgment calls for careful market analysis, evaluation of your own posture in the market and probable trends in the future, among other things.

PARTICIPATION IN THE ANALYSIS

On occasion you may think that you alone make the decision or that you alone recommend and someone else decides. Rarely is this the case. The principals may be reduced to two or even one, but you cannot ignore those who are affected or who must carry out decisions. You may take them quite seriously or you may dismiss them lightly, but even then you will have taken them into account.

One may say, with some truth, that decisions are shaped in

the long run by the forces of the environment, rather than by
individuals. However true that may be, individuals do exert a
personality influence. How does this affect the preliminary
aspects of decision-making?

In the first instance you must think of those who would be
affected by the probable or possible actions. You won't know
the final decision, yet you must try to anticipate actions, reactions, counteractions and interactions of the parties. A knowledge of these may cause you to bring uniquely affected individuals into the earliest stages of problem study.

Initial assignments for study may be to one or more people.
Questions such as the following will help you to make the
assignments:

1. *Who will make the ultimate decision and what kind of
presentation will he expect?* What clues to his probable reaction
can you find in the history of his past decisions? Whose judgments is he most likely to seek? What are his known preferences
and predispositions, his known prejudices and resistances?

2. *What technical or specialized functional responsibilities
are implicitly involved* in the making of the decision? At what
stage should the people involved be brought into consultation
or review? Should outside technical or specialized participation
be obtained?

3. *Who is affected by the possible action?* Should such people
participate in decision-making or should their participation be
obtained by survey or similar techniques? Should you obtain
the participation of people who are *not now* directly involved
but eventually will be, when new aspects of the problem come
into play?

4. *Who will carry out the decision?* Since his attitude will
influence the effectiveness of action, should he be brought into
the decision-making process as participant and at what stage?
If many people will carry out the decision, in or out of the
organization or both, how can their actions be anticipated and
taken into account?

5. *On what critical or strategic factor is the decision liable
to hinge?* What points of view, attitudes of inquiry, knowledges,

experience and influence are thereby suggested to be brought
into consideration?

The usual way to identify the interested parties is to review
past history. Names of people or organizational units will crop
up in old correspondence or interoffice memoranda. Preliminary discussions will also bring up names. The manual of organization defines the responsibilities of the heads of activities
on the basis of "who does what." The various manuals of procedure identify the responsible parties on the basis of "what is
done by whom."

Conceivably you could have another *Mayflower,* so overloaded by its improbable passengers that it never could leave
its moorings. These questions are intended only to help you
make sure you do not overlook anyone who should be listed in
the *dramatis personae.* Finally, you will probably need to keep
the active participants limited to a few, to prevent unwieldiness
while you find other less direct means of satisfying the desires
of others to participate, possibly at later stages.

STRUCTURING THE SITUATION

Merritt Williamson, writing of his experiences as acting
chairman of the Pennsylvania Turnpike Commission, said that
before he could begin making decisions of any kind he had to
steep himself in the situation. He had to learn the personalities
both inside and outside of the Commission and what they represented as forces of action. He had to learn the Commission's
goals and specific plans. He had to become quite familiar with
its physical resources and its financial problems. Only when he
had fully mastered the ground plan — and it is never really
fully mastered because of changing conditions — could he then
make his own independent judgments.

This kind of structuring of the situation prepared Williamson for decision-making as a continuing executive activity.
Over and above this, however, he needed to go through more
intensive analyses of specific problem situations, as they arose.
His knowledge of the total ground plan made this much easier.

Some generalized outlines of analysis now follow. To render

these more tangible, they will be followed by an analysis of a hypothetical problem. Again I must emphasize that it is neither necessary nor desirable that you follow the particular sequence which is given below. In actual practice you may be filling in the outline categories item by item just as you might go about solving a crossword puzzle. That is, you would select a convenient starting point and follow it as long as the approach is fruitful. If you are blocked you move on to the next item. In analyzing a situation, however, the sequences are not that neatly structured. As you follow through along one line of inquiry you pick up collateral information which may fit under other headings. Then you must decide whether to pursue these new threads of analysis or whether to record the information for further and later reference while you continue with the original line of inquiry.

Another caution to keep in mind is that if you were to pursue exhaustively each item of analysis, you would probably wear yourself down and get nothing else done, let alone solve any problems. How far to go in analyzing any situation is a matter for personal judgment.

In embarking upon these analytical approaches, you would *carry forward any preliminary information which you may already have acquired,* bearing in mind that you will be reassessing this information as you go along.

Some of the questions now listed may have been encountered before. Like the refrain in the musical rendition of Scheherazade, you will meet them again. In making important decisions on matters of complexity, you may re-examine earlier observations and conclusions, as you move forward, to verify the answers to questions raised previously. As in solving the crossword puzzle, you may be able to fill in spaces that previously were left vacant.

Attributes of the Situation

1. *Kind of situation*

Is it a problem of general management, engineering, marketing or some other aspect of enterprise? This is an identifying question to localize the kind of problem and to suggest responsibility for it.

2. *Tangible qualities*

What measures of the problem are now available? Is the problem quite clear and are all agreed as to this? Does the problem seem great or small, routine or unusual, urgent or not urgent? Are there any criteria or measures of effect which can be used in evaluating alternative actions and their consequences?

3. *Realization of problem*

Do the responsible persons realize that they have a problem which requires action? Are they aware of the significance of the problem and of the consequences of taking action? Are the responsible parties ready to consider the problem, to decide upon an action and to put it into effect?

4. *Unique properties*

Is this an entirely new problem or does it have a past history? Does the probable action represent a substantial departure from past practice? If so, is the effort necessary to overcome resistance and "retool" for the future sufficiently offset by the benefits?

Is this a recurring or one-time matter? If it is recurring, can you identify the elements of guidance for the future? If it is a one-time problem, is it deserving of attention in the light of the possible loss or gain?

5. *Relation to other problems*

Is this a situation which exists of and by itself or is it related to other situations or problems? Is action on this matter dependent on other pending actions which must be taken first and what are they? What kind of other action would be precipitated?

What competitive demands are there for the decision-making time of the responsible parties? Are they too preoccupied with other matters to give proper attention to this one? Is this one of such importance that other matters must be subordinated or set aside?

6. Organizational breadth of problem

Does the matter involve the enterprise as a whole or does it have implications for specific segments or components? What are these? Does it involve many people or few people?

7. Magnitude of problem

What resources are affected and what must be committed? How much money, equipment, personnel, time, space, etc., are at stake? What proportions of the enterprise do these represent?

Is the decision reversible? Must the action be effected all at once on a massive and an incisive basis or is it one which can be put into effect on a sampling basis or a little at a time, to permit correction of action, as you go along?

What estimates of gain or loss can be assessed against the proposed or anticipated action? What are the probable consequences of taking no action?

Operating History

1. Previous experience with this problem

Is this an old problem? What action has been taken up to now? Why does the problem arise once more? What can be learned from past behavior?

2. Experience with similar situations

What decisions were made in the past under *similar* circumstances? Did past actions in similar circumstances succeed or fail and why?

What has been the experience of other companies? What unexplained factors were there in the past? Are any of these still present?

3. *Changes in conditions*

What differences are there now as against past circumstances in such key factors as environment, magnitude of problem, time available for decision, payoff and risk, financial resources, personnel resources, key personalities, insight into the problem, experience in making such decisions, etc.

Motivations

1. *Organization goals*

What contribution to goals of the organization is intended? What operating disadvantages would be relieved? What are the long-range advantages as against the short-range ones?

2. *Origin of the problem*

How did the problem find recognition? Did it come up as a consequence of other actions, did it arise naturally out of normal management awareness or was the problem sponsored by a certain person? If the latter, what is his interest in bringing the problem up? Is the problem clearly related to operating needs or is there an element of fad or emulation? Does an outside salesman lurk somewhere behind the situation?

3. *Dramatis personae*

Who are the people principally involved? What is the stake of each, both gain and loss? Who are the controlling personalities? What possible changes in the balance of power might result from the proposed action? What possible counteractions may be expected?

Competitive Situations

(Note: The next questions relate mainly to situations in which two or more parties are arrayed against each other, such as in competitions for awards, business competition, war, international politics, domestic politics.)

1. *Counteractions*

What do you expect the other parties to do as the result of your action or decision and how must you be prepared to advance further?

What do you expect the other parties to do independently of anything you might be planning and is there any competitive action which you must therefore take?

What actions have taken place or what indications are there which point to possible actions by your competitors which may affect your position in the situation?

2. *Vulnerabilities*

What are your strong points by comparison with those of your competitors? What are your competitors doing to make up for any of their weaknesses or deficiencies?

What are your weaknesses as compared to those of your competitors? What can you do to place yourself in a stronger position in the light of these strengths of your competitors?

HYPOTHETICAL EXAMPLE: HIRING THE OUTSIDER

The following "case history" illustrates how attention to a problem in its early stages will bring out the key factors which require the most careful consideration. While the analysis proceeds in accordance with the outlines given above, you will note that some questions are not covered and that some sequences are changed for purposes of narrative continuity. This is typical of an analysis of a real situation. As you go down a list of questions you find that succeeding questions may be answered in whole or part before you get to them.

Attributes of the Problem

This is an entirely hypothetical case of an enterprise in which the general manager is faced with hiring a personal assistant. It is a medium-sized industrial organization. The major departments are product development, manufacturing, marketing, finance and administration. The problem is one of general concern because it has implications for everyone.

The need for some action arose with the disclosure that the assistant to the general manager was to move on to the parent corporation. The question of how the position would be filled drew the attention of practically everyone in the plant, either as a matter of personal aspiration, concern from the standpoint of relationships with the several department directors or mere curiosity.

The general manager had for some months been privately evaluating all possible successors from within. He had concluded that, while there might eventually be someone who might come up through the ranks, there was no one who now possessed the diversity of skills which he required in the position.

The general manager was quite aware that his problem was how to hire from the outside without disrupting morale. His decision was not known to the others. Consequently he was beset with recommendations and with the efforts of a number of hopefuls to advance their candidacy. He was well aware of the general consequences, although he could not, naturally, foretell the precise ways in which the reactions would manifest themselves. He was aware, also, that he would need to create a climate of acceptance for the newcomer. Having made the decision to hire an outsider, his decision-making problem then became one of determining how to win acceptance for his judgment.

The long-standing policy had been to promote from within unless there were no satisfactory candidates available.

This action stood by itself. It was not dependent upon any other action. The general manager had many other things on his mind as executive in charge of an active plant. Nevertheless he felt this of sufficient importance to devote much of his time to it.

He knew, also, that he had to sell not only the hopefuls on the wisdom of his judgment but all others as a condition of maintaining his leadership role and of safeguarding the effectiveness of the man he would bring in — a man whom he already had tentatively in mind.

The decision was one he could not delay nor could he take it without consulting his people. The prime decision, already reached in his mind, would not be a reversible one. Once it was announced, the effects would begin shaping themselves, for better or for worse.

As the time drew close for some kind of an announcement he sought the advice of his superiors in the parent organization as well as of key subordinates who were not themselves candidates. Some of them advised him to talk individually to all department directors and to each of the hopefuls in order to get them to accept his choice. This would be no easy task because the self-appraisals of the hopefuls would rarely coincide with his own appraisals of them.

A second approach was that on the day of the new man's arrival he should assemble all concerned and explain his actions at that time. This would get the pain over quickly.

The general manager felt that individual conversations and explanations would be desired by the hopefuls if for no other reason than to obtain some recognition of their legitimate aspirations. On the other hand he preferred not to have to cope with unpleasantry, nor did he relish spending the time. The easy way out, certainly, would be to get it over quickly. This was the crux of his problem.

Previous Experience

The last time he had had this problem was shortly after the plant had been organized — when it was about a year old. At that time the organization accepted the decision with scarcely a murmur of dissent. The only reaction was one of curiosity in view of the sensitive nature of the position and its impact upon all concerned.

The problem arose again because, although the organization was now almost five years old, it had been so busy growing up and shaking itself down that there had not been ample opportunity to expose some of the up-and-coming hopefuls to the varieties of experience which would have been prerequisites to qualifying for the position.

Looking outside, he found both practices. Some companies went so far as to include in their want ads the statement "Our employees know about this ad." As to an abrupt notification to the staff, he found instances where this was done without repercussion. Apparently this happened where the management had a continuing relationship with the affected employees who thereby became fully aware of the need and propriety of the action. The abrupt notification did not work out so well in other cases where it came as a complete surprise. This was not the case in his own plant. There were a number of people who now felt themselves in line for the position.

The Goals and Motivations

For the immediate, the general manager wanted to resolve the new appointment with as little rancor or flare-back as possible. He did not want his own superiors to think that he could not manage his human-relationship problems. More constructively, there was a posture of executive leadership which he had to maintain in the eyes of his own staff. This, coupled with the need for protecting the promotion-from-within policy, constituted the long-range aspects.

Actions Taken

As mentioned above, the problem was not who to appoint; rather, it was how to break the news. As to this, the manager had now reached a conclusion.

It remained then for him to go down the list once more of all key personnel and hopefuls in order to be prepared with the counsel or encouragement that might be required for each in the light of his self-estimate and feelings. He called in the director of personnel and assigned to him the task of accumulating the necessary notes for a strategy conference. He realized that the director of personnel would have better access to employees' opinions whereas the top man is subject to planting, pressuring and filtering.

All the decisions were now made. From this point on, the general manager would be concerned with helping his new man become acceptable and with salving the feelings of the bruised ones, through words and compensatory actions, as warranted.

WORKING TECHNIQUES

In summary, three techniques stand out as important in these early stages of decision-making. They are:

1. Assess the whole situation, looking to the experience of the past and the present and projecting into the future.

2. Get as close as possible to the facts and materials of the problem itself and the environment in which it exists.

3. Keep an open mind, reserving judgment until all of the significant information has been accumulated.

Chapter III

THE TECHNIQUES OF FACT-FINDING

The facts of the matter on which you will depend for your decision are always in existence even though you may not be aware of them or recognize them. Sometimes they stare you right in the face and you do not know it.

The facts were on the radar screens during World War II when the German capital ships, *Scharnhorst* and *Gneisenau,* escaped through the English Channel. They made no impression, however, writes Sir Robert Watson-Watt in his book *The Pulse of Radar.* And in spite of all the facts beamed in on American intelligence officials at home and at Pearl Harbor, the Japanese came through for a surprising and smashing victory.

In both instances, even when the facts were routinely perceived, they made no impression. The greatest single reason for not finding and recognizing facts is that we don't set about collecting them systematically. In spite of tales of sudden inspirations and glorious discoveries, most fact-finding is a labor of perseverance and tedium. It involves deciding beforehand (1) what stones to turn over, (2) who is to turn them, (3) how they are to be turned and in what sequence and (4) how the substance we seek may be recognized when finally the right stone may be turned, if at all.

And so in this chapter we concern ourselves with this methodology. I cannot overemphasize its importance for economical operation and prompt decision-making. Poor fact-finding, in the initial stages especially, is the source of much poor decision-making.

ENGINEERING THE APPROACH

A small investment of effort before the work of fact-finding is begun will be well repaid. This is particularly the case when you must explain to others your intent so that they will produce what you actually need, rather than what they think you need. Because fact-finding may be influenced by one's own experiences, interests and preferences, some attention to the matter beforehand may help you make the best assignment.

Who Is to Get the Facts

The assignment may be given to one or a number of people, depending on the size of the problem, the time available, the expert knowledge involved and questions of possible bias, among others.

Fact-finding responsibility could be assigned in one of the following ways:

1. Do it yourself.
2. Select the most qualified person.
3. Give the identical assignment to more than one person.
4. Split the assignment up among a number of people.

You may handle the assignment yourself when you have no one to whom you may delegate it, when it is just as convenient for you to do so or when the matter is one of privacy. If you are not thoroughly conversant with the type of situation involved, get the counsel of people who will guide you to appropriate sources in addition to such facts as they themselves might furnish. If your own status is to be affected by the outcome of the matter or if you have any other subjective interest in it, protect your judgment by seeking independent counsel.

If *you have a choice of people* to whom to give the assignment, select the one who is most knowledgeable, who has sufficient time available and who is found, by previous performance, the most dependable in doing this kind of work. If complete independence of judgment is important, you must ascertain that the person selected does not have a previously demonstrated bias and that he does not have a personal interest in the outcome of the decision.

The identical problem may be given to two or more people — assuming that it is important enough to warrant this and that the people are available. It is important to do this where there is a high degree of subjective influence even on the selection of facts or where the matter is of a highly controversial nature or where the understanding of facts may be different with each reporter. It is not uncommon for several people looking at the same problem to come up with an equal number of different reports.

Assignments are subdivided and given to a number of people, whose work must later be coordinated, when (1) it is important to get the work done in less time, (2) the assignment is too great for any one person, (3) there are a number of skill or knowledge specialties and (4) the problem embraces two or more areas of organizational responsibility. While it is important to assure objectivity even under this arrangement, group interaction tends to offset or nullify bias.

Mapping the Problem

You may already have done some preliminary work in mapping out your approach to fact-finding, during the stage of initially recognizing and defining the problem. Your preliminary examination may have identified areas of seeming knowledge and areas of ignorance. If this has not been done already, you must now identify your informational needs.

Now take your informational targets and subdivide them into manageable chunks of activity. This has several advantages: (1) it enables you to catalogue the information you acquire, (2) subdivision of the body of facts may bring out relationships that otherwise might not be seen, and (3) the more precise specification required also results in more precise fact-finding. Psychologically it seems easier to reach the end when you check off successive bits of completed activity. It is like taking a long motor drive: the goal seems to be reached more swiftly if you aim at mileposts along the way than if you count the miles remaining toward the final destination itself.

As a result of your preliminary planning you will begin sensing the various possibilities of action and the probable pros and cons attaching to each. Blocking these out on paper will tell you the kinds of supporting or clarifying facts you will need. At this stage don't look for facts that prove or disprove. Try only to shed light.

The results of your preliminary mapping may take the form of a schedule of questions. Following is a check list used by E. I. du Pont de Nemours & Company, Inc. in analyzing a proposed public-relations project. Note that only a few of the questions can be answered directly. Most of the questions require further subdivision and scheduling of the facts needed.

PUBLIC-RELATIONS PROJECT-ANALYSIS FORMULA

SECTION A

1. What is the objective this project is designed to gain or approach? Is the objective sound and desirable?

2. If the project succeeds, will it reach or approach the objective? Are there collateral advantages?

3. Is the project feasible?
    a. Is it reasonable to expect it to succeed?
    b. Can it be done with existing personnel?
    c. Does it involve cooperation outside the department?

4. Are there disadvantages to the project?
    a. Is it counter to sound public-relations policy?
    b. Is it counter to company policy?
    c. Is the expense too high in relation to possible gain?
    d. Can it embarrass top management? sales? production? research?

5. How much will it cost? Where is the money coming from?

6. In what ways can the project fail? What are the foreseeable difficulties?

7. What are the penalties of failure?
   a. Will it embarrass the company if it fails?
   b. Will it embarrass the department if it fails?

The answers to these questions should add up to the answer to the first question in

SECTION B

1. Why do it at all? Is it worth attempting?
2. Why do it now? Is there any reason for moving fast?
3. Why do it this way? Are there other methods of approach that promise more?
4. Is this the best way that the amount of money involved could be utilized to promote the public relations of the du Pont Company?

If it passes all these tests, there are two more questions in

SECTION C

1. Who, if anybody, outside the department must approve the project?
2. Who, if anybody, outside the department must be informed?

Pegging the Informational Sources

While it is one thing to know what information you want to find, it is another to know how to get it. The holders of information are sometimes quite loathe to give it up. Within an organization the reluctance may be a matter of bureaucratic competition or professional hesitation as to the accuracy or completeness of the information. Even more insidious, actually, is the slanting or concealment of information in an effort to make one's situation seem as favorable as possible.

Outside-company information is more difficult to obtain. First, you run into company secrecy. Second, when the information is forthcoming you cannot be sure it has not been doctored by acts of commission or omission, motivated by a desire to protect one's position.

People who do not know you or your purposes are usually reluctant to give information. A manufacturer of earth-moving machinery wanted information on product use from the actual users. He sent out some of his smartest fact-finders, attired in their smart-looking business suits. When they called upon the earthy operators, they clammed up. They were leary of strangers. So another crew went out, dressed in the clothes of the operators. They went to the taverns and social retreats where the operators relaxed and this time talked freely of their experiences with their equipment.

Before generating a lot of work, make sure the information is not already available in some form. You must pinpoint your informational sources or you will waste time and effort. Consider the following:

1. *Regular informational reports generated within the organization.* In addition to the regular reports of which you have official knowledge, people who generate information often keep subsidiary records and tabulations which may contain valuable information.

2. *Information derived as a by-product of work operations.* By putting your finger on the pertinent steps in a work operation, you can have tabulations or observations made as a by-product of this work.

3. *Reports of previous experience.* Check the librarian, the file room, people who have wrestled with the same problem in the past and the specialists in the problem area to ascertain the results of previous experience or previous consideration of a similar problem.

4. *Opinions and judgments of specialists and experts.* List all of the knowledgeable people and experts, in and out of the organization, who might be able to provide useful information, additional leads and authoritative judgments. Put down what you might hope to get from each. They, in turn, may suggest additional leads.

5. *Outside organizations and informational centers.* Government agencies, private economic foundations, trade associations, professional organizations, trade-magazine publishers and consultants may have pertinent information but it is likely to be secondary or even tertiary. A great deal of it is likely to have been screened or slanted before release to them so you must be prepared to do your own screening and careful evaluation. Attendance at professional workshops, clinics and seminars on specific topics may stimulate lines of inquiry. Look mainly for basic principles in the experience of others. You must still find your own unique approaches and solutions, because rarely will the practices of others be directly applicable to your own needs.

Instructions to the Fact-Finders

The person or persons given the assignment must be carefully briefed as to what is expected. This briefing should include:

1. Background information on the problem.
2. Statement of the problem or goal.
3. Specific description of the information required.
4. Description of any related fact-finding assignments given to anyone else.
5. Tips on problems that may be anticipated as well as guidance on any confidential aspects.
6. A target date for completion.
7. Format in which the information is to be compiled and presented, especially if it is to be integrated with other information.

GETTING THE SALIENT INFORMATION

The next task in fact-finding is to be able to extract from a situation the significant information and relationships which bear on your problem. The difficulty of doing this will vary with each situation depending on how new it is and how much experience you've had with the type of problem.

The ability to get to the heart of a problem is one of the hallmarks of the good mind. It is sometimes said that you must be born with such an ablity. This may or may not be true, but it is certainly safe to say that one can acquire and improve this ability by mastery of a number of simple techniques.

Getting into the Problem

There is no better way to get an intimate understanding of a problem than to come into direct contact with it. Inevitably something is lost when information is filtered through others before it gets to you. Nevertheless the executive must rely upon subordinates to get the facts. Hence, as already suggested, the first thing to do is to choose the best person to do your fact-finding.

Thus, when the Merchandise National Bank of Chicago decided to explore the computer industry to see what kind of a data-processing system to install, it realized that the quality of the investigation that would be made would largely decide the issue for the Bank. It realized the magnitude of the pressures for business among the computer manufacturers. H. F. Tubergren, Jr., vice president and comptroller, said: "We had in mind definite qualifications that had to be met. The candidate had to have an analytical mind, be a quick thinker, keep level-headed under pressure, have a knowledge of bank operations, be easily educable and be young. Equally important, the candidate had to have an understanding wife who would not object to his constant traveling." The choice in this case narrowed down to the manager of the planning and research department who met all of these qualifications.

Over a period of some years of conducting inquiries, fact-finding surveys and research of all kinds, in various capacities, I developed the following formula for getting the facts:

1. *Get into direct contact with the facts.* Whether you work on the problem or someone else does, get away from indirect reports. If you must rely upon others, ask for samples of their supporting materials. Make sure they got into direct contact

with the materials of the problem. Nothing can substitute for the realism of direct contact. Kings have traveled incognito to find out what their subjects thought. A news reporter joined the police force to get the inside story of the actual life of a policeman. Social investigators have posed as prison convicts in order to get a feeling of the realism of that kind of life.

2. *Discipline your study.* Keep the material you accumulate in notebooks and file folders, as appropriate. Do not trust to your memory; you are bound to forget much of what you learn unless you put it on paper immediately or as soon after an interview as is possible. Keep to the main lines of your inquiry; if you develop sidelines of investigation, make notes of these and attack them later if pertinent, unless you must get them this one time or not at all.

3. *Start with a broad look.* Before immersing yourself in details or in one aspect of the total problem, get a broad overview. The really experienced fact-finder may obtain all he needs to know in this way. No matter how experienced you are, however, the over-all look will (1) identify areas of greatest difficulty, (2) bring out relationships, (3) suggest a logical sequence of attack and (4) assure a balanced inquiry.

4. *Think of how other people index their thoughts.* The headings under which you expect to find your materials are not necessarily those which would be chosen by others. In a face-to-face contact a discussion may bring out what you seek, through rephrasing of questions. If you must look in file cabinets, indexes or card catalogues, think of the topics that others might use as well as those most meaningful to you. Sometimes the subject is treated collaterally with another. Facts are often found in the most unlikely places; a memorandum or report on one named subject might include related aspects not suggested by the heading. You actually need to imagine the illogical thought processes of other fact-gatherers and reporters.

5. *Exploit one lead to find others.* A knowledgeable person is likely to know of other sources of information on the same topic. Ask him for further suggestions. When you rummage through file documents, make notes on references to previous

studies, reports and memoranda. When reading in footnoted or scholarly works that give source references, use these as additional leads. Sometimes information uncovered in this way is more valuable than the document in which you found the original reference.

6. *Group related information.* As you accumulate information put things of like nature together. This will tell you whether you have enough and it will also bring out contradictions. Classifying the information will bring out patterns of information.

7. *When you're frustrated do something else.* Let your subconscious take over. A more fruitful approach may suggest itself when you're not straining to find it.

Finding the Right Depth

These two things are clear about facts for decision-making: (1) rarely, if ever, will you find 100 per cent of the facts; (2) if you wait to get all, the chances are you'll never make a decision. Yet much of the insecurity of decision-making hinges around this very question: "Do I have all the facts?" The following techniques aim at getting enough facts while conserving effort:

1. *When you're far enough along to make a tentative decision, do so and then see if your facts support you.*

The Parker Pen Company once went a long way toward marketing a new product — a tiny camera about the size of a package of cigarettes. This camera was never actually marketed although a test quantity was manufactured. The company avoided a costly error by pretesting its conclusions. It might have saved even more through better fact-finding at an earlier stage.

A study had first been made of the probable interest of consumers. This was encouraging, so product research then centered on ways of making the camera foolproof in the light of amateur picture-taking habits. After preliminary product tests in the laboratory, a full-dress market test for a single city was mapped out. This included selection of test stores and preparation of advertising copy and layouts, instruction booklets, retail-clerk training and photo-finishing service. Sample cameras were then distributed to amateurs in the Chicago area as well as to employees. The results were highly encouraging. Abruptly, however, all activity on this product was discontinued!

Somehow the designers and marketers had not reckoned with the problems of an off-standard film. The film was of unique size and was packaged in a special daylight-loading magazine. There was no such film on the market. The Parker Pen Company would either have to make and distribute this film nationally or it would have to induce a major film manufacturer to do so — an unlikely event. There were other reasons for abandoning the project, but the film obstacle was the main one. Thus, all this costly effort could have been avoided by earlier verification of the tentative decision against the availability of supporting facts.

2. *Do not go more deeply into the facts than is profitable.*

The economics of decision-making require that you develop the skill of excluding the unnecessary. Now, it is a peculiarity of the descriptive process that it requires more effort to describe or depict a limited situation than a broader one. For example, you must cover more particulars to differentiate one man from all other men than to describe all men in general. Hence, don't assume that a more limited scope will correspondingly limit the fact-finding.

There may be some situations which require minute specification, but, for most purposes, the executive wants only the key facts. An analogy may be drawn to the skill of the caricaturist who brings out the personality of his subject with a few well-placed pen strokes. Do you not recall the toothy grin which stood only for Theodore Roosevelt, the jutting jaw, smiling lips and upturned cigarette holder which meant only Franklin D. Roosevelt and the few roundish lines and a stubby cigar which could mean none other than Winston Churchill?

A purchasing manual issued by the Rockwell Manufacturing Company emphasized, among other things, the potential sources of savings through "value analysis." Purchasing officers were given check lists to guide them in finding ways of cutting costs. All materials, parts and operations were to be put to the following tests before a requisition would be approved:

(1.) Does its use contribute to value?

(2.) Is its cost proportionate to its usefulness?

(3.) Does it need all of its features?

(4.) Is there anything better for the intended use?

(5.) Can a usable part be made by a lower-cost method?

(6.) Can a standard product be found which will be usable?

(7.) Is it made on proper tooling — considering quantities used?

(8.) Do material, reasonable labor, overhead and profit total its cost?

(9.) Will another dependable supplier provide it for less?

(10.) Is anyone buying it for less?

This is an excellent check list for decision but it must be used with some discretion in each case — as undoubtedly it is. The check list would be used in a different way for a single part that would cost $10.00 to purchase than for a part that would cost $10,000. Furthermore the cost of fact-finding becomes more evident when you note that each question requires its own subsidiary set of questions.

3. *The duration of fact-finding will tend to be underestimated so be sure to include a safety factor.*

When you start on a problem with which you have not had previous experience, you are likely to underestimate how long it will take. Your schedule should therefore include a safety factor. In addition, you should provide for an early reappraisal of the time schedule after a brief overview of the situation.

As an example, the study of data-processing systems undertaken by the Merchandise National Bank, mentioned above, was originally estimated to require six months. It took two years. One thing which prolonged the study was the unanticipated vastness of the area of inquiry. Another delaying factor was the need to acquaint the equipment manufacturers at that time with the problems of bank paper-work handling. Finally,

Merchandise National had not anticipated that the design of computer hardware would be undergoing change even during the course of the survey. In fact, the final conclusion was to select a system which would anticipate, as far into the future as possible, the trends in the state of the art. All of this, however, required more time than had been anticipated.

4. *At some point you must call a halt to the pursuit of facts which still elude you and then bring into play your best estimate of the unknowns.*

One of the objectives of fact-finding is to narrow down the areas of uncertainty and not to try to eliminate them completely since that is rarely feasible.

Aiming at Significance

When the final decisions are made they will hinge on significant facts or conclusions distilled from all the supporting facts. Sometimes you have no time for exhaustive fact-finding. You must gather and weigh facts on the run. You must be able to judge the situation from a few key facts. This is the highest of decision-making skills — a task not to be given to an amateur. One is reminded of the blind men, who, touching the body of an elephant, thought it to be a mountain, touching the leg, thought it a tree, and feeling the tail, said it was a rope!

Here are some techniques for aiming at representative or significant factors:

1. *Seek the few elements that account for the greatest part of the situation.* In most cases a few per cent of the items or elements will have the greatest significance in the light of the total situation. Thus, in any organization, only a few people will have the best ideas. Most accidents in a factory seem to be concentrated in a few accident-prone personalities. Dr. Joseph M. Juran, the noted management consultant, calls this an adaptation of Pareto's Curve after the economist and sociologist Vilfredo Pareto, who noted this kind of behavior in a distribution of wealth. Dr. Juran points out that a few per cent of the thousands of items in a catalogue will account for about 80 per cent

of the aggregate value of the inventory. A corollary to this is that about 80 per cent of the items would account for only a few per cent of the total. There are about 35,000 post offices in the United States. The bulk of the business is concentrated in far less than 100. One post office alone, New York City, accounts for about 10 per cent of the total. If you wanted to localize the problem of budget control, you would concentrate on relatively few, for greatest return on effort.

2. *Rank your facts in order of greatest importance to most trivial.* If you followed the first suggestion you will already have isolated the most important items. Continue doing this on down the line so that you will have identified those things which should command most of your attention. (*Do not discard anything.* What may seem unimportant today may assume greater significance on reexamination in a new light. What seems to be a bit of trivia may have a critical relationship to one of your major points. You should consult the informational discards and set-asides when you run into frustrations.)

3. *Seek the one critical factor upon which the decision may turn.* This may be something known or unknown. This may also be called the limiting factor or the strategic factor. If there is more than one limiting factor, the combination may be regarded as a set of limiting or strategic factors. "The limiting [strategic] factor," said Chester I. Barnard, former president of the New Jersey Bell Telephone Co., "is the one whose control, in the right form, at the right place and time, will establish a new system or set of conditions which meets the purpose." In brief, find the shoe for want of which a kingdom may be lost. The strategic factor may not be the one which accounts for the greatest number of cases. In magnitude, of and by itself, it may not be the greatest element.

4. *Determine the characteristics of groups or categories of related information.* If you have been classifying your information on the basis of similarities and differences, you will already have begun noting the significances represented by the informational grouping. As you proceed with your fact-gathering and analysis you will discover additional meanings as you ask

yourself questions about the characteristics of the informational groups.

5. *Look for the relationships among elements in the situation.* Look for things that happen whenever two or more conditions occur simultaneously or in a certain sequence. Test this by finding out whether the same things recur under similar conditions. The reverse of this, equally important, is to discover whether something exists or occurs only when two or more elements are not simultaneously present. For example, productivity in a certain office drops on Mondays, which also happens to be the day when the supervisor regularly makes certain outside calls. Productivity is generally higher when he is present. When the supervisor is on vacation, productivity is also at low ebb. Your first hunch, then, is to link the presence or absence of the supervisor with productivity of workers. Having done this, you would look for other contributory causes.

HOW FACTS CAST LIGHT

In the course of fact-gathering you do not wait until the very end to begin reaching conclusions. Actually you begin formulating ideas and tentative decisions as your findings begin shaping up. If you have gathered your facts well, as we have seen, they often make your decision for you. This may be noted in the next two case examples.

The Chipped-Lens Problem

The "chipped-lens problem" offers a good example of how opinions and notions are often confused with facts and of how facts, ultimately, must govern. This is an actual case from the experience of the Bausch & Lomb Company, manufacturers of a wide variety of optical products.

The symptoms of the problem centered in the losses of labor and materials due to high incidence of lens damage. Over the years reliance had been placed mainly upon the manual skills of expert lens blockers, grinders and polishers. Quality controls through the media of management and machine had not been applied in this area. When supervisors and operators were asked why the defects occurred, they came forth with almost as many different answers as there were defects. The human element still reigned supreme.

Accordingly, unable to learn the basic causes, the management launched promotional campaigns to bring its facts to the employees and thereby make them quality- and cost-conscious. Displays were set up in the affected areas of the plant, showing the extent of the losses and the impact they had on costs of operation. This "eye-opening" approach was supplemented by the posting of bulletins suggesting additional care in handling, processing and cleaning. The effect, relatively, was as though one might have been shoveling water against the tide.

A new approach was inaugurated. The management established a fact-finding group under Dr. Joseph M. Juran. This group, gathering the facts methodically, in a very short time determined the true causes of lens damage and the lines of attack for eliminating them.

The first step was to compile loss reports and feed them into data-processing equipment. This yielded a statistical display of the kinds of defects that were being made. The machine data also put the spotlight on the particular division that had contributed most of the costly defects. Narrowing the search further, attention was then focused on one heavy contributor to losses: chipping of lenses. Instead of asking for opinions, the materials were analyzed before and after each processing stage.

Quite counter to the opinion-based reasons for chipping, the fact-finders learned that 60 per cent of the chips occurred in diamond-milling the second surface of the lens. Another 27 per cent was pinned down to the chilling of lenses to $-40°F$ in order to separate them from the pitch-blocks to which they were attached during grinding and polishing. Finally, the remaining 13 per cent of chips occurred in the cleaning stage.

Now that the origins of the chips had been localized, it was necessary to identify more specifically the causes of damage.

To bring this story to a close, from a high of 27 per cent, chipped lenses dropped to 5 per cent of total defects.

The interesting thing about this case is that the course of action in each instance was determined clearly and solely by the facts. Actually the only decision that had to be made was the choice of the analytical approach, which was to replace reliance upon opinion with reliance upon facts.

The Case of the Shrinking Profits

This same approach can be used on the smallest as well as the largest of problems. An automobile dealer whom I know had enjoyed another year of high volume sales. In spite of this, his costs seemed to have gotten away from him so that he was making very much less than in the preceding year. He decided he would compare his costs by category and by item for the two years. This brought to light many little operating luxuries which he had allowed to creep into his cost structure which, when eliminated, restored his favorable position.

One example was the license-tag attendant. This employee had been added for the main purpose of attaching license tags to new cars. The dealer asked his salesmen if they could dispense with this service and, almost to a man, they insisted that they could not assume the burden because it kept them away from working on new prospects. The dealer decided he would get the facts. Before the attendant had been hired, the salesmen themselves had attached the plates. Now, when the customer came in for his car, he usually asked for his salesman. That personage would take him out on the lot where he would look for the license-tag attendant. This worthy aide was not always available, so, while some salesmen would excuse themselves and leave the customer to wait, others would wait with him. Finally, while the plates were being attached, the salesman might sometimes stand around talking until the customer drove the car away.

Again the actual facts did not correspond with the opinions of the salesmen. Adding the attendant to the payroll had not actually saved any time for the salesmen; instead, it had merely raised their comfort and convenience levels. Had they sold any more cars? No! The license-tag attendant went looking for another job.

How to Provoke More Fact-Finding

Those who generalize or conclude from insufficient facts usually do so because they are not aware of the depth of a problem and of its range of implications. When one is not aware of the facts, the natural tendency is to oversimplify and to jump to conclusions prematurely.

It is almost useless to argue the proposed decision on the merits. Argument by itself tends merely to solidify the counterarguments.

For the immediate situation, an approach that seems to work well is to provoke your "adversary" into a feeling of insecurity. Bring up situations that are not covered by the proposed solution. Show how the proposal would be in conflict with another action or situation. Carry the effects of the action to their ultimate absurdity. Your purpose is to make him feel he is stepping off into a greater unknown than he had realized. Then you can throw in constructive arguments and supporting facts.

CONCLUSION

If we could collect all of the pertinent facts bearing on a decision, within a reasonable time, we'd have very few problems of difficult decision-making. As we have seen, however, the quality of "all" is too elusive; we can afford neither the time nor the cost. We must therefore concentrate on obtaining the key pertinent facts. This brings in the element of personal judgment in the determination of need and relevance. Different people at work on the same problem may be expected to bring in different sets of facts, different interpretations and different conclusions. The risk which this entails may be mini-

mized by a procedural approach which assures that the right
people are assigned to get the facts and that they have a method
for obtaining them which is most likely to produce what is
needed. On the last point, moreover, it is critically important
that the fact-finders get as close as possible to the primary
sources of information.

Chapter IV

THE CRITERIA OF CHOICE

The fact-finding phase brings out the various possibilities of action (including taking no action). Then the decision-maker compares the expected outcomes of these and, from among them, chooses that course which he believes will bring the most desirable return.

He can make his choice by his "intuitive" sensing of the situation or he can use a variety of techniques for making more tangible and measurable comparisons. This chapter concerns itself with the latter.

The techniques presented here do not require any special knowledge beyond simple arithmetic. Actually very few executive decisions require the use of advanced mathematics.

The executive must know when to choose a course which may not be indicated by a quantified analysis. An example is given which points this up.

In making a choice we try to limit the risks. We will take up means for doing so — for choosing courses of action which preserve our maneuverability if results do not go as anticipated.

Finally we will examine the motivations, limitations and strategies of the key personalities who influence choice.

YARDSTICKS AND STRATEGIC FACTORS

Most commonly a selection is made of that alternative which is expected to yield the greatest return, as you define it — long

51

term, short term or otherwise. In short, what is most profitable?
It would be convenient to be able to make all decisions in accordance with some financial yardstick, but this often is not
practicable. The human decision-maker is still supreme: he
must make his own selection of yardsticks from among the
many which may or may not be pertinent. He must evaluate,
also, those aspects which do not lend themselves readily to being
quantified.

The Bouncing Ball

What may be the governing element one time may not be
the next time. A change in only one element in a situation may
alter the balances enough to make the decisive difference. It's
a matter of the interplay of forces. To illustrate this, we'll explore a common decision situation: whether to "make or buy."

The pressures to make something within the house seem
much greater, generally, than those to buy from outside. Apart
from reasons of personal preference which people may have
for wanting to do work inside, the usual justification is one of
cost. All other things being equal, you get the work done at
least cost. As we shall see, however, even this is not easily established. As we shall also see, the sheer necessity of getting a job
done may outweigh other considerations. In fact, in the long
list of considerations, which follows, any one of them might be
the deciding element under one set of circumstances and not
be worth even considering under another.

1. *Cost*. The general rule is: All other things being equal,
do that which is cheapest. There are, however, many opportunities for self-delusion when it comes to cost. You may talk
yourself into saying that the work costs little or nothing because you have scrap or because you have idle equipment or
personnel. For managerial consistency you should avoid defining cost for the convenience of the moment. Thus cost may be
figured as direct manufacturing cost on an incremental basis
and it may also be figured on a fully allocated basis (sometimes depending upon what it is you want to show). Cost studies

in themselves are often not precise and hence may require verification from other data.

2. *Know-how.* Do you actually know how to do this work? This is more than mere knowledge of basic work processes. Is your experience broad enough to cover the variety of unpredictable situations which may arise? This is analogous to the man who built the boat in his basement. If he had done it before, he never would have made the mistake of assembling it indoors. You may even be willing to pay a premium in order to learn how it is done from someone with undisputed know-how.

3. *Capital outlay.* Notwithstanding the desirability of doing the work in the house, from all other standpoints, you simply may not have the working capital in your budget with which to acquire the necessary equipment and facilitation.

4. *Equipment obsolescence.* Specialized machine tools may be required which may go "out of style" very quickly. To justify procurement of such equipment you must have a sufficiently great work load with which to write off the equipment cost very quickly. Otherwise you may be saddled with a disadvantage compared to a competitor who is able to use the very latest equipment.

5. *Discontinuity.* The work to be done by the specialized equipment or personnel may be irregular, seasonal or cyclical. You may be faced with idle time as well as with an encumbrance of space which could be put to other uses.

6. *Work-load policy.* The work-load level must be maintained in order to assure a steady state of employment and to avoid peaks and valleys.

7. *Timetable.* A production plan or a delivery commitment may require that the work be done by a given time. You may have some of your inside shop people begging for work a few weeks later, but if you're going to be able to honor your commitments, you may have no choice but to send the work outside.

8. *Self-sufficiency.* Apart from matters of cost, your policy may be to achieve an independence from outside vendors. You may not want to be in the position of having to depend upon

others for the meeting of work schedules. Your operation may be a very sensitive one, requiring on-site coordination of all the parties with internal assurance of delivery on every phase, as required.

9. *Supplier strategy*. In order to be assured of the availability of outside sources when you need them, you may find it expedient to keep the outside vendor happy by giving him a guaranteed minimum of business. After all, he also has his problems of ebb and flow and he will be more favorably disposed toward you if he can predict a certain amount of business from you.

10. *Integration*. Performance of the work inside may be warranted when it represents one or more steps in an integrated sequence. The whole rhythm of operation would be interrupted by removal of the work in midstream.

11. *Materials availability*. When you have a surplus of materials you *may* find this to be a good time to work them off, especially if you are not likely to have any recurring use for them. On the other hand, certain materials may be hard to get or the delivery time on them may make it infeasible to fabricate inside. In those circumstances you might find it preferable to go to a vendor who has the materials in inventory.

12. *Privacy*. The nature of the work to be performed may be so private that you will not want to risk disclosure. This is especially true of proprietary work processes. It may also be true of certain work done for the government under security regulations.

13. *Labor relations*. Whether or not they are organized, your employees may not like to see work which they regard as rightfully theirs go out of the house. This is particularly true when they have undergone a cutback on overtime or when they have had any layoffs. You cannot always cater to these attitudes but there are times when ignoring them may be foolhardy.

14. *Self-check*. From time to time you may want to obtain an independent check on what it costs you to do your own work. You find this out by obtaining competitive bids from outside

vendors and then comparing actual performance with what you are able to do inside.

15. *Space.* You may simply have no place to put any additional equipment and employees.

16. *Transportation.* Transportation of raw materials or of individual parts may be one thing, but transportation of the completely fabricated and assembled product may be another. You may consider it too risky to move delicate instruments or very cumbersome instruments. Under these circumstances you may prefer to do the work inside the house.

17. *Attention conflict.* Your policy may be of one of "Cobbler, stick to your last." You may not want to have your executives preoccupied on too many fronts, whether at the present time or as a matter of general policy.

As you go down the preceding list of considerations in making or buying, you must note that the decision can be thrown one way or the other, sometimes by a single factor and sometimes by a combination of factors. Not many people within the organization will have all of the answers, nor can you circulate every make-or-buy decision to all of the specialists within the house who may have contributory views. On an exception basis you may set up safeguards so that items over a specified dollar amount will necessarily be reviewed by one or more people. As a matter of policy you may give the procurement officer a list of items or services which should be referred by him for additional review when they come from the internal requisitioning personnel. On the most important make-or-buy decisions the comptroller, the purchasing agent, the shop boss, the inside customer and others may be brought into the deliberations. The need for such deliberations may be averted substantially by encouraging full communication so that the current operating conditions and policies will be known by those who initiate the purchase orders.

Financial Yardsticks

The profit motive lies behind most business decision-making. The objective is to achieve the greatest return for the invested dollar. Any resource, including (and especially) time, is converted to invested cost. The motivation is to obtain the greatest return for the dollar invested. (The *return-on-investment formula* expresses earnings as a percentage of sales times capital turnover. In this formula turnover is sales divided by total investment. Total investment is working capital plus permanent investment.)

The accountant plays an important role in application of the return-on-investment formula. His definitions and his approaches may lead to a variety of results. Depreciation may be computed according to different formulas. The investment may be entered on the books as a straight capital investment or a substantial part of it may be entered as expenses and hence made tax-deductible. Profits may be computed on an incremental cost basis or on a fully allocated cost basis. (Both are probably needed: the incremental approach to determine net impact and worthwhileness and the fully allocated approach to assist in such efforts as pricing.)

Related to the return-on-investment formula is the concept of the *pay-back period*. Briefly this means: "This is how long it is expected to take for us to recover our investment." Usually this measure is applied to the purchase of equipment or the making of other capital investments or improvements. It may involve a substantial amount of forecasting. If the forecast is based upon an existing work load, it should be fairly easy to figure out the pay-back period, provided the estimate of machine productivity is a dependable one. If the equipment is to be purchased in the hope that there will be sufficient business, as yet not guaranteed, the forecasting becomes more tenuous with the result that the decision-maker must be more conservative before committing himself to the investment.

In the making of investment decisions, apart from other criteria of return, questions of time value and alternate use of money must be considered. If the expenditure is not made, what other use might be derived from the money and what return would there be from this alternative investment? In fairness to yourself, if you consider the effects of alternative investment, you should also consider the consequences of not making the investment. How will the immediate situation be affected? How will related situations be affected now and in the future? Is this the time to make the expenditure or should it be deferred to a later date when the cash position might be more favorable?

"Savings" is another frequent basis for decision. Savings are promised if an investment is made in new equipment or if new systems are installed or if major changes are made in work procedures. This is a kind of reverse aspect of profit-taking: profits are made or increased by reducing expenditures for the same effort or by obtaining a greater yield from the same expenditure.

The matter of defining savings can become quite tricky. When I was in government service I was troubled by management improvement and efficiency reports which claimed tremendous savings which somehow were not reflected in reduced payrolls or reduced expenditures in other accounts. Someone would claim that by eliminating a form or a procedure or by introducing a new procedure, 100,000 man-hours a year would be saved (or any other figure). Coupled with the claims of anticipated savings would usually be a recommendation for some enabling expenditure. What usually would trouble me is that I could not find the savings although the expenditures clearly revealed themselves. (Here one thinks of the analogy of the spending wife who bankrupts her husband by saving scads of money at the bargain sales!)

Estimates of expected savings should be challenged in general, but, in particular, proof should be sought of an actual reduction in a budgeted expenditure. If you ask for proof of a savings you may be told this is someone else's responsibility. ("We show the way; others must accomplish it!") If you want to be assured of the savings as a prerequisite to the decision, you must then follow it to its point of ultimate effect or be assured that this will be done by others. This is not to say that methods improvements should not be made unless deductible savings can be proven. Rather, it suggests that if savings are to be used as the criterion of expenditure, you had better be sure of the actual savings.

There are various measures of performance which can be used as the basis for financial and economic decisions. For example, the "break-even point" is used in making marketing and production decisions. Fixed and incremental costs are charted together with varying sales and production levels in order to determine the volume which will be necessary to break even at the prices which are to be charged. A variety of other techniques is available to the trained accountant, statistician and economist for the bringing together of two or more indicators of performance.

THE DECISION RULE

The decision rule is that criterion or that basis of judgment which will govern final selection of an alternative. It has both long-run and short-run implications, for it must satisfy the objectives of the enterprise over-all as well as in the immediate situation. Thus it does not necessarily follow that because something is profitable that a businessman would want to commit himself to that something. It might not fit his tastes or preferences or it might be in conflict with other commitments or objectives.

We run some risk in oversimplifying the decision-making situation when we discuss decision rules. The idea of a single basis of selection among alternatives may be convenient for making comparisons but in the real world of business a variety of considerations may influence final choice.

Many executives claim that they make their important decisions on the basis of purely personal judgment and "hunch." On surface this may seem true — and in many cases, unfortunately, it is — but a careful analysis would show otherwise. A man who has specialized in the making of judgments under pressure may *seem* to be operating on a quick-appraisal-and-hunch basis, but actually his computer type of mind assigns weights and probabilities to the various elements and synthesizes all in a burst of quick judgment.

Let's start with some general principles of selection and then we shall see how the executive begins qualifying his cold judgments with some warmer ones.

Some General Principles of Selection

A very common basis of decision is to select that course of action which is expected to yield the greatest return for the least commitment or expenditure of resources, whether financial, material, human or temporal. This is the return-on-investment principle stated in sufficiently broad terms to make it applicable to almost every imaginable situation in the realm of profit-seeking, government administration, education and the dispensation of charity, among others.

While maximizing profit is the most common of the principles of selection, any other goals may be substituted. The decision-maker must then place some value on the nonfinancial goal so that he can assess the relative costs of achieving the goal under different alternatives.

A variant of the general principle stated above is: "With the same expenditure (of resources), which alternative is expected to lead to the greatest goal achievement?"

Another variant may be expressed this way: "With the same goal achievement, which alternative would require the least expenditure?"

You will note that in the stream of decision a very high order of priority must be assigned to the prerequisite decisions as to what your goals must be.

Both Ends against the Middle

In spite of the best efforts of the quantifiers and decision scientists we are very far from eliminating uncertainties. We may have to begin our decision-making by whittling down the possibilities until all that remains is an area of difficult choice. Then we begin narrowing down further by trying to feel out the position which will yield most satisfaction with least discomfort. In essence this is the ancient philosophical problem of trying to achieve a balance between pain and pleasure.

As an example of this kind of approach, systematized, I draw now from an article in the *American Economic Review* by Joseph E. Haring and Gorman C. Smith. Using an investment decision as their example, they trace the steps through which an investor can proceed logically to a final choice.

First, we must recognize that each investor has his own standards of acceptance or rejection of an investment opportunity. He thinks of an investment in terms of possible loss as well as possible gain. On the side of loss, he has a limit — a maximum acceptable loss — which may be called the *boundary loss*. On the side of gain, the project must be worthwhile in some minimum degree so we have the concept of *boundary gain* or minimum acceptable gain. The absolute values of these limitations will vary, of course, with the financial status of the investor and the amount required for the particular project.

Now each possible project has a range of possible outcomes or returns on the investment. The investor must evaluate these and match them against both the boundary loss and the boundary gain. Thus there are two conditions which must be met:

1. The lowest relevant outcome must be more attractive than the individual's boundary loss if he is not to be scared off by a risk which he cannot afford.

2. The highest relevant outcome must be greater than his boundary gain to provide enough incentive for risk.

In the course of looking for investment opportunities the individual may find some whose lowest and highest relevant outcomes may both fall on the side of loss or both on the side of gain, which may be expressed as "Either way you can't win" or "Either way you can't lose." Then, more usually, projects may entail both the risk of loss and gain. Ordinarily, the investor will narrow the field of selection by a scanning process. This consists of matching the possible outcomes against his minimum acceptable loss and his minimum acceptable gain. For those which survive this scanning, he needs to devise a decision rule or central value (which Haring and Smith call a "certainty-equivalent approximation" or CEA). If the same decision rule is used to compare a number of attractive possibilities, the selection then goes to that venture with the highest potential dollar return.

Once more I must reiterate a caution: while this process of analysis and selection should aid greatly in guiding you to a final decision, much still depends upon individual skill in collecting, arraying and analyzing the facts. As a sidelight on this, Haring and Smith describe a means of reaching the best estimate of the actual outcome of the investment. Within the range of the highest and lowest relevant outcomes, the best estimate, they state, is the mean (or average) of the subjective probability distribution (or your guesses as to high and low). As to how you can reach this estimate, they offer no additional aid other than to say that it must be done ". . . by securing more information, seeking advice and counsel, recalling in detail one's prior experiences along similar lines and other like measures."

The Human Factor

In the range of decisions, from great to small, one can scarcely escape the exercising of moral, ethical and humanistic judgments. Businessmen, at least in the larger corporate complexes, have become more than ever aware of considerations other than pure financial gain. We have come a long way since the days of the "robber barons" whose ethics were typified by the famous cry of "The public be damned."

When social and human factors are taken into account in the daily stream of managerial decision-making, we say that we are recognizing "the human factor." Unfortunately we tend to talk more about it than to act upon it. The emergence of staff specialists and efficiency experts carries with it built-in pressures for self-justification — for the demonstration of practical economies. (Having been in the business of promoting efficiency, I soon learned to put tongue in cheek as regards many of the recommendations of my compatriots. In the vein of the famous remark on the defense of self from enemies and friends, one is impelled to say, "I can take care of the money-wasters but Lord protect me from the money-savers!")

Let us take the case of the stenographic pool in an office which heretofore had not had this centralized service. One day a recommendation was made to economize on secretarial costs by transferring individual secretaries away from their bosses into a centralized stenographic pool. The central justification for this proposal was the savings in time — the full utilization of the girls' time in the service of many people as compared to the peaks and valleys of performance for one or even two supervisors.

A number of other justifications were marshaled in support of the basic one of economy. These included more professional supervision and training in stenographic and typing work as such, enforcement of official style standards, more uniform treatment and discipline of the girls and elimination of the many personal services and chores performed by individual secretaries for their individual supervisors. It was also suggested that, from the standpoint of the girls, the stenographic pool would offer greater stability of employment since their own status would not depend on the rise and fall of individual executives.

Note that the reasons in favor of the decision were largely impersonal and mechanistic. Aside from the possible advantage of offering the girls greater personal stability of employment, no consideration seems to have been given to the personal reactions of either the secretaries or the men affected and the consequences of their reactions.

In spite of the objections of the secretaries and their executive supervisors, the management decided to go ahead with this effort to achieve economies. After several months of operation under the new plan, the continued objections and complaints from those who had lost their private secretaries caused the management to take stock.

Down to the last man, the executives complained against the new arrangement. They could not have the benefit of secretarial assistance just at the time when they needed it most. They found themselves spending more time on clerical chores and on the writing out of longhand reports and communications and less time on the more essential duties for which they were being paid. In support of this argument they showed an increasing need for clerks to assume many of the duties previously performed by the secretaries.

What seemed to bother them most — and on this they had some difficulty in expressing themselves — was their sense of a loss of personal status. The establishment of the stenographic pool had not deprived all executives of their personal secretaries; the highest layers of management retained their privileges. The loss of a secretary was considered a sharp break in status like "separating the men from the boys." They felt their status reduced even further by having to plead for priority service from the pool supervisor, who became a power in her own right through the dispensation of favors of assignment. They felt even further demeaned by the independent attitude displayed by the individual stenographers who were now less amenable to acceding to the personal preferences of executives in how their work should be done.

The girls themselves were none too happy with the new arrangement, either, with a very few exceptions. It seemed that a couple of them were quite pleased to have an opportunity to come in contact with many men rather than just one or two. More generally, however, the girls complained quite frankly about their diminution of status. They felt that they had lost their individuality and now were uniform members of a small platoon or squad. They felt that the few secretaries who remained assigned to superior executives lorded a superior status over them. As part of their loss of individuality, they resented no longer having their own little domains in which to "keep house." Then, too, they bitterly resented having to work for another woman.

In addition to these subjective complaints, which seemed to rank uppermost, they had complaints of monotony, a loss of identification with the work, an inability to perform best service and catch errors because of their lack of understanding of the work and a loss of opportunity to use their minds rather than their hands alone.

The management was not sure how many of the complaints of the men and the stenographers were legitimate and how many of them constituted a counterattack. It was decided, however, that in either case there certainly was a loss of effectiveness. Moreover the alleged savings in secretaries did not seem to materialize to the extent promised. This was shown in the payroll records. Adding this, then, to the undoubted loss of effectiveness on the part of the executives, it was decided to reform the situation. The idea of a stenographic pool was not completely abandoned; instead, it was reserved as a means of accommodating overflows and for providing service to those who had only intermittent or occasional need for stenographers and typists.

Had the human-factor considerations been taken into account earlier, the original decision undoubtedly would not have been made.

The Second-Chance Factor

The irrevocable decision, the one which must work its course once it is made, comes the hardest. It is natural that it should be worried through and pretested from many different angles before it is committed. A much speedier choice can be made if the element of a second chance is introduced.

The second chance may take on at least two aspects: one is an opportunity to alter the action course and the other is an opportunity to cut one's losses. A variation is the opportunity to commit oneself in principle but to test the decision through a limited involvement or trial run.

Managements are more prone to commit themselves to important decisions when they can assign high-confidence factors to the performance and managerial abilities of their subordinates and their staffs. They are more likely to make decisions of greater risk when they know that those who carry them out will be in full control of the situations and will be alert to the earliest signs of error, deviation or failure which may call for immediate corrective action.

Considerations such as these may not be directly incorporated into the formulation of the central value or decision rule. Nevertheless, for the practical executive, they are of the utmost importance.

PERSONALITIES AND STRATEGIES

So long as decisions are made by men, rather than by machines, they will reflect both the force and limitations of personalities. They will show a relationship to goals which, sometimes, are far distant from the immediate situation.

Reflecting on his many years of experience in working with executives of many different types, Clarence B. Randall, former president and board chairman of the Inland Steel Company, made these comments in his book, *Freedom's Faith:**

"Some very able and conscientious men never make effective executives because their approach to difficult problems is judicial in its quality, rather than dynamic. They concentrate so exclusively on the necessity for doing the best thing that they do nothing.

"They lack the sense of urgency which is required in the fast-moving routine of modern administration. Wise as counselors, they perform an important function in cautioning their impetuous associates against pitfalls that otherwise might have been overlooked, but left to themselves they will never come up affirmatively with a positive program of action. Actually, in most business situations a half-dozen possible plans are proposed, any one of which would work reasonably well; and it is far more important to select one and get on with the job than it is to prolong the debate until the last shred of doubt as to which is the perfect best can be removed.

* Reprinted by permission of Little, Brown & Co.

"Then there are some men who fail as executives because making up their minds is torture to them. They have something close to physical fear as the time for that final tough choice approaches, and will twist and turn and accept any temporary expedient that will give them a little more postponement. When they can no longer escape, such men seek instinctively to hedge the risk of failure by communicating their decision to their subordinates in such equivocal languages that they can later claim they were right no matter what the outcome.

"Over and against these must be set the men who decide too quickly and too easily. There is no self-satisfaction in the world like that of little men when they make breath-taking decisions with the utmost calm. All that their associates can do is to shudder and go quietly back to their desks, shaking their heads. Happily, by the law of chance such men are occasionally right."

Avoidance and Postponement of Decision

One of the most widely followed rules of action is to make the decision by default. It may not be a conscious rule but it is nonetheless a mode of behavior. You can see it operating in the executive who is not able to get to a problem. Somehow he manages to find something which must take priority. In the subconscious hope that the problem might go away, he refers it to others for written comments. Eventually he might assign it to a committee. Whenever the problem comes back to him for decision, he finds something else that needs to be done or some new question that should be answered, for, obviously, the staff work has been far from perfect. Failing all else, having no other subterfuge through which to effect delay, he takes the situation in hand and counsels delay as a virtue in itself.

This is a topic which it would be most interesting to explore, but I am reminded that this is a chapter on the criteria of choice so I will limit myself to some brief comments on how to deal with choice by inaction.

The central problem, of course, is one of insecurity on the

part of the decision-maker. He may fear the unknown, he may fear failure and he may fear the consequences of having taken action even though it should be a successful action. The pernicious aspect of all this is that he may not actually be aware of his avoidance pattern. Instead, he may attribute it to a desire to make "the right decision."

Corrective action lies in getting at the cause of insecurity itself, which may actually lie completely outside of the decision situation. To begin with, I think we should rule out the deep-seated psychological blockages; these ordinarily require a clinical approach beyond the capabilities of the layman. Climate is a prerequisite to good decision-making. The participants need to know where they stand personally and how far they can exercise an authority of judgment. They need to know that their superiors recognize that "he who makes no mistakes makes no progress," to quote Theodore Roosevelt. That is, they must feel that they will be judged personally on the pattern of their performance rather than on the individual failures which may occur in any series of judgments.

In dealing with reluctance to move on the decision itself, assuming a good environment for the support of decision-making, the first important step is to be sure that the decision-maker knows as much as possible about the decision and about the consequences of the action. Of course this is part of the fact-finding discipline but it must not be taken for granted.

The next step is to press the decision-maker into at least a minor engagement within the arena of action. That is, if you're going to teach him to swim you're going to have to get him into the water at some point. The icy pool won't seem so cold and forbidding once you get him into it. Similarly, if you can get him to take some preliminary or trial actions, you then can move him along to successively deeper involvements.

Finally, there is nothing that succeeds so much as success. The decision-maker can actually become emboldened by building on his experience in particular kinds of situations as well as in coping with action problems generally.

For those who are not satisfied with anything short of per-

fectionism, I recommend the 90 + 9 + .9 formula. Usually
you can surround 90 per cent of the problem in no more time
— or even less — than it would take to dispose of the remaining
10 per cent. If you can make a 90-per-cent decision and begin
putting it into effect, you will then have pinned down at least
that much. Then, as soon as you begin grappling with the environment of action, you begin to learn much more about it
and you discover facts which will help you to dispose of the
remaining 10 per cent. This, in effect, constitutes a new problem, and now, again, you can dispose of 90 per cent with relative ease, in most cases. Thus in two steps you are up to 99 per
cent. If it's important enough you can repeat this once more
and get to 99.9 per cent.

Limitations upon Discretion

We have already discussed the problem of making decisions
within the boundaries of financial loss and gain. Additionally,
all elements in the environment of the particular decision assert their own influence or limitations upon the freedom of
discretion of the decision-maker. These include governmental
and political, social, physical, economic, technological and legal
constraints. More directly and more powerfully, the decision-
maker is held in check or guided by the authorities imposed
on him from above. While these might seem quite obvious,
they may also work their way quite imperceptibly, as will be
seen in an example given below, in the discussion of the person-
guided decision.

Assuming a "normally" responsive individual, the following
is an outline of some of the principal influences on his personal
decisions:

1. Situational limits over individual choice
   a. Ability of the individual to cope with problems and
   to solve them for himself
   b. Limited physical, functional or financial means
   c. Limited time
   d. The role of pure chance and its recognition by the individual

    e. Actions taken by others which force or guide the hand of the individual

2. Factors of logical decision-making

    a. Long- and short-run goals

    b. Recognition of an actual problem

    c. Understanding of one's operating environment and its impact upon oneself

    d. A set of identifiable personal values

    e. Knowledge of the pertinent facts in the situation and understanding of their meaning

    f. Recognition of the consequences of action

    g. Satisfaction of an expectation or outcome level which is higher than that which is exchanged for it whether in effort, materials, status or money

3. Nonlogical influences on decision-making

    a. Fear and avoidance of the unknown

    b. Decision by indecision or default because of a lack of personal direction or a resistance to change

    c. Emulation, conformism and submission; social implications of choice

    d. Conditions of acute stress for which the individual may not be adequately prepared

    e. Feeling one's way between pleasure and pain rather than reasoning one's way through

    f. Wishing that something were so and rationalizing its actuality; justification of the nonrational choice.

Much more subtle constraints are those which are imposed upon the executive by his subordinates. In a purely legalistic sense they do no controlling; they merely follow orders. In a practical sense they determine the way orders will be carried out. The mature executive knows this and plans his actions accordingly, even though he cannot acknowledge the necessity of doing so.

The implication of this, it follows, is that you do not take actions which are foredoomed to being frustrated or nullified by the reactions and inactions of your subordinates.

Your subordinates, as well as your colleagues, may constrain your actions in yet another way. If you are the object of their attention in some unfriendly way, they may monitor your every action for some evidence of omission or commission which might be used against you. It is a hard thought but, I am afraid, a realistic one. It is one of the lessons which responsible government executives learn, and hence they rarely initiate and conclude actions on their sole responsibility. They may pass upon the recommendations of their subordinates and they may refer matters to them for preparation of the necessary staff work and recommendations. The executive feels that he is in a much more protected position, especially as to controversial matters, if they have involved his staff in the normal course under normal procedures.

The Person-Guided Decision

Benjamin Nathan Cardozo, late Justice of the United States Supreme Court, said: "There is in each of us a stream of tendency that gives coherence and direction to thought and action." This idea has already been covered in our previous discussions on the predetermination of individual as well as group behavior. Another aspect of this, however, is that when this stream of tendency is sufficiently powerful or when people seem to find it, whether it exists or not, their own actions may be governed accordingly.

Writing in the *Administrative Science Quarterly*, R. M. Cyert, W. R. Dill and J. G. March give an interesting example of how a decision was influenced by how subordinates believed they perceived the attitudes of their management. The case involved the choice of consultants to advise on the installation of a data-processing system. Initially the management had made a decision to hire Alpha, who had made a very convincing and attractive proposal. At this point, however, someone suggested that it might be better to receive some additional proposals in order to make sure that the right choice was being made. After some further discussion the additional invitation was limited only to Beta, an older, larger and more widely known firm than

Alpha, although not so highly specialized in electronic data processing as Alpha.

As reported by the authors, the comparison of the two consulting firms showed Alpha to have the edge on price and on specialized competence whereas Beta's advantage was chiefly one of geography supported by their greater general reputation. The final decision recommended by the staff and adopted by the management was to hire Beta. The comptroller, who accepted their recommendation, said, "I asked the boys to set down the pros and cons. The decision was Beta. It was entirely their decision." When "the boys" were interviewed they gave a different story. They had the impression that the instructions to consider only one additional firm, Beta, after Alpha had already submitted its proposal, reflected a bias by the top management in favor of Beta. Since the differences between the two proposals were not marked, it was not very difficult for the staff members to be influenced in their interpretations of the data in favor of Beta.

The lesson for the manager, brought out by the example, is that if you desire a truly impartial decision you must lean backward to avoid giving any suggestion of the kind of recommendation you expect. In fact, you might occasionally find it necessary to emphasize that you want an absolutely impartial recommendation. Even if you do this you must still avoid any indication of your personal conclusions, because if you give them, your subordinates may regard the admonition on impartiality as mere cover.

When you are selecting and evaluating the facts yourself, you have a more difficult task of admonishing yourself to impartiality. Assuming you have not already made your mind up before you get the facts, you begin shaping your judgments from the very first sentence you read. In both reading and in conversation you can absorb information only in a linear sequence. The first information and the first impressions you acquire tend to tell you what to look for in your subsequent reading and listening. It may not at all be a conscious process so you must try particularly hard, consciously, to reserve your judgments until you have absorbed all of the pertinent facts and analyzed them thoroughly.

The Strategy-Guided Decision

"The ends pre-exist in the means," said Ralph Waldo Emerson. There is no separation of the one from the other. No matter what your goal, it will always be transformed in some degree, major or minor, by the means selected. Thus, in the selection of means, you eventually become what you do and not what you purport to wish to do.

The implication for the decision-maker is that he should never consider proposed actions without referring to the objectives with which they must be made consistent. Objectives which had been previously formulated and pronounced may no longer be valid in the light of changed conditions. On the other hand, all of the logic of the current situation may point to the taking of an action which requires that your objectives be re-examined and reformulated.

Some element of strategy enters into almost every decision involving people, to the extent that you must anticipate the actions they will take to compete with you or to nullify your own actions. More particularly, this is an aspect of the theory of games, touched on elsewhere in this book. Game theory has direct applicability in the marketplace, in the stock market and on the fields of battle. The strategy of the game is to anticipate the moves of your opponents and to best them by your own moves which are selected in accordance with probabilities of not being anticipated or overcome.

As examples of tactical and strategic moves, note the following:

1. Build an image in the minds of your opponents; establish and maintain a "front"; keep this up even in the face of gains by an opponent in order to throw him off.

2. Maintain your flexibility at all costs; limit your commitments so as to preserve your flexibility for future moves.

3. Throw your opponents off by planting false intelligence,

by making false moves and by otherwise using diversionary tactics; if the going gets rough, infiltrate an opponent's organization in order to plant diversionary intelligence.

4. Conserve and build one's resources for an all-out, massive attack.

5. Bleed your opponents by delaying and harassing tactics and by shifting your approach unexpectedly.

6. Seize the psychological moment for your own attack; strike while the iron is hot.

7. Anticipate your opponents in order that you may be at least one jump ahead.

8. Seize and maintain the initiative so that the game may be played under your own terms on your own field.

9. Overpower part of the opposition by building combinations, coalitions and mergers.

Pricing Decisions — as Examples

The setting of a price on a product is one of the most important decisions that can be made in free enterprise. For every product in every environment there is an optimum price above which you starve yourself out of the market and below which you deplete yourself into bankruptcy. Many factors are brought into play before a pricing decision is reached.

If you were guaranteed a market for your product and a reasonable profit, the computation of price would be quite simple. All you need to do is take all elements of cost and add a legitimate markup. The price will then vary only as you make changes in the product and as you build up its volume to the point beyond which there could be no further reductions in price. In the real market, however, there are two additional potent elements with which you must contend: one is market acceptance for your product at a price, and the other is competition by others for the same market.

With certain kinds of products which have established themselves in the market, there is a "right" price which the consumer expects to pay for that kind of product. In this instance the manufacturer must start at the retail price and work his way back through the distribution costs, through his own gross markup and then finally to the actual manufacturing cost. Assuming a certain volume which he believes he could market, he must then figure his costs to see whether they will or will not exceed the limit established by working backward. Plainly, they cannot be exceeded so if this should come out, he must take a new look at the product to see if it can be re-engineered or redesigned to fit the price limitation without losing its marketability.

Let's take another case, in which the product is already on the market at a given price and competition is undercutting the product. Now you can make quite a few different decisions. (1) You can do nothing, hoping that you have created an image for your product under your brand name and that you will retain your following. (2) You can cut your own prices on the same product, provided you have enough margin of profit to do so. (3) You can cut your prices and take a temporary loss to meet competition while you plan your next move. (4) You can drop the product entirely, leaving the field to your competitors. (5) You can redesign your own product either to reduce costs or to incorporate superior features at the same price or at a higher price than charged by your competitor. (6) You can make no changes in the existing product and its price but you can launch an impact advertising promotion to point out the superior advantages of your product. Each possible decision you might reach will bring into play a whole new chain of subsidiary decisions, and all the time you are working on them you will be trying to anticipate the next moves of your competitors.

You might follow an entirely different strategy if you want to "buy" a market. You might consider it cheaper to drop your normal profit and even to budget a loss if you consider it part of the cost of entering a new field. It is a risky procedure, for you might be pegging yourself at a cost level which it might be difficult to exceed materially later on.

If you have a unique item which in itself has no direct competition, your tendency may be to charge what the market will bear. This is an aspect of monopolistic pricing. One technique is to sample different markets with the same product, charging different prices to see what the percentage of return is on each marketing effort. If the product is sufficiently unique, differences in price might have only a marginal effect on the purchase appeal for the consumer. Later on, if competition enters the field, you might need to readjust the price to meet both competition and the price level which the market thinks is "right."

In their book *Pricing In Big Business*, Doctors A. D. H. Kaplan, Joel D. Dirlam and Robert F. Lanzillotti cite the case of how the General Electric Company determined the price of a night light. There already were various night lights on the market selling for about 59¢ by the millions. GE decided that there might be a market for something of better construction at a higher price. The initial assumption as to a "right" price for an impulse item of this kind was that it should go for about 98¢. The product which GE engineers brought forth, however, could not be marketed profitably at that price. The situation, therefore, had to be restudied. It was found that the lowest price would be reached when production hit 100,000 night lights. Above this figure there could be no reduction in price on the unit.

Since the proposed new night light would be about twice as expensive as the low-priced units already on the market, it would be necessary to obtain a preferred display on dealers' counters and this could not be achieved readily unless there were sufficient incentive for them, pricewise, to give it preferred display.

GE's cost experts then made some additional calculations. They figured out how many units would have to be sold at four different prices — $.99, $1.09, $1.19, and $1.29 — to yield the same profit to GE. They found that it would take four times as many sales at the 99¢ figure to yield the same profit as at the $1.29 figure. Obviously, if the public would accept the price, the $1.29 figure would be the one to choose.

To find the answer to this question, GE conducted retailing

tests in several different cities. These showed that price variations in the range from 99¢ to $1.29 did not materially affect sales for a superior night light at a price of $1.29. The finally selected price of $1.29 therefore satisfied a number of important conditions: it yielded enough profit for the retailer to give a little extra push, it was profitable to manufacture and distribute, and it was not so expensive as to make it profitable for the customer to shop around for a lower-priced item of reasonably comparable quality.

DEVELOPING TANGIBLE MEASURES OF CHOICE

Most decisions lend themselves to having their outcomes expressed tangibly, if only to say "less than" or "more than" or "as much as." When you quantify you achieve greater objectivity.

Here we are concerned with the quantification of the simpler choices, where the variables are not very great in number, the alternatives are not many and the variables are not fluidly interrelated.

Ranking and Weighting

The simplest way to establish an order of preference is to rank the possible choices according to some governing rule: greatest satisfaction of a defined goal, greatest return on investment or greatest personal satisfaction. We normally think in terms of positive preferences, but there are times when we choose that course which yields least pain, loss or inconvenience.

Actually there may be many pros and cons even in a simple ranking of A is better than B is better than C, etc. They are often recognized and computed quickly in the mind — at least in those situations where the wrong choice does not matter too much or where the distinctions are sharply defined.

Where the alternatives are not clearly separated — and where they are many — the separating process can be helped by grouping the alternatives, two, three or four together, and then comparing the groups of related choices. This, at least, helps narrow the choice to a cluster of marginally different alternatives. This is an approach which helps when you must choose from among many people or things. A woman might find it aids in choosing shoes or a hat — if she *really* wants to choose!

The next step in refining the ranking of alternatives is to assign weights. If I like A, B and C in that order, how much more than B do I like A and how much more than C do I like B? A lot? A little? Very much? How much more than "a lot" is "very much"? An engineer said: "When the pressure is sufficiently low . . ." To which the client retorted: "How do I know when I reach the point called 'sufficiently'?"

One method of assigning numerical values is to take the heaviest choice and assign it a value of 10. The next heaviest choice is then given a value by comparison with 10. The third may then be rated by comparison with the first alone or with both the first and second. And so on.

A variation is to rate the lowest by comparison with the highest, which, again, may be given a value of 10. Then the intermediate choices are given ratings.

This brings up the question of "Why bother?" if you have already identified the heaviest choice — the one with the greatest return. If all choices had an equal opportunity of success, you could stop there, but to each may be attached a probability value of success or failure. Accordingly, you might choose a lower payoff by coupling it with a higher probability of success. It's like betting on a horse to win, place or show.

To combine the desirability and probability ratings of each alternative, you multiply one by the other. Then you rank the new values according to their converted scores. We'll have an example of this later.

The ranking and weighting technique is also applied to evaluation of the various factors that lie behind an alternative. First, you rank and weight the factors, in general. This gives you a score card or matrix against which to evaluate each of the possible choices, factor by factor. The ratings for all of the factors are added to give you a single numerical score.

This technique can be used by anyone who is able to perform simple addition, multiplication and division. No advanced mathematical skills are required.

To illustrate, let us assume a choice is to be made from among three candidates for promotion. (The same technique could be used for leasing, selecting a new product, buying equipment, etc.) It is an important position, so an executive committee has been formed to pool judgments. The first thing done is to list the elements or factors on which each candidate is to be rated. For purposes of brevity let's limit the list to five:

> *(A.) Maturity*
> *(B.) Technical competence*
> *(C.) Personal relations*
> *(D.) Managerial skill*
> *(E.) Seniority*

Each of these elements is then given a relative weight. Because the judgments are subjective, the group mind is useful in balancing out differences. (It also helps clarify what is needed in the position.) How the weights are scaled does not really matter. What is important is that they bear the proper relation to each other. Thus they can be rated on a scale of 100 or 10 or 1 — or anything else.

The group decides (you can also do it alone, if you prefer!) that "managerial skill" is most important and is therefore to be rated 10. "Personal relations" is considered to be almost as important in this situation and is therefore given a rating of 8. These two elements are then judged to account for about 60 per cent of the final decision, so the remaining 40 per cent must be distributed among the other three elements (Since 18 is 60 per cent, you then find by simple arithmetic that the remaining 40 per cent covers 12 points.) *A* is rated 4, *B* is rated 3 and *E* is rated 5.

Now each of the weights is reduced to a proportion of 1.00.

This is done by dividing each by 30, with the following results:

$$A \ (\ 4) \ = \ .133 = \ .13$$
$$B \ (\ 3) \ = \ .100 = \ .10$$
$$C \ (\ 8) \ = \ .267 = \ .27$$
$$D \ (10) \ = \ .333 = \ .33$$
$$E \ (\ 5) \ = \ .167 = \ .17$$
$$\text{(Total)} \quad \overline{(30)} \quad \overline{1.00} \ = \ \overline{1.00}$$

Note that the elements should now be rearranged in the order *D, C, E, A* and *B,* but, for simplicity, we'll still follow the alphabet.

The next step is to rate each candidate on each element. For this purpose a scale of 0 to 10 is used, with 10 standing for "ideal" or perfect. A comparison of the group judgments for each candidate is shown in the following table. The individual candidate ratings (raw scores) are multiplied by the previously assigned weights and then added to produce the final weighted scores.

		MAN 1		MAN 2		MAN 3		MAN 4	
		Raw	Weighted	Raw	Weighted	Raw	Weighted	Raw	Weighted
Element	Weight	Score	Score	Score	Score	Score	Score	Score	Score
(A)	.13	4	.52	7	.91	6	.78	7	.91
(B)	.10	9	.90	5	.50	7	.70	6	.60
(C)	.27	6	1.62	8	2.16	9	2.43	1	.27
(D)	.33	3	.99	8	2.64	2	.66	10	3.30
(E)	.17	5	.85	3	.51	8	1.36	10	1.70
		27	4.88	31	6.72	32	5.93	34	6.78

It would seem that the decision should go to Man 4, since he is high on both raw and weighted scores. In this case, however, the management committee hesitates and decides to pass him over because of his unacceptably low score on human relations, particularly since he is only a hair's breadth ahead of Man 2. In the rather active discussion it is recognized that the ratings on each element were highly personal, subject to considerable error, so some final review of this kind is in order. The choice goes to Man 2, and a conference is held with Man 4 to point out his need for improvement.

Thus you see that the measurement tool is only just that; it does not make a decision for you automatically. Note also that Man 3 has a higher raw score but a lower weighted score than Man 2, which points up how weighting alters the results.

Balancing Desirability with Probability

A more sensitive weighting of elements is that in which you combine a scale of desirability with a scale of probability. This is the art of going for win, place or show. It is the balancing of most pleasure with least pain.

In the simpler cases you look for the most desirable results but you are willing — in fact, strongly predisposed — to take less than the best for the most probable. Thus, commonly, most people prefer lower pay in exchange for greater job security. What we try to do is select that course which maximizes the return without taking away substantially from the minimum assurances, at least. (A maximin or minimax criterion would seek to maximize the minimum gain or minimize the maximum risk.)

As a business executive you may want to ply a course of conservatism, going after "sure things." That is, you may choose the least desirable course which still yields a favorable rate of return. On the other hand, you may pursue a course of optimism, choosing the alternative which may yield the most favorable results. Or you may try for something in between.

Another approach is to ascertain the most probable result. Then, if the expected return is not adequate, you may reexamine your approach to see whether it — or the conditions — may be altered in some way to improve the chances of return. In fact, this is more likely to be the case than selection from sharply defined and fixed alternatives.

In the example given above — the selection of a candidate for promotion — we went through a series of steps which combined two different scales of evaluation where the elements are fairly well known and measurable. Now we will go through an example of the combining of probability with profitability.

Roger E. Ball and Allan A. Gilbert of the management consultant firm of George Frye and Associates, writing in *Business Horizons,* suggest a technique for relating probability to expectations. For our purposes I have abridged and simplified their case. A hypothetical case is used of a manufacturer faced with the necessity of providing production facilities for a new product. The estimated sales of the product were 125,000 units a year. The plant manager proposed to produce that many (but no more) by rebuilding an obsolete turret lathe, already owned.

The president considered other possibilities: buy a new lathe, with a capacity of 175,000 units a year, or do both. He also drew from the sales department an admission that other possible sales forecasts could be made and that, if anything, the first forecast was conservative. A new set of estimates was made setting forth the probability of different levels of sales. These probabilities are shown in the table given below.

The controller then figured the *marginal gross profit* for the production levels which would follow. These, too, are shown in the table. (Marginal gross profit is the amount remaining after deducting additional out-of-pocket production costs from total additional sales income.)

Let's now look at how this information is displayed before these two measures of probability and desirability are combined.

Reading across, the top row shows the possible levels of production. The second row is the estimated probability for

MARGINAL-GROSS-PROFIT DECISION MATRIX

Production Rate Per Period	25,000	75,000	125,000	175,000	225,000	Expectation
Probability	.12	.23	.30	.23	.12	
Alternatives						
Convert Turret Lathe	3,530	10,800	18,000	18,000*	18,000*	— — —
Buy Automatic Lathe	3,370	10,800	18,000	25,000	25,000*	— — —
Do Both	3,220	10,500	17,800	25,000	32,000	— — —

* If productive capacity were available, potential sales would support production rates at these levels. However, gross marginal profits are actually limited to the figures shown by the inadequate production capacity of the machine.

reaching each indicated level. The remaining three rows show the anticipated gross marginal profit for each alternative. Note the starred footnote which explains the leveling off at the end of the "convert" and "buy" alternatives.

This is the "raw" table. It shows, for example, that if sales were at the level of 125,000 as first estimated, either of the first two alternatives would yield the same return and either would be slightly better than "do both." (Remember that the turret lathe's output is limited to 125,000.) Beyond 125,000 units, the "do both" alternative comes into its own; at 175,000, it ties for first place; and at 225,000 it is clearly ahead.

For the president, however, this analysis had one drawback: it showed the return for any given probability but it did not show which had the greatest over-all chance of realizing the highest marginal gross profit. To find this out, he multiplied each of the marginal-gross-profit figures by the probability figure. He also added these products across the table to arrive at the totals shown in the "expectation" column.

EXPECTATION-OF-MARGINAL-GROSS-PROFIT DECISION MATRIX

Production Rate Per Period	25,000	75,000	125,000	175,000	225,000	Expectation
Probability	.12	.23	.30	.23	.12	
Alternatives						
Convert Turret Lathe	420	2,480	5,400	4,140	2,160	14,600
Buy Automatic Lathe	400	2,480	5,400	5,750	3,000	17,030
Do Both	390	2,420	5,340	5,750	3,840	17,740

The gross expectation for each alternative — the one which has the greatest dynamic potential — is clearly the third: to do both. Note that the expectations from the second and third alternatives are not so far apart that management might not let other considerations play a deciding role, including cash position, equipment, delivery and space availability, among others. Moreover, management might decide to move into the third alternative by phases — buying or repairing first. In short, quantification is but a tool for further thinking.

Bear in mind, too, that "hardness" of the results of quantification depends mainly on the precision with which initial measurements are made. In this case the potentially soft element is the forecast of sales. How is management to estimate this with accuracy and dependability? It is clear that the best advice from the most informed sources will be needed. If you are tempted to disparage the quantified decision-making because of the softness of a main ingredient, consider that without the pressure of a logically ordered process, your "guesstimate" could be much softer and wilder.

Simple Scales and Tallies

Turning now to another technique, a relatively simple way to compare alternatives or to rate situations against a standard is to set up a check list with weighted rating scales, like this:

	(1) Weight	(2) Raw Score	(3) Weighted Score
Item A	(3)	1 • 2 • 3 • 4 • 5 • 6 • 7 • 8 • 9 • 10 •	18
Item B	(1.5)	1 • 2 • 3 • 4 • 5 • 6̄ • 7 • 8 • 9 • 10 •	6
Item C	(2)	1 • 2 • 3 • 4̄ • 5 • 6 • 7 • 8̲ • 9 • 10 •	16

$$3\overline{\big)\,40}$$

Final Score 13.3

for as many items as needed. The total of the weighted scores is then divided by the number of items to obtain the final score.

A different approach is used with a tally of gains and losses. You are after an absolute value, usually a dollar value. Each item is expressed as a predictable gain or loss. There is no weighting. The total is then the estimated gain or loss.

CONCLUSION

This chapter included a presentation of techniques for rendering the basis of decision as tangible as possible. It also covered criteria for evaluating the available alternatives and selecting from among them. These would seem to be logical approaches, but, in themselves, do not go far enough. One must take into account the human factors at work within the situation and the forces and limitations which they exert upon the decision-maker. In some measure these are always present and, hence, they must be identified and evaluated when one tries to delineate the total logic of the situation.

Chapter V

HOW TO REACH AGREEMENT

A typical experience in bringing decisions to a head runs like this:

1. You have worked out a proposed action to the point where you are ready to obtain the agreement or concurrences of others.

2. You believe you perceive the problem and its solution quite clearly, but you find that others do not share your understanding of one or both and therefore will not agree.

3. You then try to reach agreement by (a) saying the same thing differently or (b) proposing alternative actions.

The second item is the stumbling block. Who can say how many good ideas are lost because of the inability of men to agree as to ends or means? The enterprise is fortunate which is able to channel its prime energies into collective achievement of common goals.

Unfortunately the road blocks to agreement can not be removed solely by procedural means. You need to reach into the bases of understanding and into the very motivations of men — both conscious and subconscious.

THE BARRIERS TO AGREEMENT

In any organization, no matter how good its teamwork, the main barrier to understanding is usually a kind of functional provincialism: a tendency to see problems from one's specialized viewpoint. Coupled with this is an inability to place oneself in the position of others whose viewpoints are shaped by the perspective of different kinds of specialized responsibility.

Overcoming Functional Barriers

From the same conference presentation or from the same written reports, different meanings may be drawn by the production boss, accountant, director of personnel, legal advisor, public-relations officer and general-planning officer, to name a few. Each wears a pair of spectacles that is tinted by his own specialized experiences and goals. Each may have a legitimately different viewpoint. The task then is to blend ideas into a common product. Often, however, there are real differences, due to actual misunderstandings, which cannot be reconciled except by changing of attitudes or positions.

To make matters worse, people who have subspecialized within the same technical fields sometimes have difficulty understanding each other. Think of all the fields of specialization in engineering, law, economics, medicine, etc., and of the subfields within each of these!

People who work in specialized fields build up a jargon of their own — a kind of technical slang. Words and expressions carry special meanings but only within the particular work context. The same words may convey little or nothing to the uninitiated. Our ability to attach new meanings to language was well put by Lewis Carroll in *Through the Looking-Glass:*

"When I use a word," Humpty Dumpty said in rather a scornful tone, "it means just what I choose it to mean — neither more nor less."

"The question is," said Alice, "whether you *can* make words mean so many different things."

"The question is," said Humpty Dumpty, "which is to be master — that's all."

To cope with differences in functional understanding, you need to bring the parties into mutual contact as early as possible. All four of Mary Parker Follett's principles of coordination seem particularly appropriate here:

1. Coordination by direct contact of the responsible people concerned.
2. Coordination in the early stages.
3. Coordination as a reciprocal relating of all the features in a situation.
4. Coordination as a continuing process.

Techniques of enabling the parties to understand each other's contributions, understandings, reactions and problems include job rotation, attendance at staff conferences and seminars, attendance at briefing sessions and distribution of copies of internal documents.

Misunderstandings can be fended off through informal communication between the parties before conferences in order to throw light on possible differences. Positive statements should be avoided in the early stages of negotiation, for they make it difficult to retreat from error. A better positive approach first identifies the goals of the separate parties and then seeks to get agreement as to these. This must be followed by progressive examination of areas of both agreement and disagreement.

Coping with Strategic and Tactical Barriers

The idealized theme of group process is teamwork: men working and pulling together for the common cause, subordinating their separate interests. It is an odd thing, but one rarely encounters anyone who is opposed to teamwork. All that he may want is *his* brand of teamwork, perhaps under *his* control, but always on *his* terms. To achieve his brand of teamwork, it might even be necessary to push someone aside — with more or less vigor. Inevitably this brings on a counterattack by those who do not feel quite ready for the heap.

Conflict and cooperation actually are intimately interrelated, for out of the two, in a wholesome context, issues progress. For this to happen, men must face their problems openly and frankly, expressing their opposing views and eagerly seeking the good in them.

Competition turns into unwholesome conflict when people substitute the pursuit of their selfish interests for the goals of the enterprise. Negotiations are then conducted on a dual plane: on one level the parties debate their official differences while subsurface they press their private interests and selfish goals.

When issues deepen, men may fall back upon personal power alignments in order to advance their positions. At the same time, they may also resort to negative obstruction. In its simplest form this is the mere withholding of consent or concurrence. There seems to be no limit, however, to the more insidious forms. Some years ago I was reading a book, *Systematic Sociology*, by Leopold von Wiese and Howard Becker (New York, John Wiley & Sons, Inc.) in which the authors had compiled an amazing catalogue of the many methods and degrees of contravening action. What follows is an abbreviation. In general *contravention* includes rebuffing, repulsing, working against, hindering, restraining, protesting, obstructing or otherwise upsetting another's plans. *Simple contraventive action* includes public disavowal of another person's statement, lampooning, putting the burden of proof on another, intentionally humiliating, snubbing or ignoring, blaming, accusing, reproaching, disparaging, challenging, defying, disapproving, imputing questionable motives, withholding assent, presenting contrary views, etc. Men's ingenuity is evidently not exhausted, for *intensified contraventive activity* includes exposing, faultfinding, maliciously criticizing, frustrating and scorning. The *secret forms of contravention* include snooping, circumventing, denouncing secretly, covertly thwarting, betraying and secretly disposing of the other party. Under a *tactical* heading come harassing, annoying or perturbing by any means whatever, provoking indiscreet utterance, starting whispering campaigns, etc.

As the executive matures he learns to recognize the crosscurrents in the interpersonal underworld of the office. The younger and less experienced ones may be unable to accept the realities of such behavior. I am reminded of an incident in my class in executive leadership at The American University in Washington, D.C. I had shown the motion picture *Patterns*, written by Rod Serling, a realistic portrayal of the inhumane treatment of men by men on the altars of corporate ambition. In the ensuing discussion my students, all of them, were unable to accept the story as a reasonable one. They felt that such things do not occur in real life. Unfortunately, unless they learn these realities as they advance to higher posts, they remain ill-equipped to recognize and cope with intrigue.

These forces of disruption can be rooted out through positive example and through forceful disavowal. The wise executive discourages talebearers and voluntary informers. He refuses to reach understandings affecting parties who are not present and, more important, he makes a point of this way of doing business.

In our eagerness to understand intrigue let's not forget the ordinary garden variety of obstruction: simple resistance to any change. We grow accustomed to the *status quo* and we will defend it against its challengers. We may not like the existing power and status lineup, but we may prefer it to the uncertainties of organizational change. The corrective for this is participation of those affected — a topic to be discussed below.

Then there is an entirely different class of antagonisms which arise out of clashes in personality — differences in temperament, predispositions to fight, the nursing of old sores, etc. The executive's approach here may be to try to bring the parties together in constructive interaction. Somehow antagonisms are often dissolved when men get to know each other better through close, cooperative relationships. (But sometimes you're better off not knowing some personalities from too close a range!)

The intrigue content of organizations tends to vary inversely with the challenge of the job content. Where people are engaged in creative work or where tasks require professional and technical insights and experience, these seem to absorb much of the energy that otherwise flows into conspiratorial activity. On the other hand, people whose job content contains no creative challenge, and whose experience has centered substantially in negotiation and interpersonal relationships, seem to be more predisposed toward intrigue.

Organizations which are not expected to have a long life seem to be characterized by an opportunistic spirit. The ambitious ones recognize that time is against them, and hence they feel they must move quickly and boldly.

Again, the challenge is to the principal executives to set a pattern by their own leadership. The spirit of antagonism can be thwarted by the challenges of activity sponsored by the leadership. Busy minds can have little time for intrigue.

Some organizations seem to be ruled by a prevailing spirit of cooperation or antagonism. Whichever it is, it grows and is handed down as a way of survival which the newcomers to the organization must learn. The newcomer or the outsider can actually feel the spirit of the organization.

THE TACTICS OF AGREEMENT

How often have you heard or used the expression "What does he *really* want?" Your experience in negotiating tells you that men purport to want certain things while they are at the same time trying to cover their personal hidden objectives. The hidden objectives may be quite wholesome, or, at least, their proponent may believe them to be wholesome. You might ask yourself: "What will it take to meet his real objectives, without compromising mine seriously and how can I present my suggestions without making it obvious that I know his true aims?" A more straightforward question would be: "What is the critical point on which agreement will depend?" You may ponder whether you will be able to obtain unanimity or whether you must agree to disagree. These are the kinds of problems to which we now turn.

The Conditions of Acceptance

In the usual decision-making situation a number of people are given an opportunity to comment on a proposed action.

After some give and take they must finally agree or disagree. Their attitudes may range from enthusiastic acceptance to violent resistance. Somewhere in between lies a "zone of indifference," to use a term coined by Chester I. Barnard in a different context. Now our question is: why do people oppose or accept proposed actions?

People are likely to accept and lend active support to decisions of the following types:

1. Actions which contribute to the reaching of important goals, where the individual identifies himself with the organizational goals.

2. Actions which further the interests of the individual, whether official or personal.

3. Actions which would seem "right" because they accord with the way things are done — the governing code — or because the facts and their logical analysis are overpowering.

4. Actions which represent the mode, the group will — especially where conformism seems important or where the individual has participated with others in achieving a group mind which now he feels obliged to support.

There are decisions which people, at times, cannot accept because they contradict certain important values. These include:

1. Actions which endanger organizational goals and organizational security where the individual senses his responsibility to the organization.

2. Actions which seriously endanger the personal security of the individual.

3. Actions which would violate what the individual considers to be an important standard of behavior or of performance.

4. Actions which violate or challenge the essential logic of the situation and which simply do not comport with the facts.

5. Actions which run contrary to the group will or the group mode, especially where the individual identifies himself with the development of the group position.

In the zone of indifference lie those decisions which do not constitute enough of an incentive or a deterrent, either way, to cause the individual to make too much of an effort. He might actually feel some marginal opposition to the proposed course of action, yet he will conclude to go along with it because he does not want to be regarded as an obstructionist or because he wants to devote his energies to things which are more important to him. He is willing to lend his support to these decisions because he hopes that he will receive the same kind of support from others on some future matter which *does* concern him very much.

This brings up the category of tactical acceptance, covering situations such as the following:

1. Where agreement on the current matter constitutes a delaying action — a matter of not showing one's hand until a more appropriate time or until a really effective counterattack can be launched.

2. Where agreement constitutes a form of trading-off — where you are willing to accept something a little bitter in return for something a little sweeter.

Acceptance of a decision should lead, naturally, to final agreement — to final, inner commitment. Otherwise one does not have true acceptance and true agreement.

The Meaning of Agreement

An agreement is not worth the paper on which it is written unless it is clear not only as to the meaning of its words but as to its spirit and intent. When Prime Minister Chamberlain of Great Britain returned from Munich waving his umbrella and crying "Peace in our time!" he believed he had an agreement which would assure the peace. How wrong he was is a matter of history; the fallacy of the agreement was that Chamberlain felt that he had bought peace while Hitler knew that he had won more ground as well as time to prepare for his next move. There are other possibilities: that Chamberlain thought he was avoiding disagreement or postponing it.

Sometimes when men are unable to reach an accord they will engineer a kind of surface agreement. They set forth broad generalizations to which they may all subscribe, followed by statements which very carefully avoid commitment on the critical elements which remain unsettled. This is sometimes referred to as face-saving, but all the parties know that they cannot really face themselves.

You should be wary of anyone who proposes specific language which he insists must be incorporated without change. The insistence may be in good faith, but caution dictates that you look for hidden meanings. Likewise you must be wary of insistence that it is not necessary to cover certain details which *you* believe to be critical.

One other aspect of the insincere agreement is built-in nullification. This occurs when one provision is set aside by another part of the written document. The second provision may either be contradictory or excessively liberal or excessively restrictive. It may even include impossible conditions.

A safeguard against vagueness is to make a "dry run" of a series of trial situations to see how they would be handled under the proposed understanding.

At some point you should reach an understanding of the matters on which you are in agreement and those on which you are in disagreement. Then you must find some basis of resolving differences without yielding on the essential correctness of the positions of the parties.

Pathways to Agreement

To agree is to "come into harmony" or to "be of one mind." In the cluster of synonyms relating to the reaching of a group mind, "agree" is listed by the Funk & Wagnalls *New Practical Standard Dictionary of the English Language* as the most general term of the group ". . . while to *concur* is to *agree* in general; to *coincide* is to *agree* in every particular. One *accepts* another's terms, *complies* with his wishes, *admits* his statement, *approves* his plan, *conforms* to his views of doctrine or duty, *accedes* or *consents* to his proposal. *Accede* expresses the more formal agreement, *consent* the more complete. One may silently *acquiesce* in that which does not meet his views, but which he does not care to contest."

One could list other synonyms but these are sufficient to show the degree of mind-reaching. Perhaps this listing may help in judging the extent to which agreement is actually reached.

In their book *Society* (New York, Rinehart & Company, Inc., 1949) Robert M. MacIver and Charles H. Page discuss four means of reaching decisions. These are:

    1. Authority
    2. Compromise
    3. Enumeration
    4. Integration

To these I would like to add:

    5. Determination

Decision by *authority* is a matter of dominance. The decision leader expresses his personal judgment as constituting the will of the group. Hence, the term *authoritarian state*. Active participation by the members of the group is not really sought even though some of the forms of participation may be observed. The role of the participants really is to acquiesce or to assist.

In decision by *compromise* there is an actual give and take. The participants bargain with each other, each yielding from his original position until some point is reached where each gets enough to satisfy him and does not give up too much to pain him. Then the participants express their formal unanimity. The reaching of a compromise is a widespread and popular means of reaching agreements. It is regarded as the "democratic way." Unfortunately the compromise often fails to reconcile the basic differences which continue to keep the parties at odds with each other. They regard the compromise as a point of departure for the future in the hope that they, respectively, will reach their divergent goals. Since one cannot ride the horse simultaneously in all directions, the consequence of compromise is often reflected in continued strain and turmoil.

By *enumeration* is meant the taking of a vote. That course of action which receives the majority — or sometimes plurality — of votes is taken as the group decision. While this is common practice in legislatures, it is often used in boards and committees. The fallacy, of course, is that the opinion of the majority does not necessarily represent the right opinion. The majority can be wrong. The good organization man will accept a decision in which he is outvoted and try to put it into effect, but this may not deter him as well as others who are less compliant from seeking to upset the decision in the future. Admittedly it is difficult for the leader to overrule the majority vote. This is why I suggest the fifth category, below, of "determination."

The method of *integration* has been proposed as the ideal means of achieving sweet harmony. The motivation of the group is to find the course of action which best expresses the group desires. There is no question of who gains and who loses; rather, the group interest, as a sort of corporate personality, is the dominant consideration. Differences are not suppressed, nor are they compromised or voted upon. Instead, they are all brought out and integrated.

This has always seemed to me to be an ideal toward which one strives but, recognizing the imperfections of man, an ideal which is rarely achieved. At least four elements tend to work against the ideal: time as a scarce commodity; the necessarily authoritarian structure of business organizations (as well as government organizations); the inability of the leading executive in the situation to communicate privileged information; and the differences (and imbalances) among the personalities.

Unfortunately for the ideal approach, at some timely point a decision must be reached. It's worth noting, as a side comment, that "to decide" literally means to cut off discussion — or so the dictionary says. Eventually, then, a person of senior authority must bring the matter to a head, reconciling the unresolved issues himself.

The role of authority in administration is often misunderstood by subordinates who may feel that the making of a decision at a higher level bespeaks a lack of confidence in them.

What they often fail to realize is that the delegation of responsibility does not relieve the superior officer or executive of any of his personal responsibility for getting a job done. It is analogous to subleasing: there is an ultimate tenant who is held accountable for the property.

It reminds me of an incident involving two vice presidents of a large corporation, one superior to the other. The subordinate had proposed the establishment of a new department; the superior went along with the idea even though he disagreed and expressed his doubts as to the wisdom of the move. The decision was carried out and subsequently it was found to be a faulty one. When the senior officer was asked why he did not permit his original judgment to prevail, he stated his belief, shared by the subordinate, that you can't overrule a man at that level without obliging him to resign. Now this may be true in some rare cases, but the issue is ordinarily not created unless the subordinate brings this about on a vital issue, making it clear that a negative decision will be a judgment of no confidence.

The superior officer is accountable ultimately and therefore has a special obligation to himself to assert his personal judgments. It is not the group mind which will be held accountable if something goes wrong; it is the leader who will be taken to task.

Another reason for the exercise of a personal judgment by the executive is the possession by him of privileged information. In his superior role he does see things in a different light. He is usually aware of considerations which extend beyond the immediate situation and he is usually better able to see it in its broader perspective. Additionally, he knows of other decisions or events or instructions which have been communicated to him in confidence. Although he will not want to appear arbitrary — or stupid — he may not be able to explain his decision satisfactorily.

The idealized pursuit of agreement by integration seems not to take into account the highly variable outputs of the participants in a decision-making situation. Some will be passive and some active. Some will argue from facts and some will press their opinions or even their prejudices. Some will speak their minds independently while others will align themselves with the prevailing strengths of judgment. Anyone who has had any substantial experience in getting work done through others cannot help but be impressed by the remarks of Dr. Robert N. McMurry, president of the McMurry Company of Chicago, industrial psychologists, made in the course of an interview conducted by *Management Methods* magazine. Dr. McMurry said:

". . . Twenty-five years of work in the management field have proved to me that members of lower, middle and even top management are dependent, insecure and ineffective. They don't want to — and won't — think for themselves.

"Most people will produce because they are bossed by a strong, driving executive who defines and structures their jobs for them, who makes his expectations clear. The sooner top executives recognize this fact, the sooner they'll be able to communicate effectively."

For another point of view in support of executive strength and decisiveness, this is what Professor Douglas McGregor of the School of Industrial Management, Massachusetts Institute of Technology, had to say upon retiring from his position as president of Antioch College:

"I believed [before coming to Antioch] . . . that a leader could operate successfully as a kind of adviser to his organization. I thought I could avoid being a 'boss.' Unconsciously, I suspect, I hoped to duck the unpleasant necessity of making difficult decisions, of taking the responsibility for one course of action among many uncertain alternatives, of making mistakes and taking the consequences. I thought that maybe I could operate so that everyone would like me — that 'good human relations' would eliminate all discord and argument.

"I couldn't have been more wrong. It took a couple of years, but I finally began to realize that a leader cannot avoid the exercise of authority any more than he can avoid responsibility for what happens to his organization. In fact, it is a major function of the top executive to take on his own shoulders the responsibility for resolving the uncertainties that are always involved in important decisions. Moreover, since no important decision ever pleases everyone in the organization, he must also absorb the displeasure, and sometimes severe hostility, of those who would have taken a different course."

The executive has a unique contribution to make which is different from that of ordinary participants. He is the one who is held accountable for results and he, accordingly, must monitor and shape the making of the decision in that light.

I do not suggest that the executive or manager must accomplish his tasks by asserting an iron rule or by being quite peremptory in his judgments. Quite the contrary, if he is to develop initiative in his subordinates, he must encourage them to voice their opinions and proposed solutions to problems and he must get them to feel that their contributions are both desired and taken into account. Otherwise he will fail to develop his staff and he will tend to lower their morale.

This brings us to the method of reaching decisions by *determination*. The executive (or accountable decision-maker) seeks out and encourages full participation by all appropriate parties. He brings them together, if necessary, and he encourages the exchange and synthesis of views. He seeks ideal integration but he also brings the issues to a head, finally, and resolves them according to his own judgments, in line with his superior authority. This is participation and it is consultation. It is not democratic administration nor is it authoritarian.

Obviously, in decision by determination the accountable decision-maker must be able to exercise an authority over all the participants. If this is not the case he cannot make a determination. Instead, his role is to get the group to agree as to the areas of disagreement so that these may then be resolved under one of the procedures covered in the subsequent discussion of the mechanics of agreement.

The Value of Constructive Conflict

Early in World War II, when the War Department was almost as much concerned with the Battle of the Potomac, fought with paper, as with the Battle of Europe, a general officer struck a mighty blow for better staff work. His aim was to conserve executive time by assuring that a better job was done before referral of a staff paper to the executive. This blow was struck by Major General Archer L. Lerch, then the Provost Marshal General, in the form of a memorandum with the subject "Completed Staff Work." This became one of the most famous and important contributions to staff doctrine to have come out of World War II.

Unfortunately the doctrine of completed staff work, as applied to the problem of obtaining concurrences, encouraged excessive compromise and a consequent watering down of the quality of the actions recommended.

"Completed Staff Work," said General Lerch, "is the study of a problem, and presentation of a solution, by a staff officer, in such form that all that remains to be done on the part of the head of the staff division, or the commander, is to indicate his approval or disapproval of the completed action."

This doctrine does not suggest the possibility of differences among the various staff officers who need to be consulted prior to the completion of the document itself, nor does it suggest how these differences should be treated. The implication, in fact, is that all these differences should be worked out before the chief is presented with the paper.

I believe this aspect of the doctrine of completed staff work has generated incalculable harm. It does not always produce the best recommendation; it yields a product which has been compromised and watered down to satisfy the imperative that completed staff work must produce a paper which the chief can sign with his approval or disapproval. Thus the doctrine plays into the hands of the many, many people in industry and in government who are reluctant to acknowledge formally that they have any differences of opinion. In fact, it encourages a play-it-safe attitude, especially where the consequences of failure may be serious. Under such circumstances the proponent of action or the person who approves it tends to want as much support as possible. He prefers unanimity so that, if the decision goes wrong, he is not likely to be singled out as the sole responsible party.

Along the same line no one likes to make decisions that fly in the face of objections. True, if he does and he is right, he becomes a hero, but there is always the gnawing feeling that the majority or a substantial segment of opinion may be right and he, consequently, may be conspicuously wrong.

Conflicts of ideas, under wholesome motivations, should be encouraged. What we need is progress based on truth, rather than a playing down or concealment of the basic issues in order to avoid the hazards of controversy. Conflict is found throughout all nature as a competition for scarce means and scarce opportunity. Nevertheless nature finds and strikes its balance, evolves and moves forward to a more advanced state. In the grand order of things nature structures a symbiosis, which is a bringing together of dissimilar organisms for their mutual advantage.

The enterprise which encourages independent thought and which provides a means for resolving differences of opinion, without loss of face, is a dynamic one; it can face challenges with vigor and confidence, secure in the feeling that the best thought will come forth to meet any challenge. By contrast, the enterprise which is forever compromising its own judgments in order to maintain the form, if not the spirit, of unanimity is at a disadvantage in dealing with crisis. It plods along, achieving agreement only after a series of postponements. Its thought-products lack a crispness. They are, rather, characterized by a flaccidity.

Two essential ingredients are needed in order to derive benefit from conflict: a climate and a mechanics. As regards climate, the participants must feel that their independent views are desired, provided they are offered in good taste, and that there are no penalties for expressing ideas which are not accepted fully. The role of a mechanics or procedure is to depersonalize the process while assuring that the best ideas are brought into common focus and resolved. When these conditions exist, the parties come closer to the ideal. Presumably they all stand to gain in some way by accomplishment of the objective. It remains, then, for them to subordinate their individuality, contributing their own best ideas and yielding in favor of the best contributed by others.

The Ingenious Way Out

When parties are deadlocked they sometimes need an ingenious, face-saving way out. First, they must want to find the strategic element. Then they must have patience — if there is time.

In 1913 Sir Hugh Lane of Dublin, Ireland, offered a rich collection of thirty-nine paintings to his city, but it refused them because it didn't want to build a gallery for them. In anger Sir Hugh willed them to the National Gallery in London, but it decided that only a few were worth hanging. Angered again, Sir Hugh changed his will in 1915 and bequeathed the paintings to Dublin. That year he went down with the *Lusitania* and his will was judged invalid because it had not been witnessed. For years thereafter the English and the Irish fought over possession of the paintings which include works of Corot, Manet, Monet, Pissaro, Renoir, Rousseau and others. The Irish Republican Army plotted to steal them from London's National Gallery, where they were being held. Verbal battles were fought over them in the press and in Parliament. Finally, late in 1959, Prime Minister Harold Macmillan told the House of Commons a settlement had been reached. One half of the paintings would hang in London and one half in Dublin. Every five years the two cities would switch halves.

THE MECHANICS OF AGREEMENT

The importance of a good climate for decision-making is covered elsewhere in this book. A few words may be said, how-

ever, on the subject of integrity. In large organizations specialization and physical separation prevent the members from getting to know each other very well. Familiarity with personalities
is usually limited to the circle of immediate and recurring
contacts. To offset the social distance which intervenes between
men in large organizations and which generates insecurities,
the leadership should espouse doctrines of administrative ethics
which must become a way of life for all. Then they can approach situations more surely without being preoccupied with
their ethical context.

The participants can also approach their problems more
confidently if they know that there is no penalty for having a
difference of opinion, and if they know that there will be a
depersonalized procedure for identifying and resolving any
differences.

Where procedures for reaching agreement have not been installed, decisions are often made on a crisis basis or by default,
because of the slippage of time. Then men preoccupy themselves unduly with the pointing of the finger of blame.

The procedure for reaching agreement involves four steps:
(1) preparation of the parties, (2) obtaining concurrences, (3)
narrowing and resolving the differences and (4) coming to a
conclusion.

Preparation of the Parties

Your first step is to select the parties who should make a review. These may not necessarily be the same people who participated in the initial study. Briefly, the interested parties now
are those who would be:

1. Affected substantially by the adoption of the proposed
course of action.

2. Expected to take some specific measures if the proposed
action is decided.

3. Functional or technical authorities on the pertinent subject matter.

4. Administratively or legally responsible for reviewing or deciding.

There is a tendency sometimes to involve everyone of the same organizational status or to invite participation along lines of official protocol. I have heard this expressed as a fear that "someone's nose would get out of joint" if he were not invited. This is a serious mistake, for, besides wasting the time of people who have no contributory interest in the matter at hand, it provokes the raising of unqualified, irrelevant and unprofessional questions. It adds a great deal of additional time to the review processes.

The organization manual, containing the official duties, if complete, should serve as a guide to determining who should take lead responsibility and who should participate at different stages. Within organizational units the distribution of responsibility may be defined in individual position descriptions which would serve to clarify who does what.

The normal rules of participation must sometimes be supplemented when this would assure a more balanced discussion, especially when strong points of view are anticipated. I am reminded of advice given me some years ago by Judge Justin Miller, formerly of the United States Circuit Court of Appeals: "When you're faced with a difficult and important legal problem, you sometimes might seek the advice of at least two lawyers. A hot lawyer might tell you to take the lead, to commit yourself. A cold lawyer would advise you of all the pitfalls and of all the reasons why you should not take the action. If you listen to both, you might find the truth somewhere in between."

The participants should be briefed fully so that they have a perspective on the matter within its total context. Depending upon the previous involvement of the participants, the material to be distributed to them should include all or some of the following:

1. The proposal itself.
2. The date of transmittal of the proposal to the recipients.
3. The name and other identity of the person who prepared

the material and is most familiar with it or who is established as the official contact point for any questions.

4. A recital of the background of the matter and the reason why it is now important.

5. A synopsis or summary of the material, if it is long.

6. A list of the people who are reviewing the proposal.

7. A statement of the consequences of action or nonaction.

8. A statement as to how concurrence is to be effected.

Some of the foregoing may be covered in the basic paper itself. If you have much staff paper work, a formalized ritual may be followed for the distribution of working documents. Usually there is a "clearance [or concurrence] form" which abstracts from the material being circulated, covering most of the items listed above, if not all, and provides room for signature as well as for an indication of the judgment reached.

The foregoing may be regarded as a "straight approach." Looking at the situation quite realistically, if you are the proponent of an action, you want to sell your ideas. You must convince others that they should *change* things around, that they should *stop* doing something or that they should do something *new*. Ordinarily you need to anticipate some resistance, whether logical or emotional. Accordingly, you should be prepared along the following lines, as appropriate:

1. Whether your presentation is written or oral, make it as professional as appropriate for the occasion. Have the pieces fit together in proper sequence. An amateurish presentation will undermine confidence in the idea itself.

2. If you sincerely believe in your proposal, show it. Enthusiasm is infectious. Hesitation and vacillation only raise doubts.

3. Anticipate questions and objections. Provide answers to these in the basic document and be prepared with additional answers in reserve.

4. Put yourself in the shoes of each man who has to be sold and imagine how he may be affected. Try to anticipate the logical objections he may raise, including personal angles which he might not express as such.

5. Bring out the beneficial effects of the proposed action and, also, bring out the disadvantages of not taking action. To be honest about it, you must also identify the arguments against the proposed action.

6. Prepare your arguments so that you will retain flexibility and maneuverability in the face of counterarguments. Have in mind the realities of the situation and set up the elements on which you may have to "trade."

7. Be prepared in depth. Don't be "roundish" with your supporting data. Show a knowledge in detail of the present situation, what has happened before and what may be expected for the future.

8. Be timely. Make sure that the time is right for consideration and that the people you must convince can give adequate attention to the matter.

When a basic change in the convictions of the participants is sought, you may consider whether to sell your ideas one piece at a time or to reveal the whole plot. I think that most people will not be satisfied if given only a piece of your total planning. Unless they can see the total picture they are likely to withhold their judgments. You must never underestimate their insights and perceptions.

Admittedly there will be cases in which the sheer mass of the presentation would prevent your going into full detail. There is a compromise: lay out the total situation in its broad aspects, get agreement on these in principle and then attack the major components, one by one.

Obtaining Concurrences

In spite of what I have just said about selling an idea, your objective in seeking concurrences is to obtain constructive comment which may improve your proposal. Unfortunately this often is not understood. Instead, the clearance process may be regarded as an additional red-tape delay. The proponent of the action has delved thoroughly into his subject matter, he has prepared his proposal and he sincerely believes it is the thing to do. He understands that he must go through the forms of clearance, if not the actual spirit, but he would like to short-circuit even the required rituals.

It is understandable. The machinery for getting papers approved often seems to grind creakily and slowly, to the point of frustration. Delays in obtaining agreement add substantially to the lead time required for the planning and execution of an action. Perhaps an extreme example of this was brought out by Colonel William F. Scott, United States Air Force, in a master's thesis, as reported in *Aviation Week*. Colonel Scott made a study of the time it took to carry weapons development from the initial stage of establishing the objectives through preparation of the operational requirements and the development plan and, finally, selection of the contractor. These four stages took a total of twenty-four months in all. An additional twenty-five months was consumed in obtaining concurrences! It took twelve months for concurrence on the objectives, six months on the operational requirements, four months on the development plan and three months on selection of the contractor.

On much smaller matters it is interesting to note the ruses and the techniques of by-passing which may be employed to finesse something through to final approval and authorization, without having to go through the complete clearance channels. A man buttonholes you in the corridor and tells you all about his wonderful idea. You are anxious to catch the 5:42 commuter train so you nod and grind out a few mild syllables. Later on you learn that he reported that he told you all about it and that you had agreed.

Another technique may be called "branching the agenda." In the course of discussing a topic some side aspects are mentioned in passing. The opportunist either has planned it that way or seizes a windfall and tries to convert it into an occasion for immediate decision on the side topic.

Then there is the technique of the "privileged ear." At golf, lunch or on the commuter train, someone gets the ear of *the big man*. Oh, so casually, he plants the thought and then uses every chance available to promote himself into being drawn out on the details and advantages of this brilliant proposal which the important man "discovered."

Far from being that much additional red tape, a system for obtaining concurrences, if properly operated, should conserve time. It limits participation on a "need-to-know" basis. It provides impersonal time checks which can be made routinely, even by secretaries. It assures ordered consideration of all the pertinent elements and it provides for adequate documentation of comments and concurrences.

While I shall discuss three main approaches to obtaining clearances — conference clearance, written clearance in sequence and concurrent written clearance — in actual practice, you may employ variations of these and degrees of intermediate informalities.

Conference clearance

1. Conferences should be reserved for use when the subjects are complex or when they involve some significant new action on which an exploratory exchange of views may be desired.

2. A conference may be used when one has an agenda of many small items which can be disposed of quickly in this manner, provided the chairman has the proceedings carefully timed and controlled.

3. The conference is expected to bring out information and nuances of feeling which otherwise might not be elicited through formal exchange of papers.

4. The conference may actually be used as a means of precipitating and bringing out conflicts of ideas. So long as these remain hidden, the reaching of agreement will be delayed.

The time-wasting characteristics of conference are well known. The chairman must move the discussion along, obtain balanced participation and bring issues to a head. He must steer the discussion away from debates over language preference, restricting it to the substance of ideas and leaving to one person the responsibility for putting agreements into words, for further review.

Participants should be given enough time beforehand to read written materials. Too much time must not be allowed or the materials might be forgotten or set aside until the last minute.

Sequence clearance

Probably the most common method of obtaining concurrences on a proposed action is to circulate it in sequence to a list of names on a routing slip. As each person receives the material, in turn, he is expected to read and approve with his initials or to raise such questions or make such comments as he considers appropriate.

As against the advantage of utmost simplicity, this technique has many disadvantages: (1) While the document is wending its way through the list of readers, you are never quite sure where it is. (2) This method takes the most time. (3) Sometimes those toward the bottom of the list tend to become more concerned about the comments of those who preceded them than with a study of the basic document itself. (4) Because subsequent comments are not seen by the earlier reviewers, the same laborious circuit must be traveled again when any important points are brought up.

Somehow, contributing one's initials in a long series tends to depreciate the sense of individual responsibility. During World War II a story went the rounds about a regulation of the War Production Board which was drafted to limit the production and use of duck cloth. Like other such regulations, it carried both civil and criminal penalties for violation. The story had it that the regulation had been initialed by some seventeen or twenty-three different people, all of whom concurred. Just before it was to be signed by the chairman of the War Production Board and thereby be enacted into law, the author showed his hand. He asked if the various signatories had indeed read it, and they, in turn, insisted that they had. Whereupon he proceeded to turn to one of the middle pages and read from it a story about that famous cartoon character named

Donald Duck. The moral of the story is that if the list is made too long, individual responsibility will be diminished.

Concurrent written clearance

The method of concurrent written clearance requires that you have enough copies for all who are to review the document, so that each may receive a copy simultaneously. This is the best method when time is limited. It is also the method to use when the simultaneous reading is to be followed by a conference. As another advantage, it definitely fixes responsibility for the comments that are made.

On the side of disadvantage, this method does not allow the various reviewers to know what each is saying about the document unless any of them think to call each other. It therefore should not be used, except for preliminary orientation, when you need a simultaneous pooling of ideas or experiences.

The method of concurrent written clearance puts certain burdens on the recipient of comments, to interpret and integrate them into the final document. He must judge when to recirculate the document, when to call for a conference and when to refer the matter, as completed staff work, to a higher level for decision, unless he himself is the higher level.

Narrowing and Resolving the Differences

When comments are received, whether orally or in writing, the coordinator must ascertain the areas of agreement, the areas of difference, new aspects not previously considered and exceptional aspects which need to be set aside for exceptional attention. If he is a perceptive man, he realizes that when he handles and manipulates the ideas of others he may be touching upon their inner personal feelings. A man's words on paper constitute an extension of his ego. When he expresses himself officially, he anticipates that in some measure he personally is to be judged, and, to that extent, his sense of personal security may be affected. While this may be recognized in the conference situation, it is too easily overlooked when written views are received and evaluated.

The basic process of coordinating ideas was well expressed by Mary Parker Follett, who wrote: "Every social process has three aspects: the interacting, the unifying and the emerging." Stated otherwise: get all the pertinent facts out on the table where everyone can get a look at them, find the bases of agreement and derive from this activity an advanced product. This is no easy task for the coordinator, who must be alert always for any idea or approach which will remove or accommodate major differences without material loss to any of the participants, from their standpoints.

The sequence followed by the coordinator will vary with each situation. For general guidance I suggest the following:

1. Make sure all of the parties are dealing with the same problem, the same objectives and issues.

2. Ascertain that the working materials and their implications are correctly understood by all the parties.

3. Begin narrowing the issues by identifying the areas of agreement.

4. Now, identify the areas of disagreement, making sure that all concerned understand fully the reasons for the disagreements.

5. Put the unlikely impediments in their proper perspective. Get the participants to think in terms of probabilities and improbabilities when someone says, "What if . . ?" Do the same when people begin theorizing or when they bring up exceptional cases.

6. Maintain a level of balanced commentary. Discourage preoccupation with subsidiary details which can be disposed of more readily once the basic issues are settled.

7. Avoid the formal recognition of an impasse so long as there is any reasonable hope of finding a basis for reconciling differences. A strategic delay may give the parties an opportunity to develop new solutions, to reconcile personal differences or to find a face-saving basis for accepting what previously might have been unpalatable.

Throughout this procedure the coordinator aims constantly at keeping the discussions or comments free of extraneous considerations. This presents a special problem when anyone brings up a point which is not really within his personal scope, merely because he believes he is making a contribution. In the face-to-face contacts of the small enterprise this may indeed be highly desirable. Quite frequently, however, these gratuitous offerings do little more than add to the delay and confusion.

The person who ordinarily does not have cognizance over a matter may impute to himself a deeper knowledge of it than he actually possesses. In a conference situation it is rather difficult for the chairman to eliminate these gratuities. He can do little more than to hear them out but not encourage further discussion, unless he believes that a real contribution is being made. Similarly, when such gratuitous comments are made in writing, the recipient must judge whether to accept them or not, depending upon how worthwhile they seem. He should not, however, feel obliged to refute them or to dispose of them if he does not feel that they are acceptable. If this principle is understood by all, then they can feel free to make any comments.

Coming to a Conclusion

The coordinator must sense when to bring matters to a head and when not to. Chester I. Barnard said: "The fine art of decision consists in not deciding questions not now pertinent; in not deciding prematurely; in not making decisions which cannot be made effective; and in not making decisions others should make."

Finally, the conclusions must be recorded as a basis for carrying them out or for presenting them to a higher authority. In a conference the chairman should recite his understandings as to agreements and disagreements. Beyond this, the situation itself must dictate whether a new document is to be circulated to those present for their review or for their information alone. In either case the general rule is that the people involved should have knowledge of the final outcome.

*   *   *   *   *

My first involvement in decision-making was in 1949, under the chairmanship of Walter K. Scott, later Assistant Secretary of State. I was given an assignment to be executive secretary of a reorganization task force which was assigned problems of top structure and of the processes of making decisions and taking actions. This obliged me to delve into all of the recently made studies on effective organization for the conduct of foreign affairs and also to acquire some degree of independent insight into the operating processes of the Department of State.

After the close of World War II many people began addressing themselves to the question of whether we had won or lost the peace. They wanted to know whether the nation was adequately prepared to deal with the new problems of foreign relations as they would evolve in the future. A stream of editorial comment was published in distinguished journals and in substantial books. The Department of State itself, as well as the Bureau of the Budget, had been going through a series of internally directed "agonizing reappraisals." Finally a grand critique of the suitability of our machinery for the conduct of foreign affairs was published by the first Hoover Commission.

Just about all of these studies, both internal and external, seemed to agree that the Department of State had failed to adapt itself to the changes in the environment for the conduct of foreign affairs. They discussed relationships with the President, the Congress, and other departments of government and the public itself. They directed searching beams of light on inadequacies in organizational structure and in the personnel mix of the Department. They dramatized the appalling weaknesses in the procedures for making decisions and taking action with the effect of paralyzing the Department. In effect, they said, the Department of State had, over a period of many years, become almost an end in itself, preoccupied with the forms and rituals rather than with the objectives to be achieved through the conduct of foreign relations.

The extent to which the broader failures of the Department of State could be traced to failures in its processes for taking action was described with brilliant insight by Joseph M. Jones in his book *A Modern Foreign Policy for the United States* (New York, The Macmillan Co., 1944). In discussing the in-

ternal procedural paralysis of the Department of State, Jones
gave his account of how an action paper was reviewed after its
initial preparation:

"This paper then made its way up through the Departmental
hierarchy for initialing by all appropriate officers until it
reached and was signed by the Secretary of State. At each stage
the paper had to be in final form. Each suggestion required
the complete redoing of a final draft and the soliciting again of
the initials of all those down the line who had already approved. Papers were rewritten and reinitialed over and over
again. Each of five to ten or more officers was privileged to
make suggestions and require revisions as the price of an
initial."

A high premium was placed upon caution and the avoidance
of mistakes which might blot the escutcheon of a career officer.
As Jones put it, ". . . to refrain from acting is better than to
act . . . the old is better than the new and . . . the sin unforgiv-
able is error." Commenting further upon the stultifying effect
of this mode of reaching decisions and taking action, Jones
said:

"The paper work, the pulling and hauling even on minor
matters, the endless drafts containing more often than not
minor and personal preferences in wording – all of this occu-
pies the long hours of the officers of the Department of State,
wears them down, saps their energies and their intellects. The
system and the unanimity rule almost invariably tie decisions
down to the views of the most conservative and stubborn among
the higher officers. That which everybody can usually agree
upon is what has been done before."

As a result of the 1949 reorganization, in which I was privileged to take an active part, basic and far-reaching reforms
were made in the methods through which decisions were
reached on small as well as large issues. The effects upon the

conduct of foreign affairs could be incalculable. Nevertheless, without doubt, the Department of State will have to go through this ordeal once again, if the reports of procedural deterioration I receive are so much as half true. The sociologists would say that it is part of the process of social disorganization and reorganization.

Jones's description of the agony of paper-pushing could apply just as well to many other government departments and to industrial corporations. To illustrate this, I read passages to a group of Department of Defense officials, substituting the word "Defense" wherever "State" appeared. It was in the spring of 1960. Jones had written in 1944. They chortled and smiled, asking me for the name of this new book which showed such amazing understanding of the Department of Defense.

Recognizing that such conditions can be counteracted, at least partially, by executive leadership, a new Secretary of Defense, Robert S. McNamara, said, in an NBC interview with Martin Agronsky, soon after taking office:

". . . I think that the role of a public manager is very similar to the role of a private manager . . . He can either act as a judge or a leader. In the former case, he sits and waits until subordinates bring to him problems for solution, or alternatives for choice. In the latter case, he immerses himself in the operations of the business or the governmental activity, examines the problems, the objectives, the alternative courses of action, chooses among them, and leads the organization to their accomplishment. In the one case it's a passive role; in the other case, an active role.

"I've always believed in and endeavored to follow the active leadership role as opposed to the passive judicial role."

Of course, we all wish the Secretary the best, but the Department of Defense is big to the point almost of being impervious. Mr. McNamara will need powerful support.

Chapter VI

THE DECISIVE MOMENT — AND AFTER

As you approach the moment of decision you must realize that it is only one point in an unfolding drama of action, counteraction, reaction and interaction! The decision itself is of no consequence unless the action it is to bring is carefully planned and executed.

The aftermath of a decision, with the necessary follow-ups, evaluations and corrections, is probably the most sadly neglected aspect of decision-making.

The topics covered below are:

1. *The moment of judgment:* how the decision-maker himself must find his own way.

2. *How to blueprint action:* the subdivision of action; the key points to control; the scheduling of action; and the follow-ups needed for control.

3. *The taking of action:* how to achieve clear understanding; how to tell people; the mood of action; the timing of action; techniques of limited commitment; the stream of reaction; and the lessons of failure.

4. *Emergency decisions:* the criteria for emergency decision-making; informing others of emergency decisions.

THE MOMENT OF JUDGMENT

The decision is a moment of climax. At some point the palaver must come to a halt. A choice must be made. This can be a moment of exhilaration or a moment of numbing fear. It matters not whether the decision is one of great or small importance in the eyes of others. What counts for you are your own feelings. While we turn our attention to the more glamorous levels of decision, we should not forget that decision-making holds its excitements, its difficulties and even its terrors at all levels throughout enterprise.

The Guidance of Truth

I first met the Governor of Ohio, Michael V. Di Salle, when he served in Washington as Director of Price Stabilization during the economic emergency period of the Korean War. I was impressed then — and still am — with what seemed to be the fearlessness of his decisions in the face of great resistances and pressures. During a visit to the Governor's office in Columbus I asked him how he felt about courage as an element in decision-making.

He replied:

"At all levels of public service decisions must be made that require more perception than courage. The public official needs to have the ability to know what is right. Then, the fear that he may yield to pressures contrary to what he knows is right outweighs the fear of political consequences.

"May I offer an example? When I was a member of the City Council in Toledo, we were at one time faced with the question of a change in the routing of a bus line. Streetcars had used a certain route for almost a half century. The change from streetcars to busses gave some people at the upper end of the route a chance to come before the City Council to demand a change in routing for the expressed purpose of saving time and rendering more efficient service. It soon became apparent that the real cause was to keep the bus from running through a neighborhood that had changed from white to colored. This was evidenced by the emotional reaction of the people involved.

The white people were in fear of a spread of the colored neighborhood if transportation continued. They felt changing the route might be helpful since most of the colored persons depended on the mass transportation facilities.

"They enlisted every force in the community: neighborhood churches represented by their pastors, businessmen, labor organizations and veterans' groups. All told of the stability of the neighborhood and how improved transportation would assist in their desired objective. None of them emphasized what would happen if the bus skirted the other neighborhood. Thousands of signatures were secured on petitions demanding the change. Many proponents had been personal friends of mine. The neighborhood that they were seeking to protect was one of the highest percentage Democratic districts in the city. Many of these people had been political supporters of mine. They first tried cajoling, then threats, and then they became vicious — anonymous phone calls, anonymous letters. I received one picture that had appeared in the paper in which half of it had been painted black, the other half had been left white.

"I had lived in the old neighborhood right by the car tracks when I was a boy. One woman called to tell me that she took her life in her hands when the street car traveled through that neighborhood; that little colored boys would run out at the corner and pull the trolley, necessitating the motorman coming out and restoring the trolley to the overhead wire. I told her that I remembered a little white boy that used to do the same thing and that she never felt that anybody's life had been endangered. I didn't tell her who the little white boy was, since I was having enough problems at that time.

"Finally, the change in the routing was defeated 5 to 4. As a result, the white people became tremendously vociferous and hostile. One fellow that I had played ball with for many years and I considered a very close friend passed me on the street without speaking. In a subsequent election, my vote in that area dropped to almost nothing. But I suppose it was offset by an increase in other areas of the city, because I led the ticket. Since that day, every time that I ran for office the vote kept increasing until, when I was elected Governor, we got practically every vote that was cast.

"If I had yielded to the pressure, I would have lost the respect of the people in that neighborhood over the long run, but more important, I would have lost respect for myself. But I must not understate the fact that there wasn't a real fear that this might cost me the next election, and I must not say that I did not consider the possibility before making the decision."

I suggested to the Governor that an entirely different kind of situation might prevail on legislative and administrative issues which were favored or opposed by professional lobbyists — people who were paid well to obtain desired results.

Commenting on this, the Governor said:

"As you will recall, we met this kind of representation many times in Washington. The cotton lobby was a particularly strong lobby. It consisted of merchants, shippers, growers, brokers, warehouse people and all the other elements that had some interest in earnings from cotton. These groups together could marshal a great deal of legislative support. But the decision again had to be made on whether or not the price-control program could continue if we were to exempt one particularly well-lobbied commodity. It was actually easier to make a decision to retain controls on cotton than to anticipate fighting the losing battle on the balance of the program. Strangely enough, the day after that hearing many of the people who participated and who spoke in support of decontrol for the record called to congratulate me on my stand and the way that I presented my case and on what they called my courage. The same situation occurred in meat, in wool and manufacturing items.

"In a political campaign, one of the methods of applying pressures is through questionnaires that are sent by a myriad of organizations: trade associations, organizations for a particular purpose, labor, etc. Here the candidate gets a very early opportunity to state his position, always with the request that the questions be answered 'yes' or 'no' and always leaving the impression that, unless you favor that position, you will be haunted and destroyed by the senders of the questionnaire. I usually answer the questions — some yes, some no, some with many modifications, depending on what the particular issue might be. I have been rated unsatisfactory by many of the organizations, my opponents have been endorsed in many cases, but I doubt that there has been any large impact on the election."

"Well, Governor, what about the personal pressures — where you know the people who call upon you?"

"Yes, this is a powerful force upon one's judgment," he said, "especially because of the subtle and intimate ways in which it operates. For example, legislative lobbies who are old at the game and who have strong local people, people who are active in community affairs, people who are everywhere and who are able to exert influence on the basis of friendship rather than on the basis of pressures, make it extremely difficult for a legislator to turn aside his friends as opposed to what some frowsy-haired person terms the public interest.

"Among the most difficult of all decisions to make is that which flies against the social pressures. If everyone that you come in contact with in your church or in the country club favors a certain position, it isn't easy to become the oddball of the congregation or of the club and to support a position which you feel is based on reason rather than on emotion. This type of decision is among the most difficult because not only do you fear the opinion yourself, but you fear the result as it emanates from the family. They, too, are subject to it and sometimes they are convinced by it.

"I do want to make this point quite clear, though: in the long run, if you have reasons for the decisions you make, they are not difficult to make nor are they difficult to adhere to. They are easy to remember because you know the reasons from which they resulted."

The Lonely Decision-Maker

"Decision-making is a lonely business," said Clarence B. Randall, former head of Inland Steel Company and advisor to Presidents, "and the greater the degree of responsibility, the more intense the loneliness. It is human to wish to share the risk of error and to feel the comforting strength of outside support, like the flying buttresses, along the wall of a medieval cathedral. But the strong man, the one who gives free enterprise its vitality, is the man who weighs thoughtfully the entire range of available opinion and then determines policy by relying solely on his own judgment."

To help put this point across, Mr. Randall recounted a story about the first P. B. Armour of Chicago. He was not quite sure of the truth of the story, but it was appropriate enough not to make any real difference.

"In the early days of Armour & Company, Mr. Armour had an admirable plan for training his second and third echelons in the techniques of management. He organized about a dozen men into a junior board of directors and, from time to time, submitted important company problems to this group.

"One day, after a particularly lively discussion, a young man said, 'I move that we go ahead with this.' There was a second for the motion, and then Mr. Armour — who was, of course, chairing the meeting — called for a vote. Every man said 'Aye.'

"Whereupon Mr. Armour said, 'The motion is lost,' and went on to the next order of business.

"And he was so right. It was he who had to make the decision, and there were times when the depth of his experience and the breadth of his knowledge were more important than the initial impressions of men considering the matter for the first time."

I am inclined to believe that this actually took place, for in my much more limited experience I can recall similar instances. During the Korean War period an enforcement case came before me for decision which involved the imposition of a penalty of almost one-half million dollars. The facts were all there: they told of undenied violations of the regulations. Now it is not very easy to pen one's signature to a document that imposes so heavy a penalty. In this case the corporation involved was one of the largest and its head was most influential in the very highest levels of the Executive Branch. Members of my staff, while performing their duty well in presenting the case to me, also expressed to me their fears of the possible consequences of imposing this penalty. After all, I did have some discretion in the circumstances.

I considered the matter briefly — very briefly — and then I signed. I think everyone was really pleased, although some uneasiness still persisted. There never were any consequences, and this penalty turned out to be the largest imposed during that crisis period.

To me the issue was quite clear: it was not a matter of whether I could forgive this company or find mitigating circumstances. Rather, it was a question of whether to carry out the enforcement program or to abandon it. If I had excused this one company in this conspicuous case, I would have had to excuse practically all others.

In another situation, in a meeting with four members of my staff, they unanimously took a position contrary to mine. I felt, nevertheless, that I was right and that I should have decided in accordance with my own judgments. The matter was not very important, however, so I took a calculated risk and I yielded to their collective judgment. As it turned out, they were wrong and they came to me and admitted it, with an apology. Out of this situation I took a gain, for they were much more prone to take my judgments in the future.

A final example: I was confronted with a difficult problem of ruling on the eligibility of certain flood victims to receive additional compensation under the terms of the wage and salary freeze. I called in the chief counsel, who said, "This is really an economic problem, for it is not covered by the rules." So I called in our chief economist, who said, "This is not the kind of economic problem for which we presently have any precedents under inflation economics. I think you've got to decide this one within the latitude of your legal authorities."

Having had a balance of views, I then made up my own

mind. I decided to respect the need of the displaced people for additional, emergency compensation and I also recognized that there were legal limitations on my authority to do this directly. I therefore let it be known that if action was taken by the employers and if the facts of the action were not brought to my official cognizance, I would not be obliged to consider the legal implications. Everyone was happy, including my chief counsel.

Reflecting on these experiences, I concluded that on the really important issues the executive had to feel that he was right in the judgments that he would take; he had to follow his own instincts — his own logical and ethical judgments. At the same time, he could not be flying in the face of the recommendations of his subordinates without some risk of losing their devotion and loyalty. Accordingly, he might find it expedient to defer to them on the decisions whose consequences were not very great and where the certainties of judgment — at least on his part — were also not very great.

Although subordinates are supposed to be extensions of the personalities of their superiors, a few are not above taking advantage of the insecurities of the latter. Depending upon the particular circumstances, they manipulate either the hopes or the fears of their superiors. If they want something approved, the emphasis is on achievement of dearly cherished hopes; disapproval is sought through the painting of verbal pictures of the awful consequences of acting or not acting. I have seen this done successfully to Cabinet officers, college presidents and company presidents alike. It's really a commonly used technique: salespeople try to create pleasure thoughts in order to get you to choose one product as against another which they associate with pain thoughts.

The Hesitant Decision

A source of great frustration and demoralization is the executive who is constantly reopening decisions or who permits his people to convince him to do so. It is not wrong to reopen a decision occasionally, where new facts or new perspectives warrant doing this. Where this is a chronic condition, however, it should be a cause for real concern. Here are four of the more common reasons why decisions are reopened, together with suggestions for correcting the conditions.

1. *New perspective.* The morning after the decision brings a cry of "Hold everything; I have a better solution." Who can say no to this? Again, if the next morning brings its further improvements in what to do, who can deny those? At some point someone must say, "We're constantly improving but we're not getting anything done." If this is a recurring pattern of delay and postponement, it may be symptomatic of procedural failure: inadequate consideration of all the pertinent facts and insufficient development and review of all of the reasonably possible alternatives.

2. *Incomplete decisions.* "There's something else we didn't think of," cries the decision-maker, thereby rallying his flock to a new round of conferences. This is a more general kind of procedural failure. It might have started with a failure to define and subdivide the problem sufficiently. The initial fact-finding may have been too limited. The points of view brought to bear on the problem may have been too restrictive. The following of check lists for analysis may minimize critical omissions.

3. *Fear of action.* A decision has been made; for the sake of argument, a very good decision. The executive delays taking action, asking, "What if . . ?" or, "Did we consider . . ?" or that catchall blockbuster, "Is this what we really want to do?" The particular question raised really does not matter; the man looking for a way out will think of a new one if a reasonable answer is made. Where there is a recurring pattern of this kind of delay, it suggests a deep-seated fear of exercising responsibility and facing the possible consequences of failure. The man really hopes that by invoking new delays "This, too, will pass." The prescription is a difficult one. Each situation requires its own solution. Perhaps, with proper guidance, the executive may improve. It is more likely that he will not and that a change in leadership will eventually be necessary. Still, it might not be

that man; it might be the man or men above him who make it impossible for him to live with his decisions.

4. *The end-runner.* Because of the way they operate, you may not know the end-runners until you become the executive who has them within his purview. Then you are bothered by some few people who, after the decision has been made, get at you privately to have it changed or set aside. These are the people who want a private second bite at the apple. When their motives are of the highest, they suffer from an inability to get themselves on record before their colleagues, when the decision is in the making. There are also those whose motives may be impure, to say the least. In either case the executive imperils his finer judgment when he submits to the suasions of those who care nothing about the regularized processes of conducting business. Compelling though the arguments may seem, the executive is best off in the long run by discouraging the end-runners. One test of their sincerity is to ask them whether they would like to present their views before the entire group of those who had previously contributed openly.

HOW TO BLUEPRINT ACTION

The Elements of Action

A decision is a point reached in the stream of action. It triggers the making of subsidiary decisions and implementing decisions. Sometimes to be able to make a decision you must "dry run" the follow-through, in advance, to ascertain feasibility and to identify the critical unknowns and points of sensitivity.

The decision assumes certain conditions. The action encounters them. When you are actually up against them they usually look different. But then something else happens: as soon as you do something you change the conditions which may, in turn, require a change in the original action. In a long chain of actions this may find you doubling back constantly. When the action is subdivided for simultaneous execution, you find yourself checking back on each separate task and on the effects of change on some or all of the others.

The rational approach to effective control of action is called program-planning. In a big program thousands of individual judgments and choices may be made before the action is decided and completed. Such a program may involve:

1. Problem recognition
2. Study period
3. Decisive period
4. Program-planning
5. Installation
6. "Debugging" and revision
7. Operation
8. Review and
9. Redecision

In a smallish action you may not recognize these elements as having separate identity but they are there, whether combined or disregarded. Actually you cannot disregard *any* elements in the natural evaluation of a decision and the action that follows. Somehow you must pay the piper. Thus, if you proceed without adequate problem definition and facts, the chances are you'll take them into account later — when you correct the action which won't stand up.

At the lower end of the list we encounter something more serious — a tendency to make the decision and then to fail to follow through to render it effective. This, really, is the proving ground of the decision. It deserves better.

Elaborating the Decision Goals

When you have made a decision you have not yet really changed anything. You have yet to lay out the steps in detail which will get you from where you are to where you want to go. The difficulty of the task will depend on whether past experience is available, on whether you are breaking new ground and on the availability of skills needed to carry out the action.

The first step in elaborating the decision goals is to identify the key subsidiary actions, and their sequences, interrelationships and interdependencies. This information will later be necessary for assignment and coordination.

If the magnitude and complexity of the task require it, the activity being developed may need to be split down further and further in its refinement. Contributions of effort may be required from people throughout the enterprise at many different levels, from the least clerical to the highest executive and managerial.

Identifying the Points of Sensitivity

The unknowns which preceded the act of decision will be carried forward in some measure into the details of the plan itself.

You must identify the major calculated risks and the major areas of breakthrough, for these two are pivotal points upon which success or failure must depend. *They* are the items which may require a greater use of resources than at first anticipated.

For each of the critical points of action, you must establish criteria of successful accomplishment.

Program Requirements

As you elaborate your decision goals you begin evolving the outline of your operating plan. This plan must be expanded further through the assignment of resources (personnel, funds, facilities, materials, time, etc.) to specific tasks.

Resource requirements should be developed by those who have the greatest familiarity with the tasks to be accomplished. Early in the game you must identify those who are to be responsible for specific assignments. This is done in major blocks of activity so that those responsible for each may make subassignments. (Some of these assignments may have been made when you first began to subdivide the goals and elaborate them into a plan of action.)

The estimates of resource requirements must also be translated into financial needs. These tend, at first, to be excessive, but a review is expected to bring the costs within allowable financial ceilings and other operating limitations.

Initially you avoid reducing cost at the expense of limiting the basic objectives. It is amazing how many items can be trimmed for lack of basic utility. If this does not bring you within spending limits, however, you may need to re-examine the basic objectives and requirements with two possible outcomes in mind: (1) redefinition of objectives and requirements, to bring them within reach of your dollar capabilities and (2) abandonment or postponement of the effort as something you cannot now afford.

As you proceed through the successive stages of installation, you may find it necessary to re-examine estimates and commitments in the same light. The need for this will depend on the extent to which you depart from the original plan.

Assignments, Schedules and Priorities

Assignments of responsibility are laid out in varying degrees of detail in the operating schedules. These may need to be supplemented with written and oral specifications of tasks to be performed and their relationship to what others are doing.

The schedule is the visible blueprint of action. It takes everything that is to be done and lays it out in a time frame. It shows the successive unfolding of steps needed to achieve subsidiary goals. It shows how these become the major components of larger goals which finally merge together into the total end-product. Some of the steps must be plotted in sequence while others must be carried out simultaneously. The inputs and outputs of all of them must be threaded together so that they will all fall into place at the right time. To add to the complexity of this blueprinting effort, all outputs must be in balance; none can contribute less than is required of it nor must any contribute more than is needed.

The actions must be planned so that resources are not assigned prematurely or excessively. Thus an activity may require ten men at its peak but in its make-ready stages it may require only one or two. During the phasing out of an activity it may be possible to take people off, so that they may be assigned elsewhere. In other situations it may be necessary to assign more effort in the initial stages because of reduced productivity during training. Experience with learning curves will provide some guidance in the initial assignment of personnel to new tasks.

Experience with the particular operational processes will provide clues to the plotting of critical lead times and priorities. If it takes three months to procure a piece of equipment, this procurement must be scheduled long in advance and not when the equipment suddenly must be put into operating use.

Program Control and Evaluation

Once the plan is activated it must be monitored and coordinated until it is finally completed. There will be slippages. There will be unforeseen contingencies. There will be failures in communication so that different people will get out of coordination. There will also be some tendency to veer away from the previously assigned goals and criteria of performance.

Normally performance is assured by the hierarchy of direction and supervision, but there is also some impulse here for the rationalization of one's own failings. The disclosure of difficulties is delayed — sometimes beyond the point of remedy — in the hope that there will be improvements or self-corrections which will make it unnecessary to report failure. As an offset to this, it is usually necessary to have an independent control center which monitors performance against the scheduled targets or milestones.

The reporting of accomplishment against previously assigned and defined targets is the principal means of assuring compliance with the master plan. The reporting system must clearly show whether the target is met or whether it isn't. The reporting system thus operates impersonally to advise the management that a trouble spot exists so that corrective action may be taken. The fact that one is obliged to report his progress or the lack of it, specifically, in itself acts as a major incentive to avoid failures by all possible means. As a corollary to this, the achievement of targets must be verified against previously defined criteria of accomplishment and acceptance.

While the procedures of regular reporting will show up any

deviations from plan, it is usually desirable to supplement this at major junctions of activity by conducting a broad program review. After all, it is possible that conditions may have changed or that your experiences in going through with the plan of action suggest to you that major or minor revisions could be made. Sometimes these are shown up through the identification and reporting of the failures or defaults. At other times it is necessary to take a broad over-all view of the activity as it is moving along. This prompts a whole series of new decisions which then must be translated into changes in the master plan and schedule.

THE TAKING OF ACTION

For program-planning to be realistic it must be based on intimate knowledge of conditions. In most cases this must be achieved by the participation of a number of people, working in concert. This is easier said than done. The big obstacle is the complexity of the program-planning process itself.

For one thing, the work is divided in parallel: those aspects that can be done simultaneously by different people, with co-ordination among them at key intervals. Then, for each of the parallel lines of effort and for the program as a whole, the work moves forward in a sequence of events.

A flow diagram of the program would show each separate line of effort moving forward and then looping backward to correct and adjust original assumptions in the light of experience. At key junctures parallel lines would merge, and the combined effort would then be seen as an alternately progressing and back-looping effort. Each juncture requires decisions and actions as does each point of back-looping and forward movement.

Over the whole of such a program plan is imposed a fine network of intercommunication. Operating information is transferred among the doers. Pieces are added in sequence. Reviews and examinations are made. Trouble signals are transmitted to control points. Progress reports are made. Any of these can also trigger the need for decisions and actions.

The total effort calls for clear understanding by all of the tasks expected of them. Now for the rub: it is one thing to tell people that they have certain tasks to do, as part of a greater effort; it is another to have them perform exactly as intended. Obviously this calls for some considerable skill in communication. Clear instructions are not enough; you must make sure that separate departments have clear understandings of their respective roles in the situation so that they will be able to interpret instructions and accept responsibility correctly.

How to Achieve Clear Understanding

Joseph M. Juran noted one approach to clarifying this kind of situation.*

Taking the matter of responsibility for finished-goods inventory, as an example, he shows how responsibility can be subdivided to cover, among other things, the following seven points:

1. Developing the basic economic formulas for ordering points and lot sizes.

2. Approving the final formulas to be used.

3. Applying the formulas to determine order points and economic lot sizes for specific catalogue numbers.

4. Ordering goods so as to maintain the inventory.

5. Caring for the physical goods.

6. Keeping the inventory records.

7. Taking physical inventory.

While acknowledging this as too fine a subdivision for some small companies or work situations, Juran points out that the process of getting a group of affected people to analyze responsibilities together does generate the unity needed for subsequent carrying out of decisions.

His technique was to list each of the elements, as brought out

* "Production Planning and Control as an Interdivisional Responsibility," in *Successful Production Planning and Control,* Special Report No. 5, American Management Association, New York.

in discussion, one after the other, across the top of a blackboard. Down the left-hand side he listed the names of those available to make the decisions. Next, each participant was given a copy and asked to mark an "X" under each responsibility heading to show (opposite the name) who *then* had responsibility. He found that before this was done he had to distinguish responsibility for *making* a decision from "is responsible" and from "takes action," both of which are separate matters.

The collated forms showed marked disagreement in understanding as to who *had current responsibility*. Juran therefore tried again with another set of blank charts, asking this time for a listing of who *should have responsibility*. Once again there was substantial disagreement (although the distribution of marks was not greatly different).

Now Juran got them to talking. Rather quickly the group realized that terms such as "requisitioning" and "inventory records" had been misunderstood. Another area of disagreement was in the desires or preferences of the several departments as to how the operations were to be performed. Not until these conflicts could be resolved would it be possible to get agreement on distribution of responsibility.

And so the talking continued until the points at issue were all resolved. When this was accomplished the members of the group were then unanimous in registering their views as to how responsibilities for decision-making should be distributed.

Thus we see the value of participative explaining as a way of clarifying goals and actions. Those affected will challenge the proposals, in the light of their special and varied interests, from many angles. Inevitably this leads to modifications and, usually, to improvements. A deeper and more lasting benefit is that common understanding and common acceptance are the most effective means for ensuring progress toward goals.

This kind of discussion is costly and hence is apt to be used only on important occasions, such as the inauguration of a new program. While some elements of consultative direction will be found in almost all situations, the ordinary case is one of the intelligent giving of orders with the expectation that they will be carried out.

How to Tell People

Order-giving is an aspect of instruction-giving. An order carries with it some element of authority and therefore invokes reactions of both logic and emotion; how you feel about the order-giver and how his order affects you may determine the manner in which you carry it out, apart from considerations of pure merit.

Accordingly, I suggest two sets of rules for giving orders. The first has to do with *clarity and consistency*.

1. Give orders only to people who are prepared to understand them.

2. Express orders in the language of the recipients.

3. State the purposes and limits of action.

4. Provide detail appropriate to the responsibilities and needs of the recipients.

5. Verify that the order has been received and executed as intended.

The first and second points are somewhat interrelated. The recipients of instructions must be tuned in on the same wave length as the sender, else nothing will be received as intended. On the matter of being "prepared to understand," they must understand the problem from a technical as well as from a situational standpoint. They must have the same sense of goal and direction as you. The terms and ideas you express must convey identical meaning to them.

Stated otherwise, your preliminary task in conveying instructions is to match the men and ideas. This is not always accomplished so handily. Usually you must work with the people "on deck." If those to whom you would logically turn are totally unable to absorb the particular ideas and plans, you must either make readjustments or — in serious situations — bring in additions or replacements. It often happens that the timing of a new program may be governed by staff availabilities.

Assuming the usual — that a program is to be carried out by the available executives, supervisors and employees — an inventory of the situation will tell you what information, explanations and training will be needed to make it possible for your orders to be executed effectively, as intended. This may include correcting misapprehensions as well as providing positive guidance. It may also include the taking of preliminary "stage-setting" actions.

Preliminaries aside, we are now ready to make things clear — a topic worthy of a book in its own right. To begin with, you must structure the field of action. Explain where you're heading and delineate the boundaries of action. Here is another opportunity to use Kipling's six honest serving-men: What, Why, When, Where, How and Who. Clarity is aided by telling not only the positive but also by hedging it in with the negative. "Do this, but don't do that."

The amount of detail needed for clarity must necessarily depend on each situation, taking account of the newness of problem, degree of complexity, qualifications and caliber of personnel and relative status and working level of the participants. How this works in a chain reaction may be seen in an example of a president of a canned-foods company who wishes a survey of the market for a new spaghetti sauce, one which would be superior in quality to others on the market and also more costly. The president assumes that he need only say that much to his marketing vice president to get the job done. For his part, however, the marketing v. p. must give more detailed instructions to his own subordinates, especially as he subdivides the assignment. Since their tasks are interrelated, each must know the total mission, his part in it and how he relates to the others who have individual assignments. The conduct of the study may require participation in depth, down to a clerk who is asked to tabulate information. The more the over-all task is subdivided and the more limited the individual assignment, the more explicit must be the instructions.

Delegation of authority plays an important role in order-giving. The president did not have to tell his marketing v. p.

how to make the study. Sufficient was it that he state what he wanted accomplished. Since the normal duties of this v. p. included the making of market surveys and analyses, the president could assume a knowledge of procedure. Moreover the president himself might not be capable of giving more specific instructions. It is to be remembered that a superior executive is not expected to know the *how,* in detail, of all operations under his scope.

In the well-run organization the execution of decisions is accomplished with a minimum of specific order-giving. Partly this is achieved by assuring that everyone knows what is expected of him under both recurring and special circumstances. Participation in the making of decisions accounts for another part of the achievement, for a knowledge of the situation acquired in this intimate manner serves automatically as guidance for carrying out the judgments reached. Permeating the whole effort, though, must be a feeling of interest and motivation which expresses itself in the form of constructive initiative.

Finally, order-giving requires verification to assure that all is proceeding as intended. "The best laid schemes o' mice and men Gang aft a-gley," wrote Robert Burns, "And lea'e us nought but grief and pain, For promis'd joy." The execution of a decision is, in some measure, at least, a journey into uncertainty. Verification is not merely to assure compliance. It goes beyond to ascertain that prior assumptions were valid and that courses of action taken will actually produce desired results. Even though it be in the smallest manner, verification usually points to some modification in original plans.

The second set of rules for order-giving has to do with *acceptability.*

1. Give orders only when carrying them out is directly feasible and would not lead to conflict with other instructions, procedures or actions.

2. Show regard for the self-interest of those who must execute the orders.

3. Give orders courteously and impersonally.

4. Give orders only at a rate that can be absorbed.

One might think that the first point — not to issue orders that are infeasible — is only too obvious. Yet this is a common cause of self-entrapment and is due to poor fact-finding and poor planning. Under cover of ignorance any kind of absurd order might be given. The effect, naturally, is to demean the order-giver in the eyes of the recipients. Sometimes, also, irreparable harm may be done to the action program itself. The preventative prescription is, of course, only too obvious.

"There is no principle of executive conduct better established in good organizations," said Chester I. Barnard, "than that orders will not be issued that cannot or will not be obeyed." Anyone who is at all sophisticated in the behavior of organizational man will know the many ways in which management intent can be nullified when the desired actions are not welcome, notwithstanding the most autocratic exercise of authority. Barnard points out that management cannot admit to this, formally. "When it appears necessary to issue orders which are initially or apparently unacceptable, either careful preliminary education, or persuasive efforts, or the prior offering of effective inducements will be made, so that the issue will not be raised, the denial of authority will not occur, and orders will be obeyed."

Quite apart from the content of an instruction, "who says so" and how he says it may make all the difference in how it is carried out. An identical order from each of two executives or supervisors may be received and carried out in markedly different ways with the reactions provoked solely by attitudes toward the sources. The effort should be to have the situation govern, rather than the person. How is this achieved? Wherever possible, participation in development of the action program is urged, for self-involvement is a powerful force for self-commitment. Effective communication of goals and purposes and of the effects of the pending action also promotes self-involvement, for it enables one to identify activities with his self-interest.

When the personal element is an uncertain one, it may be expedient to make the proposed action part of a larger situation — one which will not in itself be challenged. Thus a decision was made in one company to curtail overtime payments made to senior personnel. Everyone in authority agreed that the situation had gotten out of hand but no one wanted to be the one to give the orders. The impersonal solution was found by annexing this problem to a broader situation — the making of an over-all compensation survey by an outside consulting firm. Some may argue that the situation should have been faced frontally with full understanding and acceptance of responsibility by those concerned. Refuting this, the actual case was that no one really missed the point. Rather, all wanted a face-saving way out. Along this line, major changes in organization, personnel, program or physical or geographical arrangements often afford opportunities for covering many unpalatable actions under the broad umbrella of change.

Acceptability of an order depends in part on current absorption capacity. Any individual or work unit can take on only so much change or new activity before it rebels against further increments of such load. Be conscious, therefore, of this absorption factor before you decide to order any new activity.

The Mood of Action

When you explore the situation for guidance in giving orders, you must become aware of other conditioning factors which may have a bearing on either the strategy or timing of action. One of these is the mood of the group and its leadership. Both are sensitively interrelated. Their effect upon performance can be profound. Additionally, you must take account of factors of timing, of the environment and of task difficulty.

You have seen instances where all the odds were against success, where the people did not know this and where they carried the day brilliantly in spite of incapabilities and inefficiencies. Sometimes the magic of this success lies in the enthusiasm and ebullience of a young group which feels it is on the rise. Its very mood invests it with an action momentum which overrides obstacles. You have also seen less dynamic and more straightforward situations which present a pattern of successful action compounded of (1) a high-confidence factor, (2) good organization and (3) experience in getting things done.

When these elements are present you can feel the mood of success. It operates on a momentum of its own, carrying the day for its adherents against all odds. Wise is the executive who takes advantage of this even as the pilot rides with favorable tail winds. Conversely, the pilot of the plane or ship knows the greater effort required to move against the winds or ocean currents.

The mood of the leader may, in itself, be sufficient to carry the issue — or vice versa. He must be able to appraise the situation and sense whether, even in the face of adversity, his actions might bring the results desired.

I recall an incident in Baltimore about twenty years ago at a complex street intersection. Traffic was at a standstill; cars approaching from several streets were stalemating each other. There were no traffic lights. Sensing the situation, I jumped out of my car and, taking command, I directed traffic until the jam was broken. Then I ran back to my car to drive off before I could be charged with obstructing traffic!

People tend to accept the confident assertion of authority by the leader. This will carry initially, only, for the leader must continue to impart to the group a feeling of his own effectiveness and his own enthusiasm if he is to retain its confidence. He is the pace-setter. Beyond merely setting an example, he may need to motivate and convince his people, making use of persuasion, incentives and even discipline.

Many elements enter into an appraisal of the mood of (or for) action. The following list may suggest others:

1. Agility, enthusiasm and energetic drive of the group, usually (but not always) associated with its youthfulness.

2. Recent record of performance, as an index of a mood of success or failure.

3. Group support of objectives and goals.

4. Group attitude toward its leadership.

5. Demonstrated effectiveness of the leader in getting results in the past under similar circumstances.

6. Receptiveness of the group to change as evidenced by reactions to previous changes.

7. Attitude of group toward undertaking new assignments, in light of its existing and previous loads.

8. Existence in the environment of obstacles to success, which may affect group mood.

9. Ability of leadership to carry group in the existing situation.

The Timing of Action

In the taking of action, timing is very important from a strict engineering standpoint. Using a production line as an analogy, components of action must be in place at the right time or the entire operation will be disrupted. This aspect of timing is not of concern here. Rather, we should explore the more subtle aspects of psychological timing.

Your reading of the situational mood or climate should give you a feeling of the psychological timing of action: when to announce the decision or begin putting it into effect so that it will be most acceptable (or least unacceptable), provided you have any discretion as to timing.

Psychological timing is important whenever there is to be a significant alteration of the pattern of vested personal rights and work ways. It is also important to choose the right moment when interest and zeal can be maximized for that extra burst of drive toward accomplishment.

Here are a number of techniques for achieving good psychological timing:

1. Annex the action to another activity or program which will more certainly carry a strong action imperative. For example, a planning assignment can be annexed to budget preparation.

2. Take action at a time when a new situation itself dictates change. For example, a new key official usually is recognized as having the prerogative of effecting important procedural and personnel changes, *during his early days in office.* An accident justifies pertinent operational or physical changes. A turndown

in the financial picture gives protective cover for drastic personnel changes or reductions.

3. Pave the way for the action of taking preliminary steps. For example, remove procedural obstacles or fill operational or procedural gaps. Win the confidence of key individuals whose acceptance and example will bring others into camp. Take action on a nominal or break-in scale, to let people have a taste of the major action to come.

4. Wait for the situational climate to change, either of its own accord or through precipitating actions.

Now you won't always be able to choose your own timing. It's still important to get a feeling of the mood of the situation so that you can then do whatever is necessary to minimize the disadvantages and maximize the gains.

Techniques of Limited Commitment

When the costs or consequences of a failure may be substantial, you want to "hedge your bets." You want some opportunity for recovery in case things don't work out as planned or desired. Consider another case: you approach the taking of action with some hesitance, for you are uncertain of much of the effects of your action. Aside from trying to peer into the veiled future, what else can you do?

One thing you can do is divide the action, where feasible and practicable, so as to commit a minimum of resources while you observe how things shape up. The trial run or sample installation has been mentioned as an important approach. It constitutes a sort of microcosm of the full activity which, after "debugging," is then expanded.

Another approach, when you cannot release a trial balloon, is to divide the effort in sequence. You monitor your experience with each subtarget and use the intelligence derived therefrom as a basis for correcting both preceding as well as succeeding steps. This technique avoids full irretrievable commitment. It is applicable also to the small-scale trial installation, so as to limit even its commitments.

The underlying principle here is that until you take real

action in its normal (or at least closely simulated) environment, you are limited to assumptions and guesses, however educated they may be.

Now we come to one of the key aspects of planning: the building in of flexibility and maneuverability. For each of the critical steps you must set forth the conditions of successful performance (or the probable response patterns). Then you ask: "What do I do at this stage if things don't go as I planned them?" You answer by devising alternative courses of action.

As the plan of action takes real form you then keep on the alert for any signs of nonperformance. The trick is to detect these well in advance of the actual default or slippage. When you can do this you avoid unnecessary commitment and expenditure of resources. You also find time for corrective action before an actual crisis develops.

The key to perfecting a plan which has uncertainties, therefore, is to move from the stages of conjecture and planning to the ultimate one of operating in the "real world."

Actions and Their Reactions

I have tried to bring out how proceeding from the activity of the mind into that of the real world enables you to encounter — and encompass — factors you had not previously anticipated. Now this actually is an oversimplification. Anything you do will alter the conditions in the environment of your action. In many cases you provoke counteractions from people which oblige you, in turn, to revise your own approach.

This brings to mind an interesting passage I came across in a paper given me by the late Dr. N. Sulzberger, originally published in July, 1920 in the *Medical Review of Reviews*. He said:

". . . By law of nature, every process, be it biologic, chemical or physical, produces, in the course of its action, just such bodies, conditions and effects as are hindering and detrimental to the undisturbed continuance of the process itself, such process being finally terminated if these bodies and effects are not, from time to time, removed or counteracted. . . ."

This point is particularly pertinent in both competitive and hostile situations and environments. One significance is that you must anticipate the reactions and counteractions from people which may affect your achievement of the results for which you had planned. The frame of mind and approach for this are covered in Chapter XII, "Crystal-Balling the Future."

Another implication is that you must check into the effects of your actions, from time to time, to see what antibodies may have come into being.

The Lessons of Failure

However much failure is to be avoided, when it occurs, you should take your gains from it. This is an entirely different attitude from the more familiar one of "Who struck John?" This favorite post-mortemizing sport is an utter waste of time unless it aims at correction of errors which may recur, rather than at the mere condemnation of the error-makers.

The aftermath of a decision is action, and the aftermath of action often brings out some measure of error or failure. In a sense anything short of perfection constitutes a fraction of failure. Where the effort as a whole is successful, the minor failings are tolerated. The same slippages may be looked upon in a meaner light when the over-all outcome is bad. The good executive is not concerned with the context of error so much as he is with taking constructive gains.

Two other thoughts I'd like to interject at this point are:

1. The error-maker should correct his own decisions and actions, whenever practicable, unless he has demonstrated an incapability of doing so. The human value is important here: he does not feel put aside because of occasional error. Constructively, he is given an opportunity to learn from his experience.

2. He who errs makes a greater hero of himself by admitting

it than by trying to conceal it; the onlookers will know who
did it anyway.

EMERGENCY DECISIONS

In the real world there are always emergencies when it is not
possible to go through the procedures of orderly fact-finding,
digestion, consultation and selection from among carefully engineered alternatives. To insist on ordered decision-making
under true emergency conditions would reflect a naïveté, to
say the least. There would, however, be cause for real concern
if emergency decision-making were the rule, rather than the
exception.

Criterion for Emergency Decision-Making

The judgment as to whether or not to make the emergency
decision — or whether to defer — depends mainly on the consequences of not acting. Because of the risks of such peremptory judgment, the advantage must be more than marginal.
That is, the probable gain or advantage must not be offset
greatly by the probable risks.

I would not attempt to lay down a set of rules for emergency
decision-making. Each situation has its own law of action which
can be derived only from an understanding of the interplay of
elements in the situation. This does not mean that all reason
must be abandoned. Insofar as he can do so the executive must
go through all the steps in problem analysis and decision.

The existence of an emergency means only that there is less
time for fact-finding and consideration. If anything, there needs
to be a higher order of thinking and acting than under normal
conditions. The action and its effects must be monitored closely
to identify quickly the need for corrective action. As soon as
possible, normal handling of the matter should be restored.

Informing Others of Emergency Decisions

One of the first things to do, after the emergency action is
taken, is to inform those vitally concerned. Obviously any

superior officers having a responsibility in the matter would want an explanation as to why they were not consulted. So would colleagues and responsible subordinates.

Apart from merely "briefing" the others, by bringing them into the act, even belatedly, you avail yourself of their counsel for the improvement or correction of unfolding phases of the action. Conceivably you might need to retrieve the situation — that is, to pull back — and as to this you would need counsel.

CONCLUSION

If we accept the premise that a decision must be that which is demanded by the situation, then the role of the decision-maker is really that of agent of the situation. This does not mean that he is not supposed to exercise his personal influence in the reaching of a decision, for he, too, is a part of the situation. As agent, however, he must be conscious of the legitimate points of view of all who are interested in the matter, especially of those who are affected by the decision or who must contribute in some way to putting it into effect. Those who are experienced in directing the activities of others know well the ways in which people can negate programs and activities with which they are not in sympathy.

One of the weak links in the chain of decision-making and action is the planning of the specific means through which decisions are to be put into effect. In many cases this should be done tentatively before the final decision is reached. That is, you should have a good view of the effects of a decision before you actually make the decision. Then when you put it into effect you can be more confident of results.

PART TWO

The Personal Skills of Decision-Making

Chapter VII

DECISION-MAKING IN MEETINGS

A consultant, James O. Rice, once studied the conduct of meetings in one hundred of the country's top industrial firms over a period of eighteen months and concluded that only one-tenth of about 300,000 meetings were effective. He estimated the lost time at about $250 million a year! Most of the failures he blamed on poor preparation, while a second big reason was that many of the meetings should never have been called at all.

To corroborate Rice's findings, you have only to look through the pages of any general management periodical or most trade journals and you will find that articles on meetings and conferences rate high in popularity. So do cartoons and quips like "A committee is a group that keeps minutes and wastes hours."

In spite of the complaints, most business still gets done by people talking to each other. If the walls and ceilings of office buildings were made of clear glass and you could look in, you would see a mammoth talkathon. Of all the forms of conversation, formal and informal meetings would rate high, especially among managerial and professional people. A survey by the American Management Association of a group of representative executives showed that they spent, on the average, 25 per cent of their work week in conferences.

THE PROPER USE OF MEETINGS

Sooner or later, if your company or organization is like most, you may order an appraisal of what you're getting for the time invested in meetings. When you get to this point you might want to compare notes with the findings of the Ansul Chemical Company. A survey of top and middle management executives showed that they were consuming anywhere from 10 to 50 per cent of their time each week in meetings.

These were some of their findings:

1. Meetings were being called without any real or generally understood criteria for calling them.

2. Agenda for meetings were not prepared fully and often were not followed properly.

3. Criteria seemed lacking for the choosing of participants in meetings since the wrong people seemed frequently to be in attendance.

4. Right or wrong, the actual participation in meetings involved too many people.

As reported in *Dun's Review & Modern Industry* by Grover Amen, the Ansul top management concluded that since meetings were an organizational necessity, they had to be improved instead of eliminated. This is like the famous cry, "If you can't lick 'em, join 'em!" They concluded also that since managers are more often participants rather than chairmen, they should be trained in both conference leadership and participation.

To accomplish the last item, Ansul instituted a training program from top management on down through lower-level management personnel. This study program covered the formal aspects of planning and conducting meetings as well as dealing with personal psychological factors which were obstructing effective communication.

As a result, many dramatic improvements were achieved: meetings were taking less time or they were getting more accomplished in the same time. Participation was limited only to those expected to make a *definite* contribution, regardless of protocol. Those invited knew in advance what was expected of them.

The Pros and Cons of Group Decision-Making

Some of the principal advantages of using conferences and committees as the medium through which to reach decisions are:

1. Problems are brought out into the open — whether known and held under the surface or actually unknown and identified only through a frank discussion of the symptoms.

2. Varied expert knowledge, opinions and judgments are brought to bear on matters of some complexity or intangibility where group interaction will generate a common understanding and solution.

3. Matters which have been stalemated in the course of handling through ordinary administrative channels may be brought out for re-examination in the hope that a face-to-face approach may help clear the air.

4. Acceptance and enforcement of decisions by the participants is sought through the procedure of enabling them to share in the responsibility for the decision.

5. A "court" of judgment is provided for action on matters affecting people intimately, when executives acting alone would otherwise be subject to pressure or censure.

6. Opportunities for development for higher responsibility are afforded the participants through their exposure to various assignments in the meeting and through the opportunity which they have to observe the solution of problems at close hand.

On the other side of the ledger you can find many notable expressions of dissatisfaction with committee work as opposed to what can be done by well-trained individuals acting through channels. Ralph J. Cordiner, chairman of the General Electric Company, has been quoted as saying, "If you can name for me one great discovery or decision that was made by a committee, I will still find you the one man in that committee who had the lonely insight — while he was shaving, or on his way to work, or maybe while the rest of the committee was chattering away — the lonely insight which solved the problem and was the basis for decision." With this tongue-in-cheek observation in mind, let's now look at some of the disadvantages of group decision-making:

1. *Most* meetings are a risk. Most meetings are run poorly and are a waste of time in spite of years of strenuous effort to improve them.

2. The aggregate return to the participants for the amount of time they spend in meetings is low compared to the aggregate amount of time spent by them in meetings. Thus, if five people are in a meeting, the average time spent in discussion is 20 per cent per person. Even counting listening as a form of participation, the pay-out would still be low. Moreover topics and discussions tend to come up which do not involve all of the people and sometimes do not interest anyone other than the speaker.

3. Decision-making by committee or conference tends to weaken or bypass administrative responsibilty unless the chairman is in full control and uses the conference as a consultative body. Committees are often used deliberately as burial grounds or as means of passing the buck in order to avoid administrative responsibility.

4. Some people use conference sessions as convenient media for the advancement of their personal aims rather than for the advancement of organizational aims. Committees are sometimes used as public forums, by subordinates, as a means of finessing their superiors.

5. Taken away from their ordinary work places, the participants often find themselves without adequate information on aspects of the problem that could not have been anticipated. To avoid being caught without their facts, they tend to bring along their more qualified subordinates, armed with bulky folders and notebooks. The combination of increased participation and mixing of work levels tends to stultify the proceedings. On the other hand, the absence of facts and analyses, not previously anticipated, may cause postponements, delays and loss of continuity in the decision-making activity.

6. Some people who would not hesitate to express themselves fully from behind their desks, when they have a chance

to think through what they are going to say, may freeze in the face of the need for spontaneous give-and-take discussion. The extent to which this occurs may vary with the climate of participation encouraged by management.

7. Meetings often lack an incisive quality because of an excessive preoccupation with feelings, personalities and protocols.

Suitable Occasions for Meetings

The five points which follow should be considered in the light of the pros and cons just described. A positive judgment should be made that the ordinary exercise of administrative responsibility would not be so satisfactory as the calling of a meeting. Also, as a prerequisite to calling a meeting, you should be satisfied that the committee will have the capability and authority necessary to accomplish the mission to be assigned to it.

1. The group has the collective knowledge and experience, through contact with related or similar situations in the past, which would not otherwise be available through ordinary administrative channels.

2. The subject is such that it requires the several contributions of the participants simultaneously, so that they can be interlaced and brought to bear on a complex or highly intangible topic or one requiring the simultaneous exercise of diverse technical judgments.

3. Time does not permit the referral of a matter in sequence through the ordinary administrative channels. A matter is of sufficiently pressing nature that it will exert its own time-leverage on the proceedings.

4. The participants need to become thoroughly briefed on their respective and mutual roles in a subsequent series of actions so that each will know just when and how his part is to be brought into concert with those of the others.

5. The matter is of a "privileged" nature, requiring referral to a senior group which is privy to the private matters and business secrets of the enterprise.

Boards, Committees and Work Groups

Up to now we have used such terms as "group," "conference" and "committee" rather interchangeably. In the sense of process, they are all quite similar, but some fine distinctions can be made among them. As compared to individual conferences and discussions, boards, committees and work groups have a more advanced status. They usually have consistent membership and defined missions or objectives. They usually operate under prescribed procedures and are expected to maintain some degree of formal documentation. In a sense they constitute a kind of cross-section of organization to which is delegated a specific responsibility apart from those made through ordinary channels. To coin a term, they are "activity organizations."

In spite of all that has been said about committees and meetings and their ineffectiveness, the *Management Review* found, as a result of a survey of companies of varying size, chiefly manufacturers, that the use of management committees was increasing. Even in the smaller companies, three out of four reported that their companies had more committees than five years previously. The most frequently named committee — reported by 40 per cent of the companies — was the executive management policy committee (under this or some other name, naturally).

The degree of permanency varies. A fully permanent committee will have an indefinite tenure while a limited term of existence may be given to an *"ad hoc"* body. Boards and committees may be full- or part-time, depending upon the amount of business to be assigned to them.

The functions of review and decision tend to distinguish a board from a committee which may have similar functions but also has more of the connotation of a working group. Boards are usually associated with higher-level responsibilities or with semijudicial responsibilities. Thus there are boards of review, boards of salvage, boards of survey with respect to lost or missing property, boards of promotion, etc. At the highest level is the familiar board of directors which may include membership from outside or inside the corporation or both. We will not, however, consider the operation of this kind of board in this book.

Committees and other formalized discussion groups have a tendency to continue themselves in office long after their usefulness has been served. Control of committees begins with the manner in which they are established. Some organizations require that advance approval be obtained for the establishment of committees or boards of any significant stature. This assures that the initial purposes are carefully thought out and set forth in the formal charter or authorization for the committee. The life of the committee and the manner of selection of its membership could be specified in this paper. In particular it is important to specify the deliberative nature of the committee: whether it is fact-finding, advisory or decisive.

The chairman and the secretary (if needed) should be selected both as to their personal qualifications and as to their ability to get along with each other. The requisites of a good chairman are described below. The secretary ordinarily functions as a staff assistant to the chairman, whom he should assist in matters of committee organization, drafting of long-range agenda, drafting of current meetings agenda, identification and solution of committee administrative problems, documentation of proceedings, follow-up, as appropriate, on committee actions and making of arrangements for committee meetings.

For current review and control of committee operations, it is often a good idea to have someone in an authoritative position outside of the committee receive copies of its agenda and minutes. This should permit current review of committee activities. For the long run a review should be made from time to time — say every six months or a year — to ascertain whether the committee's terms of reference need redefinition, whether its membership should be reconstituted and whether the committee is necessary at all. One means of keeping the committee invigorated as an effective mechanism for decision-making is to provide for a gradual rotation of membership.

The work group, in which the members have a continuing

relationship, as they start with the statement of a problem, gather the facts, analyze them together, develop alternative solutions and finally produce a group product, can be an enriching experience for all the members. In addition to learning from each other and also observing at first hand the value of cooperative activity, they have a unique opportunity to develop business friendships which may endure for years. From the standpoint of the organization these relationships yield a payout beyond the tasks of the work group, in other situations in the future.

Nevertheless committees pose a difficult problem for the administrator because they tend to weaken the autonomy of the regular departments of the enterprise. They also impute to themselves — or tend to do so — an extralegal status which they regard as transcending the ordinary administrative structure of authority. I have noted a peculiar phenomenon: it seems that the more junior the level of participation in committees, the more they seem to feel that they have a special mantle of authority. Perhaps this is a part of our democratic heritage, but employees generally tend to treat with some degree of respect the collective judgment of a committee.

HOW TO ORGANIZE A MEETING

The probability looms large that if time were not of the essence, a discussion group could eventually cover just about all facets of a problem and bring out of its discussion some useful conclusion — *provided the group actually worked at it.* The trouble is, time usually is quite scarce and concrete results usually are expected. Accordingly, we need some pretty firm ground rules for getting work out of a committee.

Advance Arrangements

Agenda and working papers. How long shall the agenda be? Shall it consist of one item or many? This question arises just about as frequently as the one raised every semester by students: "How long must the term paper be?" The answer invariably, from semester to semester, is that it must be long enough to cover the subject but no longer than absolutely necessary. Hence the number of items in itself is not the criterion; it is a matter of the subject matter and the amount of time necessary to give it adequate consideration.

The agenda, along with any working papers needed for the preparation of the participants, should be distributed in sufficient time before the meeting to allow them to be read and studied. As a matter of fact, in a well-run organization matters are not allowed to come up for discussion unless they have been given advance handling as just described.

Not all matters coming up on an agenda will require supporting documentation. Usually you can dispense with a prepared paper on very brief topics whose nature is self-evident. On the other hand, the case type of agenda may require very extensive documentation — even the circulation of a bulky file. When a paper is to cover new policy, procedure or program matter, the depth of coverage should be sufficient to make clear that the objective is being adequately pursued and served. The various issues and alternatives should be brought out whenever appropriate, together with supporting evidence or facts or a reference to their source and availability. In short, the working papers should represent completed staff work.

Size of group. The basis for selecting the participation in the meeting has already been discussed sufficiently. One limitation on participation which we ought to cover is that of size. Entirely apart from the matter of conserving staff time, the excessively large meeting inhibits an adequate interchange of ideas and comments. People seem to be less willing to express themselves in larger groups. Perhaps it is a fear of seeming to be conspicuous. At the other extreme, the group which is too small may not bring out a well-balanced discussion and this may lead to sharp cleavages.

The analogy of a poker game comes to mind: you need a

minimum number of players to make the game interesting while too many players will make it unwieldy (even though the cards do just barely hold out).

The ideal number of participants in a meeting, on the average, is five, based on findings of the Laboratory of Social Relations of Harvard University. Studies conducted by it suggest that you avoid meetings as small as two or three people, especially if there is any likelihood of a clash. On the other hand, you should avoid meetings with more than seven participants unless they are absolutely needed for adequate representation of subject matter and points of view.

When committees get very large, as with geographic representation or special interest representation, one of the ways out is to create a steering committee which does the work and then reports back to the main committee.

Bear in mind that participants may want to bring others along with them, to carry papers, to answer questions or to balance the power representation. You might need to pin down the matter of "bring-alongs" unless you already operate under a rule which covers this.

Meeting aids. For the conduct of the meeting itself you may need presentation "props." The tools most frequently used are chalk boards, easels for charts and easels for giant paper pads. Easels should be sturdy, to withstand the pressure of the hand or the weight of heavy cardboard charts. Sometimes the presentation of information is dramatized through projection, using ordinary slide projectors, overhead projectors or opaque projectors. Where meetings are held regularly in a conference room, equipment such as this is usually kept on hand for ready access.

The meeting place itself should afford the usual physical conveniences of good lighting, comfortable chairs, writing tablets and pencils and some means of air circulation, especially if smoking is permitted, which it usually is. While this does not seem to be the place in which to elaborate upon the physical aspects of managing a conference, their importance should not be underestimated. There are many good books on conference preparation and management and at least one of these should be consulted.

Chairmanship

The importance of being chairman has been given a statistical value. Researchers of the University of Michigan found that the effectiveness of the chairman can account for 35 per cent of the soundness of a decision.

The chairman is more than merely the impersonal monitor of the agenda and disciplinarian of the proceedings. His personal mission is to bring forth a tangible and selectively useful discussion product. To do this, he must plan the meeting in advance, see to it that all the necessary facts are brought out and discussed and that useful conclusions are drawn from the pooled information.

Apart from the obvious requisites of intelligence, effectiveness in personal communication, knowledge of the situation and the respect of the participants, he must be exceptionally skilled in dealing with and blending a wide variety of personalities. Seated around the one conference table, each of the participants will be different from all the others in his temperament, capabilities, knowledges, authorities, personal stature, expressiveness, motivations and personal security. The chairman must take account of all these as he senses the interplay of ideas and forces.

As reported in *Nation's Business,* the University of Michigan researchers concluded that the "good" chairman must possess the following attributes:

1. He must be active, directive and forceful.

2. He must have personal acceptance both as to his professional competence and his personal relationships.

3. He is the kind of person who, when he is a member of a group, not chairman, speaks up often and to the point.

4. He is a person of integrity.

5. He has a highly ordered approach to problem-solving and to the conduct of discussions.

An interesting point has been made by Robert F. Bales regarding the roles of social leader and task leader in a conference group. His sociometric studies led him to conclude that the man judged by the group to have the best ideas is not often the best liked person. Accordingly, he feels, the task leader who makes sure that the group accomplishes its mission should be supplemented by a social leader who acts as the softening and smoothing influence. The task leader might be a member of the group or he might be the chairman. The social leader might also occupy either role. While Bales makes an interesting and useful point, I have seen many leaders who are able to fulfill both roles commendably.

HOW TO GET THE MOST OUT OF A MEETING

As manipulator of ideas and personalities in pursuit of a verbal goal, the chairman has many things to take into account, mainly concerning personality, in addition to the substance and complexities of the topic itself. Like writers (and others) the good chairman is not just a born chairman. What he knows comes with progressive experience out of which he derives his insights, his skills in interpersonal relations, his maturity and his ability to perceive total situations or fields of activity. He can also learn from the experiences of others, offered in both serious mood and light humor.

How to Wreck a Conference

A great deal of our business humor is aimed at meetings and conferences. The *Management Review* published one series of cartoons entitled "How to Wreck a Conference." Apart from the self-sufficient satire of the illustrations, the captions themselves (by Lydia Strong) carry serious messages. Thus:

1. Call the meeting without notice.

2. If you've compiled ten pages of advance information that was sent to everyone, read it aloud and explain the footnotes.

3. Let Sam and Joe debate their personal differences for the

length of the meeting, thus providing good clean entertainment for all.

4. Or insist that Sam and Joe are really in agreement, and prove it by misquoting both of them. This will unite them in an attack on you.

5. Squelch any new approach not outlined on the agenda.

6. Don't snub any friends who may telephone during the meeting. Have your secretary put every call right through.

7. Ask leading questions, as: "You surely aren't casting doubt, are you, on the validity of the Zwibelfoos Survey?" They'll agree, to avoid admitting they haven't heard of the Survey, but the meeting will sour from this point on.

8. Answer all your own questions. It may take some juggling, but it's the only way to insure the right answer.

9. Change the decisions reached at the meeting — but don't let the others know. (It might hurt their feelings.)

10. Keep the purpose of the meeting a secret.

11. Warm up the meeting by devoting the first quarter hour to an account of your trip to the Thousand Islands. Pass around snapshots, by all means . . . souvenir matchbooks, too, if you have them handy.

12. Instead of preparing information in advance, send out for each item as needed. This gives participants time to duck out for quick phone calls, from which they may never return.

13. Track down all the fascinating side issues, lead where they may.

14. Twist other people's remarks to suit your purpose.

Obviously all you've got to do to take your gain from these sarcasms is to convert them into "don't's." The failures are those of the discussion leader.

In more serious vein, the National Industrial Conference Board made an analysis of seven hundred practice sessions in conference leadership and concluded that the following are the most common pitfalls, as reported in the *Management Record:*

1. Inhibiting free and objective discussion; influencing the thinking of the group by use of leading questions, suggesting arguments and provoking antagonisms.

2. Keeping the meeting going at top speed; talking too much himself; failing to give the group itself time to develop its own solution.

3. Excessive use of "direct" questions; aiming questions at individual members rather than at the group, except where necessary for particular reasons of balancing or stimulating discussion.

4. Lack of control; failure to follow an orderly and disciplined procedure, failure to move the meeting along to its desired conclusion.

5. Lack of preparation; failure of the leader to brief himself beforehand.

6. Embarrassing an inattentive member; failure to use more constructive approaches for obtaining active participation.

7. Failure to organize and record the group's thinking visually; failure to drive home the points made or conclusions reached through use of blackboards, paper charts and oral summaries.

In case we have omitted anything, I would now like to list fourteen frustrations in conferences as brought out in a series of meetings conducted by Malcolm Macurda of the Pacific Telephone & Telegraph Company and reported by Mrs. Gloria Fowler of the Industrial Relations Section, California Institute of Technology.

1. Lack of acquaintanceship with the other conference members — who they are, what they do and, particularly, their status.

2. Outside distractions.

3. Inability of the group to get the discussion started.

4. Distractions caused by members of the group — physical attitude (e.g., slumping, expressions of anger, excessive weariness, etc.).

5. Uncomfortable pace.

6. Difficulties in gaining acceptance of ideas.

7. Inability to understand what someone else is trying to say.

8. Interruptions by others during the discussion — lack of recognition.

9. Strong emotional disagreements, including sharp, outright contradictions.

10. The person who can "straighten the others out."

11. Interchanges localized between two members or one member and the leader.

12. Too rapid shifting from one topic to another — inability of the group to "stay together."

13. Lack of organization.

14. Pressure of time.

The Tone of Participation

The tone of the meeting is derived largely from the general environment in which the participants ordinarily operate. Within this climate, the occasion for the meeting and its urgency affect the tone of participation more directly. A good chairman senses these conditions and adjusts his own demeanor and strategy accordingly.

The tone of a conference may be created by the balance or clash of personalities. The chairman may take this into account in adjusting or modifying the participation, if he has anything to say over this, and he may also astutely arrange the seating with specific personalities in mind.

When the meeting gets under way, if any of the participants are not known to the others, the chairman should dispose of the amenities, thereby setting the participants at ease and enabling them to communicate with each other most effectively.

This is not to suggest that a conference must be a model of gentility. An article in *WE* (Western Electric Company) suggests that a productive conference must contain a desirable amount of friction. This is the kind of constructive conflict discussed in Chapter V. It reflects honest differences of opinion and the spirit of the play which impels participants to back up their opinions forcefully. To derive the benefit of such productive friction, the participants must have maturity, tolerance and good manners as necessary support for a common desire to reach a common conclusion.

Much has been said about the desirability of encouraging participation in decision-making as a basis for assuring acceptance of decisions. The theory is that when the group makes its own decision, the participants usually feel under obligation to carry out the group will. The converse is that the group resents being fed a decision.

While this is generally sound I believe the principle does not apply to the kinds of decisions which the group *expects* the leader to make under his own authority. The participation may actually consist of being consulted, with the realization that the executive may choose to accept, modify or reject the views presented to him. The leader acknowledges the value of other opinions while retaining his independence of decision in the light of his own responsibility and his own awareness.

Leading the Discussion

The chairman has one or more discussion goals to achieve within a limited period of time. He is anxious that there be adequate and balanced discussion in spite of the pace of activity which he must maintain.

To keep within his timetable the chairman may need to break into discussions with summary comments or with transitional remarks to enable the group to move on to the next point. If the discussion gets off the track the chairman must restate the discussion goals and issues. The chairman must be able to sense the "alertness index" of the group. Boredom is evidenced by fidgeting, dozing, doodling, glancing around the room, etc. This is a notice to the chairman to change pace, raise his voice, go to the blackboard, call a recess or refreshment break or even tell a funny story.

To obtain a full and balanced discussion, the chairman may need to suppress some participants while he draws out others. Part of the skill of the chairman is in recognizing certain "meeting types" and knowing how to deal with them. Following is a catalogue of some of the principal problem types, condensed from my book *Handbook for Sales Meetings, Conventions and*

Conferences (New London, Connecticut, National Foremen's Institute, division of Prentice-Hall, Inc.):

The talker: He may be anxious to display his knowledge which may be very good; he may really want to be helpful; or he may just be the talkative type. If he is actually well informed he may make some of the best contributions but you still cannot risk having him dominate the meeting. A remedy is to offset his activity by encouraging others. Take some of his ideas and throw them to the rest of the group. Stop him with some difficult questions. Don't ridicule him or be sarcastic, for then you may lose his valuable contributions.

Silent Sam: He thinks he has nothing to say; he thinks he knows the score and has nothing to get out of the meeting; or he may be timid or insecure. To draw him out, you'll have to know him better and this may be hard to do if you only have the one meeting in which to analyze him. If he seems the timid type, give him a pat on the back after you've gotten him to say something. If he seems the superior type, go after his ego. Recognize his special experience in a way that does not antagonize the others in the meeting.

The rambler: He can wreck the agenda by talking about one thing and then getting sidetracked onto another. He brings out examples which are not really pertinent. You must break into his discussion at the first opportune moment, but don't embarrass him. Make some neutral, friendly remark very briefly, but move quickly to another topic or another participant. Be on guard for him to prevent recurrences.

The aggressor and heckler: He is probably frustrated. He might not feel recognized or rewarded. Whatever is bothering him may actually be far away from the meeting or office itself. He must be brought under control because he can disrupt the meeting if allowed to cut in constantly. Give him the recognition or satisfaction he craves, whenever he deserves it, but don't give him too much. Get him to feel he belongs but also make him conscious of the needs of the others. If he is wrong in what he says, avoid being the one to put him in his place. Channel this to the group instead. Don't lose your temper.

The initiator: This fellow is in the same ball park as the talker. He is chock-full of ideas but forgets the other participants. Again your main remedy is to get the others to participate. You can also channel his energies by giving him special assignments such as summarizing or recording.

The complainer: He is negative from the word "go." He may have some good points but they are pretty hard to separate from the illegitimate ones. You may not really be able to solve his problem in the meeting. Ignoring him won't help because he'll be even more determined to have his say. One remedy is to refer his complaints to other participants for them to answer. As a last resort, tell him cordially that the issue he raises is too big to solve in the meeting but you are anxious to discuss it later to see if a solution can be reached.

The side operator: He may be doodling, talking or working on his own papers. He may have other things on his mind which seem more important to him. Keep him in the act. Fire direct questions at him from time to time. Be careful not to make a public spectacle of him. Try catching his attention and then, if you bring him into the discussion casually, he'll know what you're up to and will probably play along thereafter.

The opinion-holder: This man can see only his own point of view. If, after a good try by you and other participants, you still can't get him to come around, leave him alone for a while. If he is adamant you may need to suggest cordially that the group view will have to prevail — or you may not need to say anything at all.

The inarticulate: He is a man who can't express himself. He may fumble his idea sequences as well as his words. The others can be pretty rough on him. Before he gets too far you may need to step in and help him out. Steer him toward a logical sequence or help him find the words or expressions that will convey his meaning. If you don't handle him well you might lose him as an active participant.

If the discussion lags it may be stimulated by asking questions. These should stimulate controversial discussion. They should not be framed so that they can be answered by a "yes" or "no." On the other hand, the discussion must not become so controversial that tensions develop. Arguments must be kept on a friendly and constructive plane. The chairman should pick up a thread of controversy and convert it into constructive talk.

The good chairman is one who has learned to be a good participant. He is qualified then from both points of view.

How to Be a Good Participant

The good participant needs to work at it. He starts by doing his homework and informing himself before he comes to the meeting. He contributes to the proceedings when he has something worthwhile to say. Otherwise he lets others have an opportunity. He pays careful attention to the discussion, he listens and absorbs and he raises reasonable questions. His questions and his remarks are germane to the topic under discussion. He does not expect to have all of his views accepted and if he meets with conflicting points of view, he acknowledges the sincerity of others and their right to express their own views. Throughout the proceedings he maintains a good temper and refrains from personalizing his own remarks.

The Hidden Agenda

In business we grow accustomed to looking for hidden motives behind the expressed or ostensible motives. These may be found also as a kind of hidden agenda in conferences. The chairman may recognize that a game is being played, but the circumstances may be such that he will have no choice but to monitor this game. At least he should have the sophistication which will enable him to keep the affair within bounds.

An interesting example of the hidden agenda is brought out in a story told by the late Dr. Edward C. Lindeman before the Council of Personnel Administration in Washington which I heard in 1944. Dr. Lindeman said:

"I remember a long time ago I was asked to go to Geneva to make a study of the committee system of the League of Nations, and I selected for my observation what I thought was the best committee, the Economic Committee. It was composed of the leading economists from all over the world. I had three assistants, and we worked out very elaborate charts, and our job was to sit in the background and all four of us were making marks, symbols on the charts so that afterwards we would be able to reproduce the entire proceedings of the committee and then analyze it.

"For two and a half days we sat there making these symbols on the charts, and what do you suppose these men were discussing for two and a half days? I know this sounds absolutely incredible to you, but I vouch for it. For two and a half days these men discussed, Shall we have three meetings next year or five meetings next year? Obviously that wasn't an issue. You can't spend two and a half days discussing three versus five, can you? So it was quite clear after some exploration that that wasn't the issue at all.

"The real question was this: If we have three meetings, then all the small nations will have big delegations, but if we have five meetings, the small nations will not be able to send big delegations and the big nations will be able to run the show."

Critical Control Stages

By way of a summary recap I suggest the following critical points of control for the chairman, with notes on what to do about them:

1. *Floundering:* Restate objectives, agreements reached thus far, residual goals; throw out challenging questions.

2. *Dissension:* Pick up the argument and convert it or shift it to someone else; intervene with an analysis of the issues and then bring another viewpoint into the discussion; throw some oil of humor on the troubled waters.

3. *Deadlock:* Identify and state the issues on which there is disagreement; relate these to objectives and areas of agreement

reached thus far; to avoid deadlock, use informal test votes on minor, indicative issues and then, if so indicated, back off from the issue until more facts can be obtained; if emotions are flowing over, find some means of graceful retreat for the parties at issue.

4. *Hasty conclusion:* Before concluding too quickly, make sure discussants have had adequate opportunity to express themselves; review adequacy of facts in support of the conclusion; make sure all understand the implications of the conclusion and that they all fully accept it.

5. *Wrong decision:* If the chairman does not have authority to decide in his own right but feels the decision is wrong, find some excuse to delay — some hypothetical question, some new facts or someone else who needs to be consulted. If the chairman has decisive authority in his own right, if his conviction so dictates, he must stand against the group and decide contrary to their recommendation.

6. *Conclusion:* Express the positions reached, making sure no one takes away an understanding not shared by the others; identify the mechanics of carrying out the decision and translating it into action.

BRAINSTORMING

Brainstorming is a technique for getting participants in an idea-seeking conference to produce an unrestrained flow of ideas. No ideas are ridiculed, for one of the basics in brainstorming is that you must throw off all of your inhibitions and all of your preconditioned assumptions, for they may be false. Brainstorming as a technique is attributed to Alex F. Osborn of the New York advertising agency Batten, Barton, Durstine & Osborn. We discuss brainstorming in this chapter because essentially it is a conference technique, but there are pros and cons to consider.

Brainstorming in Brief

One of the leading exponents of brainstorming, Charles H. Clark, said of brainstorming that "it is a technique which encourages people to stick their necks out so that radically new ideas will be constantly produced."

The size of the group can be larger than the ordinary problem-solving conference in which there is a great deal of interaction among the members. In a brainstorming conference the group can range from not less than six people to not more than twelve. If you have too few the results might be limited while too many will produce unwieldiness and will tend to cut off individual contributions.

The main rules are: (1) don't criticize while ideas are flowing; (2) encourage the wildest ideas, for it is easier to tame them than to grow them; (3) obtain as many ideas as possible, for you then have a broader base for successful selection, and (4) encourage brainstormers to add to ideas, combine them or improve them — but not to disparage any. Afterward you can have evaluations.*

From a conference standpoint you might consider three different kinds of groups:

1. A vertical group, including people from all levels of the organization.

2. People who operate on the same status level, including a mixture of specialists as well as generalists.

3. People whose understanding of the problem is at about the same level but who have different points of view.

Note that in some situations you may need to recognize the importance of operating according to the official status pattern, without mixing subordinate and superior levels of status. In other situations you want to have some homogeneity in the maturity level of thought, although you want to have a variety of thought patterns. Above all, it is important that the membership be mutually stimulating and that this should lead to some competitive flow of ideas.

---

* These rules and many constructive suggestions for conducting brainstorming sessions are contained in a number of books on group creativity. One, by Clark, is *Brainstorming* (New York, Doubleday & Company). Another, by Osborn, is *Applied Imagination, Principles and Procedures of Creative Thinking* (New York, Charles Scribner's Sons).

The Group Versus the Individual

Many reports have been published on the tremendous results — the many new ideas — that have been achieved as a result of brainstorming sessions. Nevertheless some people believe that the individual working by himself can produce more than when he is thinking as part of a group. Carried further, the argument states that the aggregate number of ideas of a number of people working alone will exceed that of the same people working together.

This was the conclusion drawn from a study conducted for the U. S. Office of Naval Research under a grant to Yale University.

Professor Donald W. Taylor, who conducted the study, suggested that one reason why group participation might limit creative thinking is that the members cannot help but feel that they are subject to some criticism or censure when expressing new ideas, in spite of all the admonitions to the contrary. A second reason is that the group tends to channel the thinking of its members. That is, they tend to acquire a degree of group unity. Perhaps they mesmerize or hypnotize each other.

The doubters of the brainstorming approach may make such criticisms as this by President A. Whitney Griswold of Yale University: "Could *Hamlet* have been written by a committee or the "Mona Lisa" been painted by a club?" This question is really not relevant because it pertains to a single, unified product whereas in brainstorming you produce only a series of separate ideas, listed one after the other.

Where the unified product is the object, the brainstorming session may not be desirable at all. This may be borne out by the findings of Professor John Jewkes of London University (J. Jewkes and others, *The Sources of Invention;* New York, St. Martin's Press, Inc., 1958). Studying the history of sixty-one important inventions of the twentieth century, Professor Jewkes and his associates found that over half came from men who worked alone without organized research backing.

It might be easy to say that since there is some doubt as to the efficacy of brainstorming, one should not bother. By all means, if there are better approaches, use them. Still, bear in mind that brainstorming provides a discipline; it assures that a group of people will be brought together for a specific purpose and that there will be a result of this effort. Under the pressures of everyday business life you cannot be sure that people left to their individual efforts will set aside a "meditation period" during which they will think up new ideas. The realities tend to argue otherwise. Maybe this is what the critics have overlooked.

A Combined Approach

Perhaps the truth lies somewhere between the group and individual approaches. James R. Adams said, in his book *Sparks Off My Anvil* (New York, Harper & Brothers):

". . . For many years I have used the group method of creating ideas, but with a different twist. I usually gather a group, explain the problem, then send them back to their offices for two hours, where they can think alone. Then another meeting to accept and reject, and another two hours in solitude. Of course, somebody has to pick and choose after the group discussions. Sometimes this method is productive of ideas and sometimes it fails miserably. For most of its work, the human brain is an individual unit and works best alone. It is an idea factory all by itself."

CONCLUSION

The proper use of meetings for decision-making, we have seen, is to bring people together whose knowledge and views need to be intermixed simultaneously. Unfortunately many or most meetings turn out to be delay points in the path of reaching a decision, because of the poor management of the meetings. Better results can be expected from decision-making meetings if:

1. Meetings are called only when ordinary administrative channels cannot be used effectively in reaching a decision on the particular matter.

2. The chairman and participants do their homework, including the preparation and distribution of agenda, the reading of pertinent materials *before* coming to the meeting and the reaching of tentative positions before entering the meeting.

3. The chairman adheres to the agenda and monitors participation to assure that all appropriate contributions are made and that participation is balanced.

4. The chairman makes sure that all discussions are brought to a head in some way, whether in an agreed position, an agreement to disagree or an agreement to continue discussions.

5. All decisions reached are confirmed after the meeting and follow-ups are made by appropriate persons to assure that intended actions are taken.

Chapter VIII

HOW TO HELP OTHERS MAKE DECISIONS

There are certain people who make their living by helping others make decisions. They include staff specialists, professional consultants, lawyers, economists, technical specialists, personal assistants and psychological counselors among others. The better and more successful ones develop personal skills which enable them to help in a tremendous variety of situations, often covering many fields of subject matter. Their secrets are easily learned, for they embrace certain common elements of procedure which should govern most advisory situations. These are:

1. You must acquire an understanding of the total problem situation in which the decision-maker finds himself, whether or not he himself recognizes the extent of the situation.

2. You must be able to perceive the personality of the decision-maker at work in the particular situation. This extends to a recognition of his motivations, his personal values, his operating assumptions and his mental blockages and blind spots.

3. You must be able to win the confidence of the decision-maker.

4. You must guide the decision-maker through the steps that assure that he will understand the situation and the alternatives of action and their consequences in relation to the satisfactions he desires to achieve.

Oddly enough, a knowledge of the subject matter is *not al-*

ways necessary. It can, in fact, be detrimental if it is too deep.
It is more important that you enable the decision-maker to
find his own solutions. Of course, this does not apply to situations in which the decision-maker seeks purely technical consultation.

Assuming that you master the procedures — and they are not
difficult to learn — you will always be operating under one great
handicap: as soon as you enter the decision situation, even as
counselor or assistant, you begin losing objectivity. You cannot
entirely eliminate your personal reactions to the situation. You
cannot be totally impersonal in your reactions to the operating
personality of the person you are trying to help.

The purpose of this chapter, then, is to suggest techniques
for maximizing your beneficial assistance to the decision-maker
and minimizing any purely personal influences on your part.

GENERAL RULES FOR HELPING OTHERS

Some people cannot be helped except on their own terms,
which means that you cannot really help them. Once I worked
for a man in a top executive post whose usual practice was to
listen to my recommendations or proposals and then reject
them by substituting an opposite course of action. He seemed,
in fact, to respond in this way almost automatically. In due
course I learned that the shortest road to alternative A was to
present alternative B. I could depend upon him to squelch B
and to order action on A!

I mention this only to emphasize that some people are really
not susceptible to being helped. In this kind of relationship
you will not be able to rely solely upon the logic presented in
this chapter. Rather, your skill will need to prove itself mainly
in your ability to anticipate nonlogical and emotional reactions. If you can conquer these, then you can bring into play
the more straightforward procedures.

How to Understand the Need for Help

The fact that someone else may need assistance in reaching a decision — whether he be subordinate, colleague or superior — does not in itself reflect a lack of competence. Among the legitimate reasons why any of us may need help in reaching decisions are the following:

1. The decision-maker may want merely to use an individual or a group as a sounding board for his own thoughts and tentative decisions. He may want to clarify his thinking, to find new ideas or to validate his conclusions.

2. There is a need for expert counsel, skill or experience in estimating the situation and drawing conclusions from it, particularly when the expertese lies outside the ordinarily expected capabilities of the decision-makers.

3. Certain information may not be available except from specially privileged sources.

4. The generalist may need the more particularized view of the specialist and the latter may need the broader view of the generalist.

5. The decision-maker may be pressed with other duties to such an extent that he must willingly yield to the judgmental assistance of others.

6. The human element may constitute an important part of the decision itself — typical of personnel decisions — so that more than one judgment may be desired.

7. The problem may be overloaded with uncertainties and intangibilities to such an extent that the executive would feel most comfortable in having the inputs of other people.

8. The action that is to be taken should be acceptable to those whose assistance is sought in deciding upon it.

9. The matter under consideration is of such great importance as to dictate that no single person take upon himself the responsibility for making the final decision.

There are two other conditions which, *if occasional,* may be considered to be legitimate. If they are chronic there is more than a suggestion that the decision-maker should be replaced.

10. The decision-maker may be insecure and want others to share his responsibility so that they may also share in the blame if anything should go wrong.

11. The decision-maker may actually be incapable of managing the problem situation.

Are You Qualified to Help?

The fact that you are called upon to help — or that you want to do so — does not in itself qualify you. It should be obvious that if you are not qualified you should withdraw, but this is more easily said than done.

In the first place, the subdivision which characterizes industrial organization compels the rendering of mutual assistance. You must advise *me* as to the implications of what *I* intend to do as they bear upon *your* related responsibilities. Also, *I* must advise *you* in like manner. Both *you* and *I* and other of *our* colleagues must all advise *our* common superior. And so on. In this fabric of interplay you are supposed to be qualified by the very definition of your responsibilities. This does not mean that in fact you will be well informed or experienced on every matter which will arise.

The big fallacy in self-evaluations is that when we are not sufficiently informed on the particular matter, we lack even the prerequisites to self-evaluation. We tend to oversimplify and rely upon our individual "common sense." When I was with the Federal Government I never ceased to be amazed at the lack of qualifications of many claimants to high office. Especially when there was a change in administration, mere clerks would bring political pressure to have themselves appointed as heads of divisions or chiefs of bureaus. The more amazing thing was that sometimes they would actually win the support of their congressmen and senators!

Here is a self-evaluation check list:

How good is your background in the problem area?

1. Have you had actual experience as well as a "theoretical" background in the matter?

2. Has your experience been specifically limited or does it cover a diversity of situations?

3. How relevant has your experience been to the particular situation now being studied?

Are you a party at interest?

1. Do you stand to gain or lose from the outcome of the decision?

2. Are you likely to be so strongly biased — or be accused of it anyway — that you should withdraw from participation?

3. If you recognize the possibility of bias but still feel you have an important contribution to make, should you not strengthen your position by acknowledging this?

Will your views be given credence?

1. Do you have the personal attainments, experience and operating stature *in the eyes of others* that will cause them to put faith in your views and judgments?

2. If you conclude that you lack recognition, should you try to overcome this in your presentation or should you make your contribution through others whose views may be given more credence?

Spadework for Helpers

The techniques of situational analysis have already been covered in this book, from several different standpoints. At this point we need only review those things which bear upon the strategy of your relationship as helper to other decision-makers.

Is your timing right?

1. Is there sufficient recognition at this stage of the need, in general, for help or of the particular contribution which you might make?

2. If your help right now would be premature, do you need to work out a strategy of input?

3. Has the situation become so far committed or have events moved so rapidly that you have, for all practical purposes, lost any real chance to be of real service?

4. From your personal standpoint, can you time your assistance so that you personally derive the maximum recognition for your contribution (but never at the risk of jeopardizing the best interests of the enterprise)?

Are you helping the right person?

1. Is he the decision-maker in his own right or a contributor to the making of the decision?

2. Who is the ultimate decision-maker and how must his views be anticipated and considered?

3. Is the recipient of your aid in a position to make effective use of it?

What are the goals and personal values of the decision-maker?

1. Try to outline a framework of goals, policies and attitudes as expressed in previous acts. This may enable you to fill in the gaps or make logical projections based upon past consistencies.

2. Present to the decision-maker the possible outcomes of the various alternatives of action. By noting those to which he reacts positively, those to which he reacts negatively and those from which he shies away, you may be able to obtain meaningful clues.

3. In this way you may also be able to find the answer to this key personal question: does he truly want your independent advice or assistance or is he desirous merely of having you confirm what he wants to do anyway?

4. If you are able to do so try to interact with the decision-maker. Remember the English proverb: "Speech is the picture of the mind."

What should be your strategy of input?

1. Should you actively press your aid or respond only to direct requests? Your approach will depend on your knowledge of the decision-maker's personality and your appraisal of his motivations and desires.

2. Should you avoid a frontal approach so that the decision-maker will feel that he is expressing his own ideas and reaching his own conclusions? Skilled advisers make use of the "forcing

technique" of playing-card magicians. That is, they steer the conversation through bringing up key words and ideas which, in turn, provoke the other party into pursuing desired lines of inquiry.

3. Should you feed the decision-maker brief reports and other informational inputs over a period of time to sensitize him progressively to the problem and its implications?

These last suggestions constitute a strategy of approach. The best research and analysis into the problem situation and the personalities will be of no avail if you cannot succeed in effectively presenting the products of your effort to the decision-maker. In large measure, this is the heart of it.

The Dynamics and Mechanics of Helping

There is an ethics of advice and assistance. In pure principle, you are supposed to assist the decision-maker in reaching judgments which are best for the enterprise. You are not supposed to be influenced by your own private interests or objectives (or even by his!). You are not supposed to have any axes to grind. Assuming that you subscribe to these ethics, apart from questions of subconscious bias, the party being helped may not know this. To the contrary, if he is a top executive, he may become quite accustomed to people trying to advance a personal cause without seeming to be doing so. Almost automatically he begins looking for hidden motivations.

The acceptance of your support is essentially a function of the confidence you build in the decision-maker. Like a lasting friendship, full confidence is not built overnight; it must be aged. Having achieved this, you must take it for granted and you must never abuse it; you will be working just as hard to maintain it as to instill it in the first place.

When you win a person's confidence you create a new danger: because the decision-maker has been able to rely upon your developmental assistance and advice in the past, he may be inclined to accept your suggestions too readily, without independent reflection and challenge. A full review of this would lead us into an analysis of the psychology of suggestion. Suffice it to say that in our everyday life we are inclined to accept as valid, and without challenge, most of the statements that we read and hear. It would be physically impossible even to try to go behind all these statements.

Applying this to the situation of advice and assistance, the burden upon you is to lean backward to make sure that the decision-maker does, in fact, reach his own conclusions. Apart from your ethical responsibilities to do so, you should want to protect your personal status; if he should be caught in a serious backfire which he attributes to your suggestions, you may impair or destroy your own effectiveness.

If you are to be "happy though helpful" you must not tread on the ego of the decision-maker. In his mind, dependence upon another for assistance or advice may imply inadequacy. While your help may be accepted at the moment of need, resentments may be implanted which may subsequently turn into hostility. This is not true of all kinds of assistance. Thus we do not resent frank statements made by a physician, lawyer, mathematical statistician or engineer, within their technical fields. As one veers away from purely technical content toward a higher percentage of preferential or judgmental content, the greater is the likelihood that the feelings of the person being helped must be taken into account.

The safest course is not to tell others what to do but to enable them to perceive their goals in relation to the total situation, the alternatives of action, the possible outcomes for each and the relative values of these outcomes. In addition to structuring the situation as a whole, you should try to bring out the underlying principles which operate in the particular situation. This will enable the decision-maker to cope with the situation even though it undergoes changes as time moves forward.

THE RECIPIENTS OF HELP

Now I would like to be more specific by aiming at the various recipients of help. Usually we think of helping our superiors but we must also take into account our subordinates and our colleagues.

Serving the Upper Level

The first thing to do is to "peg" the superior executive on the totem pole of authority and informational access.

1. What is the level of his authority, both actual and theoretical?

2. What are the higher levels of policy and information to which he has access?

3. What kinds of relationships and associations does he have at his level within the organization (and outside, as pertinent) that may have a bearing on the matter, particularly as they point up his informational sources and his possible strategic interests?

4. What are the related activities and problems which are preoccupying him at his level or which may be preoccupying his colleagues and how might any of these bear upon his handling of the current matter?

This matter of knowing his current interests should be pursued in depth if your relationship is a continuing one. Get information on the following:

1. His current projects and their origin in each case.

2. His long-term projects and specific goals.

3. The sources of his information.

4. The nature and authenticity of the information he receives from these sources.

5. His specific requests for information in recent times.

6. The record of his past experiences and interests.

7. His recent decisions and expressions of policy and attitude.

8. The matters of importance and critical discussion in which he has *not* participated.

Remember that a man's actions can usually (but not always) be predicted in the light of his past performance and expressions, if these are fully known and understood in the context in which he has operated and is currently operating.

To avoid misunderstanding: I do not advocate an "under-cover" approach. In fact, I urge against invading the privacy of your superior. Your sole purpose is to know how best to serve him rather than how best to uncover him.

In fact, if you have a direct working relationship you can do no better than to talk directly with him about his needs for information and assistance. Obviously it is better to ask when in doubt than to miss the boat entirely. On the other hand, if your superior is not accessible he expects you to become informed on your own.

Finally, the time must come when you are to make your case to your superior. Usually he is a busy executive who is preoccupied with many different matters, all of which demand more time in the aggregate than he can ever hope to have. The essence of the procedures for making a good presentation was stated well by Joseph M. Dodge, formerly Director of the U. S. Bureau of the Budget and chairman of The Detroit Bank:

"When dealing with experienced members of a board of directors, or a manager, or a management group, it is unnecessary to prove how thorough you are or how much you know.

That usually is taken for granted, if you are good enough to hold the position you do. It is not necessary to educate men of this type by going through every step of your mental processes. By the time the second step is reached, the experienced man is way ahead, looking for the issue, and probably bored and resentful.

"The practical rule is a simple one; state the problem or the proposition first — then, as concisely as possible, give the reasons for or against it, and the recommendation. Be sure the comments include the essential facts and cover the issues sure to be raised. If properly done, nothing more may be necessary. Let any further information be requested.

"In this way what is needed to make a decision becomes available and no one will be bogged down with unnecessary details. Put a high value on the other man's time. He puts a high value on his time and he thinks you should value yours."

Nevertheless, for whatever reason we do so, we frequently tend to underestimate the informational grasp and understanding of our superior officers. Have you ever had such advice as this: "Look, Joe, I've got a great many things on my calendar today. Why don't you cut out some of the details? If I want more information I'll ask you or I'll call someone in. If I disagree with what you have to say, I'll say so and you can argue with me."

Here are some additional suggestions:

1. Try to choose a favorable time for your briefing if it is to be oral (although a written presentation also requires good timing). Consider the press of other matters, the sequence of preceding and succeeding events and his mood.

2. In an oral presentation try to get some guiding interaction with your superior. Start by throwing out a "sighting shot," some kind of preliminary remark or statement which will give you a measure of attitude or mood. Seek clues to whether you're getting through and whether you need to modify your presentation.

3. Be utterly truthful and strive, also, to play down the personal element so far as you are concerned. If your superior once finds you to be opportunistic, you might not be able to regain his full confidence.

4. Don't give your superior the "emperor's clothes" treatment; that is, don't patronize him — don't give him credit for attributes or capabilities which he does not have. While some few people may fall for this, most resent it.

Helping Your Own Helpers

The ability of your own subordinates to help you will depend largely upon the guidance and leadership you give them. This necessarily must start with clearly defined missions, both general and specific. Your subordinates will want to know whether they should wait for your call for assistance or whether they should anticipate or recognize the existence of a problem on which you will need assistance. Usually we preach the latter but subordinates may want to "play it safe."

Don't hold back facts your subordinates will need — unless this is necessary for legitimate reasons of operating secrecy. If you do you limit their usefulness.

Over a period of time your assistants will come to know how you operate and they will come to know what you expect of them, if through no other means than trial and error. The trial part is all right, if it is guided, but the error part can be more costly than you can afford. It scarcely needs saying that whatever constructive guidance and channeling you can provide will be more than repaid. You want them to become thoroughly acquainted with your objectives, working programs, working philosophies and policies and operating relationships, among others. With the passage of time you will need less and less to provide informational guidance. To the contrary, you should reap a harvest of return; that is, you expect your subordinates to begin briefing you after the "break-in" period has been completed.

Subordinates also have differences in personality which must be taken into account. Some may be more reticent while some may be bolder or more impulsive. Some may need to be encouraged and some restrained. Recognizing and accommodating these differences is a straightforward responsibility of executive leadership. Nevertheless top executives must assume that by the time their own subordinates reach those heights, they must have survived many tests of competence, especially those which demonstrate their ability to interact effectively at the upper levels.

This, of course, is the ideal. You are never quite relieved of the responsibility of developing your subordinates. I do not suggest coddling, but we must not forget that there is something about the large organization which tends to restrain initiative and impose timidity. Perhaps it is the tremendous fragmentation of effort. Perhaps it is the greater uncertainty which is an accompaniment of being able to deal only with parts of problems. Uncertainties engender fear which imposes restraint. Here are some suggestions for encouraging initiative:

1. Encourage your subordinates to suggest new ideas and new approaches.

Just to ask for new ideas is not enough. The executive must set an example by his own initiative. On the other hand, if he waits for others to take the risks, he will discourage constructive initiative. Worse than that, he will, in the long run, drive away any really creative or enterprising people.

2. Encourage initiative by giving support to your subordinates' views.

Governor Michael V. DiSalle gave me this advice: "If an administrator is inclined to second-guess decisions, this will make the people under him gun-shy. If a subordinate makes twenty-four good decisions and one bad one, it may be necessary for the administrator to support that decision, or at least to accept the responsibility for it before it is altered." To minimize the hazards of error under this kind of acceptance, Governor DiSalle recommends: "Many wrong decisions by subordinates can be avoided by the type of association that will tend to reveal the thinking of the chief executive or the administrator. If there is sufficient contact, sufficient discussion on general matters, it doesn't take long to absorb the philosophies and logic needed to make decisions down the line."

3. Let it be known that it is perfectly normal for everyone to have some percentage of error.

When something goes wrong, do you conduct a "who struck John" inquiry? Do you try to affix blame and penalty or are you more concerned with understanding why the error was made so as to avoid it in the future? You cannot merely preach a policy of tolerance; you must demonstrate this in actual practice. You must let it be known that a failure is your responsibility, too. Your subordinates must feel that they are judged by the totality of their performance and not by a minority of mistakes.

Another bit of advice from my friend the Governor: "There must be a development of mutual confidence, there must be the willingness to absorb an occasional setback because of error, and this has to have with it the knowledge of the subordinate that his decision will receive support; that he will not be embarrassed by being pushed out to accept the responsibility alone; that, if there has to be a modification or revision, a method will be found which will correct without condemnation."

4. Discourage yes-men, coattail riders and those who would shield you from bad news.

An occupational disability of men in high place is their difficulty in obtaining candid expressions from their subordinates. The high executive tends often to be shielded from the truth so that his feelings might not be hurt — more likely for fear that he might hurt his subordinates. Here again, if you want your people to speak their minds candidly, you must demonstrate a willingness to be influenced by their good judgments. You must discourage coattail riders by indicating that you can move forward much faster, by yourself, without their dead weight.

5. Give credit publicly to your subordinates for their own good ideas.

When you give credit to subordinates for their own good ideas, you gain much and lose nothing. In the eyes of your colleagues and of your own superiors you are given credit for having the kinds of subordinates who will generate good ideas. You are also given credit for the final results even though the idea behind them may not have originated with you. Those who work for you will repay such recognition by their greater dedication to their work and by their intensified loyalty to you.

6. Set an example by your own promptness in decision-making.

If you take action without delay and with good timing, your subordinates will respond in kind. You will be pacing them. Conversely, you cannot expect to generate the drive and promptness you may require of them if, subsequently, you "sit" on pending matters until the timing is lost or they become crises because of delay.

Helping Your Colleagues

By the very nature of modern corporate organization none of us can work alone. Each of us, in some way, must receive and offer assistance to his colleagues who have related responsibilities. It is a straight-out duty. Unfortunately actual relationships are not always fully cooperative, even though all may appear quite tranquil above the surface.

One deep-seated reason for this is the fear of some people that if it is known that they had to receive help from any other source, except on the most technical matters, they might be considered inadequate. Another deterrent is a reluctance to become obligated. Then there is the sometimes fierce competition for relative advantage that goes on in all organizations — the struggle to gain personal ascendancy, if not merely to protect what one already has.

In this competitive environment how does one acquire that personal posture which invites requests for personal — rather than routine — assistance?

You will be judged first as to whether you are one to whom problems can be entrusted without undue advantage being taken of the confidence. You will be judged by the pattern of your actions and behavior — and very little by your mere words.

Your colleagues may conjecture such questions as these:

1. Will you take credit for giving help?
2. Will you be gracious in being helpful or will you take a smug satisfaction?
3. Will you create a sense of obligation?

Don't underestimate the importance of taking credit. This is one of the values for which people will fight dearly. Credit for ideas or accomplishments is desired in order to bolster one's sense of security in the job. It is amazing how effective you can be provided you accord full credit to people other than yourself.

In the ideal situation you should not have to operate through indirection. A desirably more positive approach will depend upon individual relationships.

Impersonal means of inviting assistance include:

1. Circulation of drafts of action documents or problem papers for comment.

2. Agreement in advance that certain matters are appropriate for conference discussion.

3. Designation, by a common superior, of problem-solving groups whose membership includes people on the same working level.

In the ordinary crisscrossing of work relationships you can find many opportunities for making your assistance available, provided you contrive your offer as the natural thing to do. Here, too, you can be more effective if you understand the goals, values and personality structure of your various colleagues. The analytical framework given above, for your superiors, may be adapted also to your colleagues.

HOW TO MULTIPLY THE EXECUTIVE

Increasing burdens of scope, complexity and pace of activity have forced the modern executive to find ways of multiplying himself. Inside the house he makes use of staff assistants, troubleshooters, executive secretariats and functional staffs. From time to time he may reach outside for expert or independent consultative assistants. Which he makes use of these in many ways to extend his effectiveness, we'll consider them here only as they relate to the processes of decision-making.

"Assistants to," Special Assistants, and Troubleshooters

The typical "assistant to" is identified quite closely with the personal interests of his superior. His precise duties may vary, depending upon the kinds of staff services otherwise available. Usually he reviews all communications going into and out of his superior's office, except for personal matters. He reviews incoming communications for adequacy of staff work, sometimes calling for additional information. He may make preliminary analyses and digests of the essential facts and he may point out implications, as he sees them. He may screen a wide variety of reports and other internal publications for intelligence which he should refer to his superior. Thus he is able to act as a sounding board and as a personal confidante of his principal. Detached from direct responsibility for decision-making, he may lend a cooler perspective on decisions or actions in the making. With a good relationship, the executive knows that he can rely upon the assistant to protect his left flank and his rear while the executive himself is engaged in action on his right.

Valuable though he may be to his principal, the "assistant to" is often highly controversial. Regardless of how carefully he observes the paramount rule that he must never take unto himself the direct authorities of his principal, he is still liable to be regarded unfavorably by others who report directly to the principal executive. If he maintains his silence, as he should, they are never quite sure how he may screen or edit their own submissions. He seems to be able to command more of the time of the principal executive than they. When they receive requests or directives they are not quite sure whether these come from that official or whether they were inspired or written by his personal assistant. If they don't like the contents they cast their eyes suspiciously upon the assistant.

Sometimes they are warranted in their hostile attitudes because now and then one finds an assistant who may be misguided by his ambition or enthusiasm. The "assistant to" holds a position of great power. If he really enjoys the confidence of his superior he is able to exercise a greater influence in subtle ways than others. If he lacks principle or simply fails to understand the distinctions which must be maintained between line authority and staff authority, he can be so disruptive to top relationships that he may become more of a liability than an asset.

In my own career I have had an opportunity to observe at first hand both points of view: when I served as a top executive and had my own personal assistant and when I served other top executives in the capacity of personal assistant. Out of these experiences I accumulated the following thoughts about the qualifications of an "assistant to":

1. Ability to grasp situations and their meanings quickly; ability to see the heart of the situation and to sense critical factors.

2. Ability to see the broad picture and to understand the interrelatedness of programs and activities, especially as they relate to the whole.

3. Ability to take particular situations, matters and proposals and to relate their implications to past actions as well as to the unfolding series of actions to come.

4. Facility for absorbing, remembering and interpreting facts; facility for knowing what additional facts are needed and where and how to get them.

5. Sensitivity to interpersonal implications.

6. Facility for oral and written communication; flair for brief expression.

7. Sensitivity to timing factors.

8. Ability either to complement his superior or to blend his personality and operating methods with those of his superior or to do both in varying degree.

9. Possessed of courage, ethics and a passion for anonymity.

The executive must be prepared to spend some time to bring about a mutual understanding of goals, operating methods and standards of performance. For his part the assistant must learn his superior's preferences in communication and the amount of supporting detail he may require. Above all, the two must enjoy each other's full confidence so that they will be able to intercommunicate without restraint.

The special assistant is a variant of the "assistant to." He usually does not have the full range and scope of the latter. He may be adviser or an aide on specialized assignments or be an extension of his principal with respect to a particular functional area, as researcher or as coordinator or as watchdog.

The executive assistant more closely corresponds to the "assistant to," but his position usually suggests a more direct executive arm — someone who is expected to follow through on decisions and directives without, however, assuming line authority.

The troubleshooter is yet another variant. His title suggests a shock-trooper, sometimes used to trail-blaze new assignments, to unsnarl tangles and to take on particular fact-finding assignments.

Executive Secretariats

The executive secretariat is a group of people who, together, perform the kinds of duties assigned to the "assistant to" or executive assistant, as described above, except that a good part of the personal element is necessarily excluded. Typically, the concept of the executive secretariat was developed by international organizations, the military and Federal Government agencies such as the Department of State. Most recently it was adopted as a means for coordinating all the paper work, at the policy coordination level, of the White House. The services of an executive secretariat would have applicability in the top offices of large corporations.

Basically the executive secretariat performs a triple function:

1. It assures that information that goes to the chief executive is presented so as to save his time. That is, the memorandum, work document or folder will contain all the information needed for decision. If necessary a covering brief will present the matter in capsule form.

2. It assures that matters presented to the chief executive for decision represent completed staff work; that is, alternatives of decision are set forth, together with an estimate of their consequences, all supported by facts. The chief executive is apprised of supporting or dissenting views. He is assured that documents sent in for action have had all necessary reviews.

3. It assures that the decisions of top command are properly recorded, made accessible for future reference and communicated to all who have need for the information.

The key to the success of the executive secretariat consists, in the first place, of assuring that it is populated with people whose abilities correspond in large part with those of the "assistant to," as described above. Procedurally, the working strength of the executive secretariat lies in the fact that it sits astride the channels of communication. Literally, it intercepts all of the action documents which are directed for the attention of the top executive.

The use of an executive secretariat is not without some danger. Like the "assistant to," only more comprehensively, the executive secretariat can become a center of power and a dispenser of patronage through its ability to assign priorities or to control the sequence in which matters are presented for decision. Of course many private secretaries have been known to manifest their power in precisely the same way, to the point of being accused of trying to run the organization. Therefore these comments are intended only to alert the top executive to conditions which he must prevent or minimize.

A greater danger is that a processing group may bring about a sameness of policy and action. To put it another way: regardless of the kind of meat that goes into the sausage machine, it all comes out looking like sausage.

One means of assuring that the executive and the entire organization do not become captives of an executive secretariat is to rotate the person of the chief, in order to bring in new points of view and to assure that they remain reasonably neutral, at least for a time.

Functional Staffs

The functional staff may be an expansion of the special assistant who has responsibility in a particular technical or professional area. Thus the top executive may have special assistants for legal counsel, finance, public relations, industrial relations, economic analysis, organization planning, etc. Where the workload warrants, these may be expanded into entire departments, although in some cases the top executive may still retain individual advisers independently of the corresponding technical departments. These specialized functional staffs both result from and contribute to the growing complexity of modern industrial organization.

The functional staff usually performs a dual service: it performs certain supporting services to the rest of the organization and it also provides a service of analysis and advice to the top executive.

The professionalization of functional staffs has gone so far that they have, in many cases, exceeded the actual grasp of understanding of the general executive. This is especially true in such fields as economics, statistics and industrial management which have tended to embrace a higher content of mathematics. As we move more toward a technological society the scientist has begun to assume a correspondingly greater role. Symptomatic of the condition this has tended to bring about is an interesting, if unconvincing, article in the *Harvard Business Review* by Stephen B. Miles, Jr. and Thomas E. Vail. They suggest that the manager must move over to provide room for a dual management with scientists who would actually make all the decisions of substance. Under this dual arrangement the managers would have responsibility for human relations and for routine administrative housekeeping and support.

I mention their argument here because it is indicative of an emerging problem of relationships within the top councils of organization with which the executive of the future will necessarily deal. The counterargument to this should, of course, be rather obvious. All those within the enterprise are there to serve its ultimate purposes. The organization does not exist for the benefit of any particular class or category of its employees (unless, naturally, they happen also to be the proprietors, through financial control). In an ultimate sense the top managers are the agents of the total enterprise. They must assess means and priorities for achieving specific goals and they must make the final decisions in the light of the over-all posture of the enterprise.

There have been instances of scientists and other professionals who, irked by nonprofessional influence over their activities, have broken loose and established their own enterprises. As soon as they did this they became entrepreneurs.

Those who run the enterprise become managers regardless of their professional origins. One may question whether they can manage as well as those who have spent their careers learning the techniques of management in itself. This is not an argument against scientific people becoming managers. It merely recognizes that only a small percentage of *any* population will ever have the attributes for becoming top-level managers, This applies alike to the scientific and management population. If you try to combine ability to be a creative scientist with ability to be a creative manager, you are asking for a small percentage of another small percentage!

The solution is straightforward: the general executive should operate as in the past, taking into account all specialized points of view before making his decisions. On technical matters he will ordinarily yield to the judgment of the professionals. If he feels the need for independent interpretation, from his personal standpoint, and if the work load warrants it, he can attach to himself one or more special technical advisers. They can both interpret to him and represent him. Another technique is to check one technical specialist off against another. Whatever the arrangement there can be no *dual* management as such. Ultimately someone must be supreme. If the scientist prevails he will then have become manager, but then he will not have time any longer to be the creative scientist.

A greater problem, in today's real world, is the failure of many corporations as yet to recognize the valuable contributions which can be made by their controllers, statisticians, economists and other professionals who happen not to be physical scientists. The role of this former group was well expressed in the *Harvard Business Review* by Clark S. Teitsworth, economist for Socony Mobil Oil Company:

"What is important to the corporation is organized attention to forward planning by the best talent available. In this age of specialization, the economist ideally specializes in trying to see the whole picture. In a business sense, he might almost be said to specialize in not specializing. No matter who makes the final decisions, forward planning must be based on organizing and analyzing the facts and the trends relating to the company, the industry, the general economy — right up to the edge of the always-misty future. They should be gathered with objectivity as well as understanding, and related to each other without fear or favor. The individual charged with that responsibility may not always win his point, but he must command the respect of management.

"Of course, forward planning involves something more than a knowledge of facts and trends. It demands the ability and the imagination to draw profitable inferences from situations which have not yet materialized. . . ."

However valuable the role of the economist and his other analytical and advisory colleagues, their full talents are frequently not put to use. Teitsworth related a favorite story of the economists, probably invented, about the corporation which hired its first economist:

"The corporation's top management agreed that a man versed in the science of business cycles and forecasts was an appropriate sort of person to have on the payroll, even though nobody was able to define his special duties with any clarity. He was assigned to a pleasant office, and thereafter was left to the mysterious devices of his profession. And for several months nobody had the temerity to approach him.

"At last, a young executive of the corporation, finding himself stumped by a problem involving freight-car loadings in Nebraska, boldly made up his mind to seek the economist's aid. On entering the man's office, he immediately sensed a strangely lifeless atmosphere about the place, but he brushed the cobwebs from his eyes and began to phrase his question anyway. Then he noticed something equally lifeless about the economist himself. . . .

"The autopsy disclosed that unmourned by anyone, the man

had quietly expired at his desk some weeks earlier — with death presumably caused by an overwhelming sense of boredom and of social isolation."

Mr. Teitsworth asserts that this caricature of the role of the company economist is no longer valid, but this protest in itself suggests that there could be an improvement generally, apart from his own company.

The Consultant

Functional staffs, as previously mentioned, serve also as in-house consultants. Unfortunately their potency in this area tends to wear down very soon. This is true also of outside consultants who are brought in and stay overlong. One reason, however trite it may seem, is that familiarity breeds contempt. Another — and probably more basic — reason is that the insider cannot completely disassociate his own interests from his recommendations. Regardless of his personal integrity, he has become part of the political system of the enterprise and to that extent may be suspect. This is substantiated somewhat by the fact that when you hire an outside consultant he often derives some of his very best ideas from the specialists within the organization.

When you buy the services of an outside consultant you obtain:

1. Specialized skills and talents.
2. Knowledge of the practices of other firms.
3. A greater likelihood of objectivity than you might obtain from within.
4. Fresh ideas and an unhampered outside perspective.
5. Undivided attention to the assigned problem.
6. Disengagement from the internal politics and a resulting ability to make rather fearless recommendations.
7. Deadlined employment which usually assures that the task will be completed on a timely basis.

If you are planning to bring a consultant into your organization, you will want to choose carefully. Following is an outline for evaluation of a proposed consulting selection, prepared
by Robert F. Dick, vice president of the Illinois Tool Works,
formerly a consultant himself, and published through the courtesy of *Steel:*

"1. *Before you start shopping know specifically what you
want the consultant to do.* 'Come in and look around, boys' assignments are often disappointing. Don't start to select a firm
until everyone in your organization who must approve and
work on the project clearly understands the objectives.

"2. *Talk to the principals in two or three consulting firms
before making a final decision.* Be wary if talk concentrates on
exploits and results with other clients instead of your problem.
If the consultant guarantees to save you a definite amount of
money, write him off; this is dangerous ground. You may find
it helpful to interview staffmen who would do the work. If you
feel they are the kind of men you would like on your team,
chances are your organization will feel that way.

"3. *Ask for recent references on assignments similar to yours.*
He may have worked for a number of blue-chip companies on
production, personnel or financial problems — and he may have
worked for them some time ago — but that's not going to solve
your marketing problem. Get the names of a few former clients
and call them. Ask what was done about recommendations.
Find out what management didn't like about the consultant
and what mistakes were made in carrying out the assignment.

"4. *Remember, both small and large consulting firms have
their place.* Some smaller ones specialize in a given industry or
function, such as marketing, compensation problems or sales
training. The size of a firm is no indication of ability, but you
should always satisfy yourself about:

a. Financial standing.

b. Background and experience of its principals and staff
members.

c. Caliber of its clients.

d. Amount of repeat business.

e. General reputation.

f. Willingness to refuse a similar assignment for one of your competitors unless cleared in advance with you.

"5. *When using a consultant for the first time, consider giving him a limited assignment.* Examples: A study of organization, review of compensation or analysis of sales territories. That gives both sides time to get acquainted. For a modest fee you can get an idea of the contribution and level of thinking the consultant offers. That's important. It's easy for the consultant to oversell his services. Some are supersalesmen in consultant's clothing.

"6. *Insist that a written proposal be submitted by each consulting firm interviewed.* It should outline:

a. What the work will cover.

b. How it will be done.

c. If a written report is to be submitted.

d. How long it will take; an estimate of cost.

e. How much time the principal will spend on the assignment. (It is annoying and unethical to have him tell you he will supervise on the spot, then do it by remote control.)

"7. *Consider the personality and background of the principal who will handle your account.* He should be a man you can do battle with verbally at no loss to your admiration and respect for him."

When you have engaged a consultant, there are still a number of things you must do in order to obtain the best use of his services. Some of these are:

1. Inform all who will be concerned, within the organization, as to why the consultant has been brought in and how he will operate. Instruct those with whom the consultant is to work that they are to give their full cooperation, as directed.

2. Designate a top-level liaison, if it is not yourself, to work with the consultant to assure that all necessary facilities, data and personal contacts are arranged.

3. Find out from the consultant what will be needed in the

form of operating manuals, organization charts, operating data, financial reports, etc., and see that these are provided at least by the time they are needed.

4. Inform the consultant as to any relationship problems or as to any other privileged or unusual or difficult situations.

5. Review the progress of work intermittently in terms of the assignment as spelled out in the consultant's proposal and in your contract with him. You may decide to modify the original terms but this should be through joint understanding and not come about as something decided upon unilaterally by the consultant.

There are two things the consultant can do to improve the likelihood of putting across his recommendations. One is to submit periodic progress reports. Aside from informing the management, this is a means for alerting it to what the recommendations might be. Without commitment, in this way, there can be preliminary exchanges of opinion.

The second technique used by successful consultants is to submit a final report which constitutes a plan of action — not merely a description of what is wrong. If you can afford to do so it is frequently advantageous to have the consultant follow through with the actual installation of the finally approved plan.

THE DOCTRINE OF COMPLETED STAFF WORK

In Chapter V, "How to Reach Agreement," I touched briefly on the meaning of completed staff work, especially as it was defined by Major General Archer L. Lerch, who popularized this term and its meaning during World War II. I touched briefly on some of the fallacy of a doctrine which tends to require that agreements must be reached among all the reviewing parties before the matter is finally presented for decision. My argument against this is that too often it tends to water down the product to the disadvantage of the organization. At this point I shall expand upon this topic, emphasizing, however, the more constructive aspects.

The Meaning of Completed Staff Work

General Lerch's paper on completed staff work is quoted below. Apart from the very first sentence with which I take issue quite emphatically, the paper contains some very fine advice.

"Completed Staff Work is the study of a problem, and presentation of a solution, by a staff officer, in such form that all that remains to be done on the part of the head of the staff division, or the commander, is to indicate his approval or disapproval of the completed action. The words 'completed action' are emphasized because the more difficult the problem is, the more the tendency is to present the problem to the chief in piecemeal fashion. It is your duty as a staff officer to work out the details. You should not consult your chief in the determination of those details, no matter how perplexing they may be. You may and should consult other staff officers. The product, whether it involves the pronouncement of a new policy or affects an established one, should, when presented to the chief for approval or disapproval, be worked out in finished form.

"The impulse which often comes to the inexperienced staff officer to ask the chief what to do, recurs more often when the problem is difficult. It is accompanied by a feeling of mental frustration. It is so easy to ask the chief what to do, and it appears so easy for him to answer. Resist that impulse! You will succumb to it only if you do not know your job. It is your job to advise your chief what he ought to do, not to ask him what you ought to do. He needs answers, not questions. Your job is to study, write, restudy and rewrite until you have evolved a single proposed action — the best one of all you have considered. Your chief merely approves or disapproves.

"Do not worry your chief with long explanations and memoranda. Writing a memorandum to your chief does not constitute completed staff work, but writing a memorandum for your chief to send to someone else does. Your views should be placed before him in finished form so that he can make them his views simply by signing his name. In most instances, completed staff work results in a single document prepared for the signature of the chief without accompanying comment. If the proper result is reached, the chief will usually recognize it at once. If he wants comment or explanation, he will ask for it.

"The theory of completed staff work does not preclude a 'rough draft' but the rough draft must not be a half-baked idea. It must be complete in every respect except that it lacks the requisite number of copies and need not be neat. But a rough draft must not be used as an excuse for shifting to the chief the burden of formulating the action.

"The completed-staff-work theory may result in more work for the staff officer, but it results in more freedom for the chief. This is as it should be. Further, it accomplishes two things:

"1. The chief is protected from half-baked ideas, voluminous memoranda, and immature oral presentations.

"2. The staff officer who has a real idea to sell is enabled more readily to find a market.

"When you have finished your 'completed staff work' the final test is this:

"If you were the chief would you be willing to sign the paper you have prepared, and stake your professional reputation on its being right?

"If the answer is in the negative, take it back and work it over, because it is not yet completed staff work."

Returning now to my argument against insisting that staff papers must represent agreed papers before they are submitted to top executives, I would like to comment on how this doctrine has actually worked out in the fields of military and foreign affairs. It is understandable that those who have responsibility for contributing to decisions on matters that commit the national welfare and national security should be reluctant to have their judgments adopted when there are arguments to the contrary on record. As a consequence, when there are basic differences of opinion the matters tend to remain unresolved, even to the ultimate detriment of the country or its economy. A fair percentage of those matters which do find common agreement have, in the process, been watered down to the point where they lack vitality and may fall quite short in their ultimate achievements. Close-at-hand observers of the Washington military and political scene have commented quite candidly about this condition. General Maxwell Taylor, for example, made this one his chief criticisms of military staff process in his book *The Uncertain Trumpet*.

Another keen observer, former Secretary of State Dean Acheson, had this to say in *The New York Times Magazine* about the fallacy of this approach, which he called "agreement by exhaustion":

"The military substitute for thought at the top is staff. Staff is of great importance. It performs the indispensable function of collecting the food for thought, appraising and preparing it. It is the means of carrying out decisions made. But, when it also performs the function of final thought, judgment and decision, then there is no top — only the appearance of one. This can happen in a number of ways, but the most insidious, because it seems so highly efficient, is the 'agreed' staff paper sent up for 'action,' a euphemism for 'approval.'

" 'One can always,' I have said elsewhere, 'get an agreed paper by increasing the vagueness and generality of its statements. The staff of any interdepartmental committee has a fatal weakness for this type of agreement by exhaustion.' But a chief who wants to perform his function of knowing the issues, the factors involved and their magnitudes, and of deciding, needs, where there is any doubt at all, not agreed papers, but disagreed papers."

Perhaps we are upon the threshold of a new era in public service decision-making. In his first State of the Union Message, President John F. Kennedy said· "Let it be clear that this Administration recognizes the value of daring and dissent — that we greet healthy controversy as the hallmark of healthy change."

At least one interesting development has come out of the Kennedy Administration: The President and other top officials have sharpened supporting staff work by delving deeply into selected staff papers. The author of a paper may be called directly by telephone by one of these officials with a request for more facts or for the authority on which a statement has been made. This has had a whiplash effect all down the line — at least in a number of departments — since no one charged with development of policy can foretell when he may be called directly. This is excellent, if it persists. It demonstrates how executive leadership and initiative can influence the character of staff activity.

Briefly, then, completed staff work must put the top executive in a position to *decide,* not merely to *ratify.* Apart from the thoroughness of the fact-finding and exposition in themselves, the staff paper should indicate agreement where all parties are wholeheartedly in accord with the proposed action. If, however, there is disagreement or there is even agreement that there are various alternatives, these differences should be spelled out and presented to higher authority for final *determination.*

Under the principles of delegation of authority, subordinate officials and executives are expected to make decisions appropriate to their levels of responsibility as specifically delegated. These statements of delegation cannot, naturally, anticipate every conceivable situation which might arise. Moreover, notwithstanding any such delegations, there will always be occasions when a subordinate official should refer the matters up the line for decision at a higher level. For example:

1. When the matter is clearly beyond your delegated scope of responsibility.

2. When the matter must be acted upon by higher authority for legal reasons.

3. When there is no established policy and you do not have adequate authority to establish policy in your own right.

4. When someone on a higher level has requested the referral, even though you otherwise would have authority to take final action.

5. When the matter is of such importance that your supe-

riors should be knowledgeable even though, under strict terms, you may have adequate authority to act finally.

6. When you anticipate adverse repercussions which may involve higher officials in the receipt of complaints or correspondence.

7. When any of your colleagues are in disagreement with your proposed actions and you do not feel that you should move forward under those circumstances.

We cannot leave a discussion of completed staff work without touching upon a technique for getting a head start on decision-making. This may be called *the doctrine of staff anticipation*. This means that the staff assumes the function of front-runner or advance patrol. While the boss is preoccupied with his own current problems, his staff assistants work ahead. They look for clues of things that may happen and they begin assembling the facts to prove or disprove their hunches.

If they do their work well they may prevent fires instead of running madly about at a later date to put them out. At the very least they can be sure to keep their principals fully informed as to upcoming problem areas so that they will not be taken by surprise.

The techniques of anticipation are not hard to learn. For example:

1. Keep a schedule of target dates on all key projects and activities. Anticipate the target dates well in advance by looking for positive assurance that intermediate targets will lead to satisfactory completion of either a full phase or the finally completed work by the target date. If you encounter a lag which cannot easily be overcome, you know that a crisis is in the making and that corrective decisions may need to be taken.

2. Accumulate a check list — at least mentally — of key indicators of probable events. This is the cause-and-effect technique.

3. Get to know the key individuals and the techniques which they use when they are building up to a default in their own timetables or the revelation of some kind of embarrassing crisis.

4. Study the operating reports for indications of probable trends.

5. Keep your ear to the ground for rumblings from any source. Check these out, however, before you jump to any conclusions.

Remember, while it is well to anticipate and thereby to protect your superior, you can also embarrass him if you throw him off on ill-considered tangents. Therefore you should always double-check carefully on your forecasts of future events. Unless you are quite certain of what you are reporting, you should make your cautions known, for the protection of your superior.

CONCLUSION

Those who presume to help others make decisions, whether voluntarily or by request, take on a great challenge. The recipient of aid may resent the obvious helping hand. In the discussion of this problem we covered many points out of which these reminders are selected, in summary:

1. Preserve the dignity and sense of personal security of the recipient of aid or guidance.

2. Never press your services upon someone who does not desire them, unless your duties so require.

3. Examine your own motives; detach yourself from your own self-interest; you are advising someone else in his interests as well as those of the enterprise.

4. Examine your qualifications; are you competent to provide assistance on the matter at issue?

Chapter IX

HOW TO IMPROVE YOUR SKILLS
OF DECISION-MAKING

We are now upon a topic of some sensitivity: how you and I as executives can improve our personal skills of decision-making. This is akin to the problem of trying to teach executives how to think. Writing on the latter topic some years ago in *Fortune* magazine, Perrin Stryker concluded that it's well-nigh impossible to achieve much success in this unless the effort seems down-to-earth and practical.

Stryker said: ". . . most executives still seem to be offended by the idea of being taught to think, since executives, like other human beings, normally cherish a high opinion of their own mental powers. An executive may readily admit that he was not taught to think systematically in school, and may recommend a technical education such as engineering for young men hoping to become managers. . . . Yet the closer to the top an executive climbs, the more likely he is to doubt the possibility of teaching so complex a process as 'good judgment.' He may not be able to articulate the problems of management thinking — or even be conscious of them — but he will probably be convinced that the problems are too numerous and complicated to be solved by any kind of schooling or by any battery of training techniques."

I do not propose in this chapter to teach anyone how to become a good thinker. I do believe, however, that anyone who already has the capabilities of being a good thinker can improve his analytical skills by acquiring practice in certain tangible skills which I shall describe. Additionally, I believe that analytical ability alone is not sufficient to become a good decision-maker. Hence, the second major topic covered in this chapter is a presentation of the personal operational skills that one needs — the skills of making the best use of one's analytical abilities. Finally I will describe some of the techniques in current vogue whereby groups of people can obtain practical experience in making decisions under simulated real-life conditions.

I started this chapter by saying that it introduced a sensitive subject. The reason it is sensitive is that when a man becomes a key executive he soon recognizes that he must create and maintain a posture in the minds of his superiors, associates, subordinates and people in the outside world with whom he has contact. If, during his tenure, he seems not to be an excellent or born decision-maker, he finds it easy to rationalize his state by attributing fault to the conditions or to the impenetrability or inflexibility of other people. The fact is, there are very few of us indeed who cannot benefit by the acquisition of greater skill in decision-making. Paradoxically those who need improvement least are among those who most seek it. Conversely, those least experienced, both academically and practically, are among those most disdainful and resentful of efforts to enhance these skills.

Fortunately the reader can resolve — in the privacy of his own study — his interest in the techniques which will be described below, *after he has read them.*

THE ANALYTICAL SKILLS OF A DECISION-MAKER

Listed below are ten key analytical skills. They are the skills necessary for drawing useful meanings out of situations. As I describe them and their practical application you will note that they overlap; they depend upon each other. In greater or lesser degree all or some of them are employed simultaneously, without consciousness of particular skills, when you devote yourself to the analysis of a problem.

I shall describe each skill separately and tell of its practical use but I shall defer until the end a set of suggestions for perfecting them. The reason for this is that certain of the techniques I will recommend are applicable to more than one of the various skills.

The Ten Analytical Skills

The ten analytical skills are:

1. Frame-of-reference facility
2. Associational perception
3. Sequential perception
4. Elaboration
5. Generalizing
6. Symbolizing
7. Organizing
8. Strategic sensing
9. Goal-mindedness
10. Objectivity and skepticism

Frame-of-reference facility. The frame of reference is an organized body of information, experience and opinions which serves as a background against which new problems can be examined. The frame of reference is acquired indirectly. First, there must be a storage in the mind of a mass of related observations, information and experience, acquired bit by bit over a period of time. The storage may be both conscious and unconscious. The frame of reference is what you retrieve from the mind in response to some kind of stimulus or instruction. This usually is in the form of a conscious observation of a problem or of a requirement for judgment. When the mind is so stimulated it automatically goes to work to draw forth the selective inputs of the past as they relate to the new situation. Thus each new problem draws forth a new frame of reference.

This may be likened to the operation of a giant electronic computer into which you have stored a mass of information. At any time that you desire particular kinds of information, singly or in combination, you have merely to instruct the machine as to your requirements. Automatically, then, the machine will comb through all that has been previously fed into it and will print out the desired information. You may also present specific problems to the machine which it will work out for you in the light of its stored information.

The practical value of being able to draw upon the mind for instantaneous assistance in coping with problems at hand is obvious; the man with built-in frames of reference is miles ahead of someone else who must start from scratch or from a low base to accumulate the information and insights necessary for the solution of a new problem. This is of the utmost significance when you need to think on your feet — when either you have an adequate working background or you do not. Also, as we shall note in Chapter XI, "How to Unravel a Problem," the well-stocked mind is a prerequisite of the ability to reason intuitively.

Associational perception. The ability to see likeness, relatedness and interdependence may be called associational perception. This is the ability to recognize things that go with each other.

The associational technique lies at the heart of a number of memory courses. When you learn something new you associate it with something else that is familiar to you. The practical value to the executive of associational perception is that it enables him to draw from one set of experiences to another. It also enables him to recognize entire situations by perceiving only some of the elements. Thus the skilled diagnostician, such as a top-notch consultant, often needs to look at only a very few elements in a situation in order to develop a working hypothesis which will lead to his solution. The amateur may need to take inventory of the entire situation before he is able to do this. The difference is that the skilled man knows that certain key elements go with others; as soon as he recognizes one or more of them, he checks his preliminary hunch with associated factors which should exist alongside of those already perceived.

Associational perception forms the basis of reasoning by analogy. When you form the analogy you are determining that it resembles the real situation before you, in its major attributes. Thus you are able to transfer the essence of experience, thought and action from other situations to those with which you are currently involved.

Sequential perception. The ability to see events and phenomena in a time relationship, reaching back to the past, progressing through the present and extending into the future, may be called sequential perception. This is the essence of understanding cause-and-effect relationships. The ability to think through the passage of time is basic to planning and programming. After all, a decision is merely a moment in time. It is consummated through an action which brings about reaction followed by some kind of interaction and counteraction. In order to pierce through the veil of uncertainty, the decision-maker must be able to perceive the probable responses to actions.

Elaboration. The ability to round out — to flesh out the skeleton — to supply the subsidiary details in a plan — may be called the skill of elaboration. (It is a form of conical perception in that you start from the small end and expand your coverage as the cone widens.) At upper levels of management one necessarily deals in summary concepts. Sometimes an exceptionally broad brush may be wielded. To assure that the broad outlines are soundly conceived, one must have an ability to visualize them in detail. This is an essential ingredient of program-planning in which you must take agreed goals and elaborate them in the form of specific subtargets, resource allocations, interrelationships, time schedules and controls. The mind which is capable of elaborating is able to think in terms of "blueprints." It visualizes the main structural elements and is able to support them in the detail necessary to prove them out and make them reality.

Generalizing. The ability to draw central principles from the mass may be called generalizing. This also covers the ability to find single terms descriptive of many related or similar items. It may apply to things existing at the same time or to a series of situations or events. The generalization is the short expression of the whole. Where the mind has this facility, however, it must also be able to test the generalization by checking individual items against it.

The skill of generalizing is fundamental and prerequisite to policy determination and rule-making. In both cases the single policy or rule is expected to cover a multitude of individual cases or situations which are alike in their central attributes although they may differ in detail.

Symbolizing. The ability to symbolize is an advanced form of generalizing. It is an ability to express thought, quantities, matter and relationships in abstract or symbolic forms. The most common example of symbolic expression in the business world is the dollar sign — the expression of resources, effort and value in financial terms. Statistical terms, expressions, graphs and charts depict magnitude, relationships and trends symbolically. Behavior patterns and operating systems are expressed through mathematical formulas which also, in their advanced form, provide the basis of developing conceptual models as aids to decision-making. Speaking by analogy may also use symbolic forms.

The symbolic expression hastens thought and communication in its most popular usage. In the interactions of people who have common purpose and relationships, certain shorthand expressions often convey what otherwise might take yards or miles of words. Perhaps it is a crude analogy, but one thinks of the old expression that a single picture is worth ten thousand words. Symbolic thinking is highly manipulable. That is, it permits grouping and combining. It permits interchange. This is most commonly seen in finance, when once you have put dollar values upon items, you thereafter have wide latitude for symbolic manipulation. The same is true in mathematics, when you apply quantitative values.

Organizing. The term organizing is used here not in its commonly understood (or misunderstood) sense of getting things done but in the more literal sense of "to arrange or constitute in interdependent parts, each having a special function or relation to the whole." The ability to organize is to take the whole and to divide — and then interrelate — logically according to a useful scheme. This may be for purposes of logically ordering the distribution of information. It may be to subdivide a total operation according to logical sequences of action with the assurance that each subdivision is in balance with every other and with the whole effort. It may be to subdivide a broad activity into its functional components while assuring that each of these is fully integrated with each other and with the whole.

The skill of organizing is a prerequisite to the division of effort. This in turn is a prerequisite to the making and defining of task assignments. As regards both program-planning and procedural planning it assures that a logical approach is taken to the distribution and phasing of action. The skill of organizing is the skill of blueprinting.

Strategic sensing. A key action skill is the ability to identify key facts, thoughts or events upon which other such phenomena will depend. In a structural sense it is the ability to see that one particular element is a keystone for an entire archway. Strategic sensing is implicit in critical timing. It is the ability to spot trends (which in turn is an ability to sense a rate of displacement). A facility for strategic sensing enables one to recognize as well as to foresee critical obstacles. These may be obstacles in being as well as new obstacles which are generated as a result of actions precipitated by oneself.

The skill of strategic sensing "separates the men from the boys." The strategic elements are the control elements upon which decisions may turn one way or another. In critical situations they are the exceptional aspects toward which management attention must be directed. In situations of competition, where great agility and flexibility are required, these qualities depend upon an ability to push aside all except the most critical elements. Strategic sensing is the basis of assigning priorities, for all things are not equal and some are more important than others.

Goal-mindedness. Goal-mindedness is an ability to relate thought and action to end purposes. It is also an ability to perceive and formulate new goals. An advanced skill in goal orientation is the ability to construct and interrelate a whole network of long-range, intermediate and short-range goals. While this involves seeing into the future, it also requires an ability to relate it back to the present. It begins with an ability to estimate the existing situation, to project from it to an estimate of both general and specific conditions in the future and then to integrate the two. In effect, the signal that you send out into the future is bounced back to your estimate or inventory of the present; the information received back is then used to formulate a more tangibly directed goal.

The ability to perceive goals helps assure that all actions are usefully related. An action which is not specifically related to a useful goal dangles without effect; in fact, it may constitute an impediment. Pre-identified goals enable you to carry on a multiplicity of activities. They provide for an economy of effort in that you are able to exclude things which do not pertain to defined and acceptable goals. They sensitize you to your future requirements; that is, they enable you to recognize information and actions which should be taken up when encountered in the stream of activity so that they can be related to your ultimate ends.

Objectivity and skepticism. We are concerned here with two personal attributes which govern the acceptance or rejection of information and propositions. The objective person is able to rise above personal, emotional or unreasoned attitudes or assumptions. He has an ability to depart from his own prior conclusions, especially to adapt his thinking and attitudes to new conditions. While he is able to detach himself from sentiment — he may yet respect but rise above it.

The attitude of objectivity runs into the quality of skepticism. This is an imperviousness to the hypnosis of suggestion. It is not quite disbelief, as such. Rather, it is a willingness to accept statements and propositions subject to demonstration of plausibility and proof. One might say it is an attitude of "show me." When these attributes are developed to their highest degree, the executive is able to recognize those matters on which he may have prejudices or predispositions of one kind or another. Recognition of the importance of this is observed in the judicial process whereby judges disqualify themselves from hearing cases under certain conditions.

How the Skills Help Each Other

You must have noted the overlapping and interdependence of

CHECK LIST OF PRACTICE TECHNIQUES FOR IMPROVING ANALYTICAL SKILLS

(For explanation of practice items, see list beginning on page opposite)

SKILL	PRACTICE
1. Associational perception	Clustering, Extended notation, Inputs
2. Elaboration	Action involvement, Extended notation, Ranking
3. Frame-of-reference facility	Inputs, Reflective analysis
4. Generalizing	Clustering, Outlining, Validating
5. Goal-mindedness	Counseling, Forecasting, Validating
6. Objectivity and skepticism	Counseling, Inquisitiveness, Involvement-detachment, Validating
7. Organizing	Clustering, Outlining, Ranking, Validating
8. Sequential perception	Action involvement, Reflective analysis
9. Strategic sensing	Gaming, Outlining, Ranking
10. Symbolizing	Training in symbolic disciplines

the analytical skills. In some of the material which follows, you will note also that a number of the practice techniques will lead to improvement simultaneously in more than one of the skills.

Here are some examples of how these skills interweave: Associational and sequential perception usually go together. The former pertains to things that go together without reference to time while the latter pertains to the sequence of actions in time. The ability to perceive and interrelate matter in both cases is dependent upon one's frame-of-reference facility. The skills of elaborating and generalizing are the reverse of each other. It depends on whether you are looking through the narrow or the wide end of the horn. Organizational ability is the visible fixing of a frame of reference. (You can also say that it is the externalized representation of a frame of reference.) The ability to sense strategically requires, first, that you be able to perceive the whole of the situation. This comes back to the organizational ability and to associational perception. If strategic sensing has to do with the progression of events, it requires a facility in sequential perception. Certain of the elements serve a universal function in blending, joining or integrating the various attributes of analytical process. One is symbolic facility. Another is the sense of purpose or goal-mindedness. Throughout, the qualities of objectivity and skepticism serve as the screen for keeping the analysis clear of impurities.

How to Acquire Analytical Skills

On the opposite page you will find a chart of the analytical skills just described. The right-hand column identifies the particular kinds of practice which contribute to the improvement of the specific analytical skill to which they pertain. Listed below, alphabetically, are these practice techniques with appropriate suggestions.

While I have listed thirteen separate practice techniques, naturally some of them are more important than the others. If you want to narrow down the list I suggest that you concentrate on the following seven:

> Action involvement
> Clustering
> Inputs
> Outlining

Ranking
Reflective analysis
Validating

Certain of these seven also go together quite well. Thus *action involvement* and *inputs* both have the same purpose of adding to your store of knowledge and experience. *Clustering, outlining* and *ranking* are means of putting related things together in meaningful groups or sequences. *Reflective analysis* and *validating* are techniques for examining data and events in order to draw meaning from them.

I offer these as tools of practical experience. I do not claim that they have been scientifically validated. Certainly I can point to no controlled experiments conducted by others or by myself to demonstrate their validity and reliability. Having made these disclaimers, I now can say that I have found these techniques to have served me mightily over the years. In no small degree they have contributed to such accomplishments as I have made. The list itself was accumulated by me as the product of many years of preoccupation with the processes of thought and analysis coupled with a willingness to experiment and innovate.

Action involvement. Inject yourself, as active participant, into as many different situations as possible. Take specific action matters and follow through actively in all phases from inception of the problem, through analysis and decision and then through the subsequent action, evaluation of effect and further action. Get your fingers into the "goo" in order to learn the feel of action, especially to learn what it takes to get things done. Observe the sequence of cause and effect. Get a feel for the causes of failure and for what it takes to correct a wrong decision and action. Look beyond the immediate situation to see how it ties in with broader situations. Examine implications for other areas of policy and operation.

Clustering. This is a pencil-and-paper exercise. Quite simply it involves putting related items together under common headings or identifications. It serves both as an analytical shortcut and as a means of bringing together related items so that they may be placed in some common focus. Similarly it obliges you to screen out the unrelated. When working with a number of items or a variety of materials, it is an easy way to get them under working control.

Counseling. To protect yourself against your own prejudices or lack of perspective — and we're all subject to such errors — develop sources of independent review and comment. Ideally these should be people who themselves are not personally involved. Do not seek counselors who will merely echo your own desires. There is a great advantage in merely having the opportunity to explain your ideas to trusted persons. As you do so, this contributes to clarification of your own mind. Having to answer the confidant's innocent questions has the same effect. In short, have at least one sounding board.

Extended notation. This is the technique of going beyond the main facts or highlights. In essence it involves looking into supporting details or getting more deeply involved into the environment of a situation. Admittedly this seems to run counter to the principle that the executive must limit himself to the basic control elements, leaving to others the responsibility for absorbing or surrounding the details. However true this may be for the generality of situations, there will be many times when the requirements of the situation dictate that the executive plunge into it in great depth. It is also something which the executive may need to do when he undertakes a new assignment area with which he does not have full familiarity. Moreover, if the executive did not go through some of this in the early stages of his career, he may need to catch up with himself currently.

Basically it is the acquisition of a habit of looking at things. When you become acquainted with people you try to note everything significant about them — their physical characteristics, their personal abilities, their relationships, their interests, etc. Things are examined both for their similarities and their differences with other things and the identification of such tucked deeply away in the mind. An all-embracing look is taken at the general environment of a situation, with notation in the mind as to the key elements. You develop an awareness of things that are present invariably with other things or you notice that when certain conditions exist others never or rarely do. When you observe actions you look for their ramifications into all related fields.

Forecasting. Since much of decision-making has to do with uncertainty, a prime skill is to be able to predict the turn of events. Skill in doing this may be achieved by studying cause-and-effect relationships, studying statistical trends, giving careful attention to the conditions represented by the trend data. Study related types of situations, covering the background, the problems, the bases of decision, the actions taken, the effects and the corrective decisions and actions. Compare your own problems with these related situations, taking particular note of similarities and differences in both the environment and the activity. To really sharpen your predictive abilities, compare your forecasts with the actual results. Take the time to write down just what you do predict will happen, in some detail. Then, after the action has been taken and enough time has elapsed, compare actual results with your predictions. Determine the reasons for variances. Experience in developing program plans and schedules, monitoring them and determining the reasons for failure as well as success will also contribute to your ability to predict the results of specific actions.

Gaming. Game-playing, in the jargon of modern management, is the working out of management problems in make-believe situations that simulate real life. (These are discussed in greater detail in the latter part of this chapter.) Competitive games provide training in anticipating the moves of others in the light of the total operating situation. There are also one-sided games which provide experience in identifying and evaluating the available alternatives, especially as they unfold as you move ahead, step by step. For experience in problem-solving even simple puzzles, problem games and mathematical problems can be helpful. They provide training in finding one's way out of a predicament, identifying a cause or achieving a goal.

Input. Your resource of information should be both extensive and intensive. Your extensive coverage should include at least a superficial coverage of all the fields of subject matter and managerial and technological developments related to your own area of activity. Your intensive coverage should embrace as much as possible about your own specific areas of activity — the matters with which you are directly concerned. In addition to the more conventional methods of learning, expose yourself to the most current thinking. Speak to knowledgeable people, attend conventions, read trade journals and other current literature, study trade literature describing new products and processes, speak to salesmen, read internal publications and reports (or at least digests of them). To make the deepest impression, write key points and ideas on paper. As you do so your mind has time to race ahead and cogitate on the material which you are putting on paper. Thus you make a triple impression: you observe what you wish to note, you write it down and you reflect upon what you are writing.

Inquisitiveness. In a social sense the inquisitive personality is one who is given to inquiring into just about everything, for his personal gratification. In the context of our present subject matter it suggests one of a searching mind, curious, desirous of going beyond things as represented on the surface or in broad outline. A first prerequisite to building one's own inquisitiveness is to have specific goals. When you are motivated you have a more specific pressure upon yourself to acquire information. Put yourself in competition with others; commit yourself to getting certain things done by a certain time: such actions stimulate a pressure from within to seek knowledge. Acquire some measure of the scope of knowledge in the field of your interest and then compare that which you already know against it: such perspective on one's limited acquisitions may spur to greater efforts. Get into the habit of asking questions which bring out motivations and causes, methods and results, quantities and dimensions and interested personalities.

Take nothing for granted. Ask why it was done, why it is needed or why it is to be done; ask how it was or is to be done and what the effect will be; ask who did it or is to do it and why; ask how many times something has happened and when last; ask how an action is related to some other condition; and so on. Whenever possible try to interact with the actual material or mechanisms which engage your interest. By handling or manipulating things you discern more clearly the cause-and-effect relationships, processes, internal systems relationships and applications of products and processes.

Involvement and withdrawal. Sometimes you must "get away from it all." When you pursue an inquiry in depth you may lose perspective on the whole. This is also true in reverse; you may become so detached from the particulars that you may fail to see the exceptions and the variations which help you frame your generalizations in proper perspective. Here is a suggested cycle: (1) pursue the inquiry up to a point of moderate saturation, withdraw from the object of inquiry and then evaluate what you have done; (2) the evaluation may assist you in organizing, reorganizing or reaffirming your approach; (3) then pursue your inquiry again, going through the same cycle. When you believe you have reached a correct judgment or made a proper decision, let it rest before taking final action. In cool perspective you might see things differently.

Outlining. In outlining, you represent the whole of your subject matter in skeletal form. The outline enables you to bring out in sharp relief the key relationships, imbalances, need for additional information and gaps in the thought structure. The techniques of outlining are described in Chapter XI, but will be summarized briefly here. The first step is to determine upon a useful scheme for dividing the subject matter. This may be according to operational sequence, categories of things or uses or origins, subdivisions of a major purpose, alternatives of action and so on. Then the main divisions of the outline are determined by reference to the random notes. The items in your notes are then allocated to the appropriate headings. If some items are left, this may indicate either that you have a faulty outline or that you have not discovered the relationship between the residual items and the headings in the outline, or that the leftovers are really not germane to your subject matter. Thus you begin immediately to derive some benefit from the outlining process. The outline may need to be reorganized or you may need to do additional research, if you find imbalances, blank spots, overlapping and contradiction. A well-designed outline serves as an excellent model of an entire situation.

Ranking. Ranking is an important tool for evaluating and judging the merits of the available alternatives of action and their outcomes. You must start with some criterion of importance or some specific contribution to value. Then screen out any noncontributory or nonpertinent items. With the remainder, you can start at any point, although an item of intermediate ranking would seem most appropriate. You can extract items visually from those listed at random on a sheet of paper or you can write the separate items on individual 3" x 5" cards which then can be arranged with least effort in any suitable combination.

Actual ranking can be done in varying degrees of refinement. You can judge an item as being worth more or less than another, thereby putting it higher or lower on the scale. You can refine this by assigning numerical weights to each of the items and then ranking them accordingly. This kind of exercise sharpens your sense of relationships and of comparative values. It obliges you to think in terms of goals.

Reflective analysis. After an action has been completed, give intensive thought to the interplay of elements in the situation and what each contributed to the final result. Try to draw from the total situation a single, governing action principle for guidance in similar situations. Try to identify at least the single most important thing which might have been done differently in order to have achieved some more desirable effect. Combine this approach with that of involvement and withdrawal as well as that of counseling.

Training in symbolic disciplines. The symbolic disciplines are those fields of learning in which numbers and other symbols are used to represent ideas, mass, quantity, dimension, relationship and force. Certain courses of study, while directly useful themselves, also develop within the student a facility for logical reasoning and for the manipulation of ideas. Financial symbolism provides a common language in the world of business. Mathematics and statistics have become increasingly indispensable in both the social and physical sciences. The study of logic, of course, provides facility in pure reason in itself as well as in ability to detect fallacies in reasoning.

Validating. Probably the most common form of reasoning is by analogy; unfortunately there is probably more fallacy in this kind of reasoning than in most others. Because we reason from this to that on the basis of similarities, we should be equally anxious to look for dissimilarities. Hence get into the habit of asking for the answers to two important questions: how is this situation similar to another, and how is it different from it? The same approach should be used when you are acting on specific situations in accordance with general rules, principles or policies. Is the situation covered adequately by the governing policy and to what extent is it not so covered? In conjunction with the technique of forecasting, get into the habit of comparing actual results of an action with your predictions. Acquire the habit of challenging assumptions and generalizations with requests for factual support. A subtler technique of validating is that of the rejection of the inconsistent. There is a rule of reason applicable to most situations which may exist even though it has never been stated. When someone comes in with an unusual or fantastic report of something that is supposed to have happened or to have been said and if it has about it all of the earmarks of being outside the bounds of what might normally be expected, you should challenge it. You will be surprised at how often the person making the report or statement will be unable to provide you with first-hand evidence to back up the information previously given you.

THE OPERATIONAL SKILLS OF A DECISION-MAKER

Analytical skills alone do not make a decision-maker. To deal with conditions in the real world, he must have other attributes.

If the ones to be listed below seem to overlap or largely parallel the general attributes of an executive, it is quite understandable that this should be so, for the executive is preoccupied in large measure with the functions of decision-making.

Preconditions for Use of Skills

The general prerequisite for the exercise of decision-making skills is a wholesome operating environment. The conditions must nurture the development of operating skills. They must enable people to operate without having their best efforts frustrated by the lack of machinery for constructive participation, final judgment and follow-through of actions. If there are no procedures or institutional mechanisms to permit decisions to be reached through teamwork, it will be difficult, if not impossible, to put into practice any of the principles described in this book.

Because the various conditions which make up a viable environment for decision-making are discussed in other chapters throughout this book, I shall limit myself here to a mere listing of them, as follows:

1. Clear-cut responsibility assignments so that people will know what is expected of them and of others with whom they must interact.

2. Adequate delegations of authority to decide and to act, consistent with the levels of responsibility at which executives are expected to operate.

3. Defined goals, policies and programs communicated fully and clearly to all who are expected to carry them out or take related actions.

4. Clear lines of communication for the dissemination of operating intelligence and decisions.

5. The establishment of sources of operating intelligence in order to bring problems to consciousness and in order to provide factual bases for decision.

6. Adequate media of communication, suitably controlled, in order to provide convenient means of disseminating and receiving intelligence.

7. Disciplinary control over communication systems and media, both written and oral, to assure adherence to the rule of need-to-know and need-to-participate and to prevent the ills of overcommunication.

8. The attainment, through good leadership, of a wholesome atmosphere that engenders constructive and positive performance without fear of the consequences of being forthright or of making an occasional error.

9. Adequate administrative support for decision-makers so that their own time is not diverted or consumed by such activity which can be provided more economically through separate arrangements.

10. A self-disciplined mode of operation throughout the organization which assures respect for responsibilities of each other and that organizational purposes, policies and directives will be carried out faithfully.

The adequacy of the environment for good decision-making will make itself apparent without the need for specific analysis. If there is excessive pressure to have decisions made at the highest levels or if there is an inability to bring decisions to a head, you may assume quite safely that the machinery for good decision-making is either missing or inoperative.

A Personal Value Structure

In addition to an environment which nurtures good decision-making, one must have internalized goals, attitudes, standards and points of view which enable him to make up his mind on specific issues. These generally come under the heading of a personal "value structure." A value, of course, is some measure of worth on some scale of preference. A value structure is the total framework of the importances that we attach to things. Things or actions are evaluated by us in the light of what we have previously judged to be of importance.

The organization as a whole develops a value structure which governs its policy-making and its activities. It also governs individual behavior.

If your values, as an individual, are in harmony with those

of the enterprise, you are fortunate, for then you can operate without the burden of rationalizing any conflicts between the two. Many men resolve this as a matter of personal employment policy; compatibility of values becomes a condition of accepting a position.

Each of us creates an image of self as seen by others. What they perceive in part is *their* view of your value structure. This characterization serves a very practical role: your colleagues are able to judge your words and your acts in the light of what is known of your past behavior. Are you known as a man whose word is his bond and whose word is integrity? Are you regarded as dependable, prompt and courteous? Are you considered self-oriented or one who is willing to accommodate the interests of others?

The building of a personal image is preceded by personal insight. This goes back to one's appreciation of the values of the various ethical imperatives which ought generally to guide behavior. Then there are the behavioral principles which pertain to various professions and industries and even to local business communities.

Note that I used the term "behavioral" rather than "ethical" principles. In certain professions so-called ethical principles are laid down to govern business-getting, among other things. The members must adhere to these or be expelled. The "ethics" are understood for what they represent: the protection of existing clientele of the older members. Nevertheless the rules must be followed as a condition of survival. The alternative is to change them, if one can be so brave — and powerful.

You learn the prevailing values in your own organization by studying its objectives and policies, generally, and by observing the judgments that go into making various types of decisions. Value judgments are most likely to come out in direct conversation, whether between two individuals or in conferences.

Outside guidance may also be found in the proceedings and journals of professional societies, such as the American Management Association, National Industrial Conference Board, American Public Relations Association and specific trade groups. The value structure provides you with an inner resource which gives you a personal perspective on new situations. In itself, however, it will not make you an effective "operator" within your organization. To cope more specifically with situations, you must learn the use of certain aditional working tools.

Eight Operational Tools for Decision-Makers

Clarence B. Randall, former president and chairman of the board of the Inland Steel Company, writing in *Dun's Review & Modern Industry*, commented on the attributes of the competent decision-maker:

"First of all, he has a perceptive instinct for recognizing that a problem exists and an ability to articulate which permits him to frame the issue with clarity. . . .

"Here, breadth of education and experience are extremely important. It is the specialist who is at a disadvantage. . . . It is the man who, by education or broad reading, has opened his mind to the widest range of intellectual experience who has the best chance of recognizing unfamiliar problems before stepping into them.

"Secondly, he has the ability to saturate himself with pertinent data about a subject before permitting his mind to come into focus, coupled with a sense of urgency that causes him to do this as rapidly as possible. . . . He must display a nice balance between the desire to know more and the necessity for action.

"In the third place, he must have the courage not to look back once his decision is made. There must be no aftermath of doubt once the commitment is made, or the morale of the whole organization will suffer."

These are more than mere inspirational suggestions. The motivated individual can expand his capabilities. The following material contains suggestions for improving one's operational capabilities. The eight tools to be covered are:

1. A broad general background
2. Adequate technical background
3. Institutional awareness
4. Self-organization
5. Resource-utilization
6. Communication skill
7. Interpersonal proficiency
8. Action personality

General background. A broad frame of reference equips you with knowledge in depth. Out of your exposure to many fields you draw experiences and insights which you can use in your own specialty. You acquire a readiness to understand new situations and an ability to see how they tie in with others. You acquire, also, a capacity for understanding men of different backgrounds, particularly the specialists to whom you must turn for analysis and counsel. This explains why professional schools now generally require students to take more liberal-arts work before they go on to their specialized studies.

To acquire breadth is no easy task. You must be willing to yield some of your time to wide reading, study and attendance at lectures. In addition to the more practical fields of knowledge, I suggest readings in economics, individual psychology, social psychology, philosophy, sociology, creative processes, public opinion, political science and international affairs.

Technical background. An executive needs to be sufficiently knowledgeable in his own field to enable him to evaluate what others bring to him and to be able to ask meaningful questions. His personal grasp of situations should be such that it wards off any effort to "put things over." The higher one goes on the ladder of executive and administrative responsibility, the less important it is that he have detailed technical competence. It's more important to know about trends and new developments and where to go for more information and assistance when needed. Hence, keep abreast of your field by reading its trade journals and current books, attending its conventions and becoming familiar with the key technical personalities.

Institutional background. General and technical knowledges, as well as other personal skills, are usable only within the context of the operating situation and its workways. Like the battle commander you must become thoroughly familiar with the field of action. You must become familiar with the organization as a whole: how it is set up and the rationale for how its functions are distributed; its long- and short-range goals; its programs and policies; operating and administrative procedures and anything else that acquaints you with how things get done. Less discernible, but equally important, is a knowledge of the environment of operation: an understanding of the history of successes and failures and the reasons for them; familiarity with the key personalities, their motivations and their methods of operation; and recognition of the existing competitions and obstacles to progress.

To become thoroughly knowledgeable in all these areas is a tall order. How you go about it depends partly upon your own personality. I recommend that you acquire perspective on the whole before you dig into specific areas. Keep a notebook in which you can jot down specific items on which later you might want more information. Don't cram, for if you do so you will lose many of the important nuances of policy, motivations and relationships. Keep an eye out for specific source documents and other internal literature which you can read at your leisure. From time to time get into specific activities in depth which enable you to get a cross-sectional feel of important processes. If you are still a man on the rise, try to get a diversity of assignments: move from staff to line and from headquarters to field — and vice versa in each case. Move into slightly different subject fields, to round out your perspective. If you're beyond this flexibility of assignment, help your subordinates get this kind of broadening exposure.

Self-organization. A friend who publishes one of the weekly news magazines and yet finds time to write a daily news column told me how he learned to get much done in little time. On a train ride to the Chicago convention that nominated Warren G. Harding for President, he talked with the late Frank B. Noyes of the Washington *Star;* Noyes told him that he rarely put things aside, other than to handle them in some predetermined order of priority. If once he picked something up he disposed of it, unless there were more important things pressing. Thus he saved the time of rehandling and rethinking.

Time is the scarcest resource of the executive. Much has been written on this topic. You'll find excellent reading in a slim volume published by the American Management Association: Carl Heyel's *Organizing Your Job in Management.* Following is a list of hints out of my own notebooks:

1. If you want something done, find a busy man to do it. Chances are he can always squeeze another task in.

2. Allocate time for the things you *must* get out of the way. Set aside time for *some* reflection.

3. Channel the time demands of others so that they do not take up more than a predetermined percentage of your schedule.

4. Don't let people take up your time while they explain complicated situations or give you long memoranda to read: ask them to write a memo or leave material with you so you can become familiar with it.

5. Line up deferrable tasks for compatible mood and energy periods. Do your creative work when your mind is fresh.

6. Accumulate small or unimportant items in desk folders labeled with different peoples' names on them. Take them up when you have enough such business or when you get together for some other purpose.

7. Know when you have reached a point of poor return, whether in conferences, fact-finding or the performance of others. Learn to sense the moment for action.

8. Observe how other successful people handle their affairs. Pick up little tricks which will also fit in well for you. Thus, I learned from Maurice Stans to put a big round "O" next to incomplete or unfinished items on lists, reports and other documents. It flags these for further attention and checkoff.

Resource utilization. If you acquire a good institutional background you will have some idea of the resources to which you can turn for aid. Don't be passive or make assumptions based on surface indications. Just about every organization has its share of people bursting to win recognition. They're eager to have their hidden skills and knowledges tapped. Be careful, however, that you don't take on an encumbrance. Be alert to evidences of special skills and abilities of your superiors. If the occasion warrants it they may be glad to help. They could be flattered!

We read and hear much about the importance of delegation. Equally important is our ability to get work done when needed. The cheapest and most effective way to do this is to let subordinates know what is expected of them and to motivate them highly. Still, you must have means for following up on the laggards. The techniques will vary with the relationship and the work load. Some of the best follow-ups are the impersonal ones, linked to other plausible requests. Then there are prods and checks built into the work processes themselves.

Communication skills. There is scarcely a skill in personal communication that does not pertain in some way to the effectiveness of the decision-maker. Some of them have been covered in other chapters. Two which rank high and only lately have begun to command deserving attention are reading and listening. And why not? Both relate to the fact-finding capability.

The listener has an advantage. He hears and absorbs and, at the same time, he has a chance to think up questions with which to guide the discussion. For a good book on this topic, see *Are You Listening?* by Ralph G. Nichols and Leonard A. Stevens (New York, McGraw-Hill Book Co.).

Whether in reading or listening, you're more likely to retain the greatest part of your information if you jot it down as soon as possible for later review. Otherwise you'll lose most of it. Outlines and frameworks should be used. Thus, if you are given fifteen facts you may not remember them all, but if you divide them into three or four categories, each of which contains four or five items, you may remember them all.

Interpersonal skill. Interpersonal skill is the ability to handle oneself effectively with many different people in a variety of situations. This is a big one, worthy of volumes. All we can do here is assert a point of view. The perception of self in the eyes of others is one of the rarest and most valuable of skills. How you *are* regarded is the real thing, quite apart from how you *want to be* regarded. Be alert, then, to demonstrated attitudes of your colleagues, subordinates and superiors. How do you compare with how they react to others? Inventory the attributes which you believe you possess. Then appraise how well you seem to be regarded in each. Look for objective evidence of this regard.

In the business environment feelings of personal security have much to do with how we feel about people. If people associate you with their well-being they are more prone to accept your company and your suggestions. Conversely, if they feel you are always pressing for some personal goal or some disturbing changes, they will tend to shy away from both your company and your ideas. These overpowering attitudes of others toward you are more important than all of the memorized procedures drawn from books on skill in handling people. If you win acceptance you need no special procedures.

The action personality. The possessor of an action personality is one able to meet and deal forthrightly with situations as they arise. Study the successful action types with whom you come in contact. Their demeanor generally is one of confidence, whether cautious or brave. Most seem to abound in energy and a capacity to carry tremendous work loads. They generally are highly motivated. They are able to shift course without being personally disoriented in so doing. I suspect that the successful action personality has a feeling of personal security which enables him to take detached views, take chances and accept the risk and fact of failure with equanimity.

You can study the successes and failures of such people and, no matter how discerning you may be, you will not be able to emulate them unless you have the same inner preparation — the same inner security. From maturity onward, if not from late childhood, the likelihood of developing new inner perspectives is not very great. Still, it is possible to ameliorate one's weaknesses, provided they are understood.

Most of the capabilities described above can be acquired through individual observation, thought and practice. The more critical skills in decision-making require experience in interacting with others under real-life conditions. On a trial-and-error basis, much of this experience is acquired as one moves up the ladder of advancement.

Managements would like to provide additional "live" opportunities for acquiring experience but they are inhibited by fears of costly errors. For this reason a number of practice techniques have been developed which are used in group training in decision-making. Many people are aware of these, sometimes in different contexts. Four which show most promise, described below, are:

1. Junior boards of directors
2. Role-playing
3. Group analyses of cases — the incident process
4. Business games.

The Junior Board

The junior board of directors was popularized by Charles Perry McCormick of the tea company that bears the same name. In fact, junior board and McCormick's "multiple management" have become almost synonymous. This is a system of subordinate boards — below the regular board of directors of the corporation — whose membership is derived from officers, executives and employees. Essentially it is a system of executive committees for the major components of the enterprise.

Membership on one of the boards offers an opportunity to formulate or review important policies and programs and to recommend them to the corporate board. The junior-board members acquire experience in give-and-take discussion on important issues. They acquire an over-all point of view through their interactions with people from all elements of the company. An incentive to learn and develop is provided through the opportunity to be elected to the corporate board.

For such a program to be successful the members must have a sense of serious purpose. They must feel that their contributions are important and meaningful. They must see the effects of their recommendations in actual practice. The management must encourage a freedom of expression. Membership should be rotated in order to spread the opportunity for participation.*

Role-Playing

Role-playing is the re-enactment of a situation. The intent is to create a sense of deep involvement on the part of the actors while also benefiting the audience. Although the technique has come into vogue in recent years under the names of psychodrama and sociodrama, its venerable status goes back into antiquity. William Shakespeare understood its value when he wove it into the plot of *Hamlet*. You will recall the famous line: "The play's the thing wherein we'll catch the conscience of the king." Psychiatrists use role-playing to bring to the surface deeply hidden feelings, attitudes, frustrations or emotions of the patient.

Today role-playing is used extensively in human-relations training. I have also seen it used extensively in conventions as a means of laboratory portrayal of some group process. It is an excellent means for developing a feeling for self in relation to others. It provides training in empathy.

Senior personnel may be reluctant to involve themselves in this activity, to defend their sophistication. For best results, real problems should be chosen, particularly those recommended by the group itself. Role-playing must never be used as a stunt, for then it will not serve any constructive use. †

* For a guide to functioning of junior boards, see John R. Craf, *Junior Boards of Executives*, New York, Harper & Brothers.

† For a further discussion of role-playing and other group executive-training techniques see Harwood F. Merrill and Elizabeth Marting, eds., *Developing Executive Skills*, New York, American Management Association.

The "Incident Process" in Group Analysis

A much more sophisticated technique, more likely to be acceptable by senior personnel, is Pigors' Incident Process, developed by Dr. Paul Pigors of the Massachusetts Institute of Technology and distributed by the Bureau of National Affairs, Inc., Washington 7, D.C. It has been used widely in corporations, government agencies, schools and universities.

The incident process is a form of learning by case study, but it differs from ordinary case examples in that it uses real-life management problems as incidents. After the incident itself is described to the participants they are given an opportunity to find additional facts by asking for them. The participants themselves must frame the issues and the alternatives of decision. They debate among themselves and compare the judgments they reach with what actually took place.

The advantage, obviously, is that the sense of realism imputes a corresponding reality to the thought processes of the participants. The typical case takes at least two hours. A desirable audience is from fifteen to twenty people around a conference table, but there should be no fewer than ten people.

Business Games

Most recent of the techniques for training in decision-making, without incurring any risk to the corporate resources, is the business game. It is a simulated business situation in which the participants make decisions and take actions under the rules of the game, with the effects of their actions calculated mathematically.

The two main types of games are enterprise games and functional technique games. Enterprise games usually simulate the operation of a competitive business — a number of firms competing in the same market for the sale of a single product. Each company is represented by a team of players. A functional game usually narrows down to more specific operational techniques such as production scheduling, sales management, personnel assignments, materials inventory and systems management. The functional technique has a broader potential in that it may be brought down to lower levels of personnel in addition to its applicability to the highest levels.

In the typical enterprise game the players are told about their own and the competing companies, including their finances, the market, marketing programs, advertising budgets, research and development, production and finance, including plant investment. Usually all companies are equally capitalized and have equal shares of the market. Teams may organize themselves along corporate lines and delegate responsibilities for decision-making. Prepared rules of play are given out to all participants. Then the teams start making their decisions, usually on a business-quarter basis, in order to try to improve their positions.

This might strike you as a kind of advanced form of Monopoly — a kind of business chess. You can also draw analogies to war games and the moot courts of law students.

Time is telescoped by feeding the team actions into preprogrammed computers. The results of actions taken by competitors are communicated promptly to all players, along with the results of their own actions. Noncomputer games are also available but as must be expected, they move along more slowly. They use monitors or umpires who do the calculating according to formulas. Obviously the computer games can be more complex because they can accommodate more variables simultaneously.

The American Management Association may take deserved credit for having promoted the idea of the business game. The AMA top-management decision game uses an electronic computer. In a few hours of concentrated game play, years of business experience can be simulated. A typical game divides into five teams or companies that are manufacturing in competition with one another. They make a single product which sells for from five to ten dollars. The game starts with each company having exactly one-fifth of the market, the same dollar assets as all the others and the same range of expenditure choices. The goal of each team is to increase its assets. The players are given twenty-five minutes to select their decisions for the first quarter. Each must decide how much to spend for production, marketing effort, research and development, additional plant investment and the price to be charged for the product.

Less than five minutes after it makes its initial decisions, each company receives a quarterly operating statement showing its sales and its costs. This is repeated quarter after quarter until the equivalent of several years of business activity has elapsed. As Harwood F. Merrill, vice president and editor of the AMA, said:

"The competitive spirit was intense as team members wrestled with their decisions — whether to cut prices and marketing expenditures or boost them, whether to put more capital into plant, whether to buy market research information on sales potential and competitors' positions. The discussion, argument and analysis voiced as the teams outlined policy, plotted moves, and tried to outguess competitors, vividly reflected the kind of thinking that the game develops:

" 'If we spend the maximum on research and development, we'll have to cut back on marketing or sell off some plant to get the money. What will that do to our sales and production?' (As one president observed ruefully, 'Limited funds are the most realistic part of this game.')

" 'That investment in sales effort and research really paid off; customers are screaming for our product. The only trouble is that somehow we forgot about plant capacity. How can we get our inventory up to meet the demand?' (One president later pointed out in a critique session, 'This game really shows the importance of keeping operations in balance; you can't afford to go overboard on any one factor.')

" 'We raised our price and yet we increased our share of the market. Was it the extra sales campaign we put on, or is this a bull market we are selling in? Maybe we should be buying more market research information; certainly we should be making our own market analyses.' (Commented one president, 'The importance of having facts — and using them properly — is one of the greatest lessons the game teaches.')

" 'Things looked pretty good for us until Company 3 lowered the boom with that price cut. Now we have to revamp our whole strategy.' (In the game, as in real life, flexibility is a key ingredient in success.)"

A number of "portable" business games are available for companies that would like to try them on their own premises. Thus C-E-I-R, Inc., of Arlington, Virginia, the largest of the independent computer service organizations, has developed a game called SESAME, short for Sales Executives Strategy and Management Exercise. This, too, is a game of competing teams whose decisions and actions are quantified and fed to a computer on a quarterly basis. The data may be telephoned or teletyped to and from one of C-E-I-R's computer centers or the game may be played at one of them.

On the specific values of the business game, I quote from Jay R. Greene and Roger L. Sisson, *Dynamic Management Decision Games* (New York, John Wiley & Sons, Inc.):

"1. The player should learn which key factors to observe in an actual on-the-job situation in order to understand the business' position. The game, therefore, should emphasize those factors or data that are thought to be most important in decision-making.

"2. The game will illustrate what facts are important and may give some idea of the approximate quantities involved. For example, the student would learn in the Retailing Inventory Game that markups in retailing range from 20 to 60 per cent and not from 5 to 95 per cent.

"3. A dynamic game should give the participant an opportunity to gain insight into the particular area of executive action abstracted in the game. Business problems are frequently too complex to permit intuition, years of experience, or even analytic tools to lead to an understanding of the over-all situation. There is no guarantee that games *will* lead to insight, of course.

"4. Playing a dynamic game forces the player's attention on establishing policies or strategies and on longer range planning.

On-the-job experience tends to emphasize the 'putting out fires' problem and the young manager very rarely gets a chance to participate in long-range planning. A dynamic game gives him this opportunity.

"5. The participant will gain practice in the use of decision-assisting tools. Therefore, he will be able to make better use of break-even charts, financial statements, Gantt charts, and even such devices as linear programming and statistical inventory control. There is presently no other educational method which gives a student so much practice in decision-making as does a dynamic game.

"6. A game can be used to illustrate the value of analytic techniques where they exist. In many business decision areas it is possible not only to develop a model of the situation but also to express this model mathematically and to solve the mathematics to give a specific rule for obtaining 'optimum' decisions. Where such an analytic approach is possible, simple games may be used to illustrate its use and value. To do this, the game should be played through once before the student is instructed in the analytic procedure. The player will presumably make judgment decisions. After that, if the analysis and solution of the problem is taught and the game is replayed, using the optimizing method, its value is usually made quite evident.

"7. Possibly games can be used as an aid in training people in operations research. The students could be permitted to play the game (as usual without knowing the game structure) and could be asked to develop the structure by using various analytic tools during the game.

"8. There is no question that players become highly involved when participating in a business game. They tend to act as if the game represents a real business situation and that the objectives of the game are real-life objectives. As a result of the involvement, the participants should learn more than from the usual static case study in which the student tends to look on the solution as a one-time decision.

"9. The type of game described in this book is dynamic. It has feedback which allows for actions taken in one period to affect future conditions and results. There is no other educational device that permits the dynamic nature of business to be illustrated as effectively to the student.

"10. In game situations a large number of interacting variables must be simultaneously accounted for by the player. This is highly realistic and gives the player a better appreciation for the difficulty of making decisions in business.

"11. Because time is compressed, the player can make as many decisions in a game in a few hours as he would make in an operating business in several years. There is no measure yet as to the direct value of this kind of experience but it should be considerable.

"12. The game offers the functional specialist a vehicle for broadening his management horizons."

The business game is not the final and exclusive training tool, notwithstanding its current, dramatic popularity. One must bear in mind that competitive positions are altered by other factors, including the force of personalities, inequalities of finances and personnel, espionage, creativity, etc. The game necessarily must be simplified, for if efforts were made to plug in every conceivable element, it would become too cumbersome. Andrews M. Lang, in charge of the AMA program, recommends that it be used in conjunction with other training tools.*

CONCLUSION

Few of us use our natural endowments to fullest advantage. This chapter covered a variety of techniques for self-training in analytical and operational skills. It also discussed a number of group practice techniques which have been demonstrated to improve personal skills in executive decision-making. None of these techniques can be expected to produce immediate results. They call for practice, reflection and more practice. The skills of analysis and evaluation must become part and parcel of the executive's way of life.

* A valuable collection of papers on management games is contained in AMA Management Report No. 55, *Simulation and Gaming: A Symposium,* New York: American Management Association.

PART THREE

Aids to Problem-Solving

Chapter X

HOW TO EVALUATE FACTS

Get the facts! This is the battle cry of men of responsibility. Facts are the solvents of uncertainty. They guide us more surely to our goals. Surely, then, we should want to learn more about their nature — and about how to evaluate them — yet our executive skills in this department have been sadly neglected.

This chapter, then, covers techniques for:

1. Assuring that facts are expressed concretely and specifically.

2. Assuring that expert testimony or opinion is really authoritative.

3. Identifying common errors in reporting facts.

4. Recognizing common statistical errors.

You may regard this chapter as a discourse on skepticism. It is so intended. As a matter of fact, we have a normal tendency to be skeptical of "facts." "I will sing of facts," said Ovid, "but there will be some to say I have invented them."

The expert or the specialist may mystify the layman because of his ability to carry arguments with asserted facts which one is not able to challenge. A fear or distrust of the unseen or unfamiliar moves us to rely on tangible things or experiences which we can examine or feel. It may be that our skepticism for "facts" harks back to a day when moneylenders and changers were held in disrepute and men would embrace such proverbs as "There is nothing so false as facts, excepting figures."

Of course blind rejection of facts can be as ruinous as blind acceptance. I do not, however, suggest a "happy medium." There is no compromise with truth. Rather, I offer a number of tests of factual validity which can be applied on a reasoned basis.

Do you know that you have facts or hearsay or opinions or wishful thinking? Do you know that the facts, if valid at the time of their observation, are valid and pertinent today under possibly different conditions? Do you know that you have all of the pertinent facts and that there do not lurk in the background some elements which, if brought forward, would materially change the view and understanding of the entire situation? Do you know how to challenge facts when they are not brought forward under the purest of motives or when, to give the devil his due, they bespeak error or carelessness in observation, analysis and interpretation?

HOW TO EXPRESS THINGS CONCRETELY

It may be a fact that Harry Denton *said* so-and-so, but *what* he said may not in itself be factual. Facts must be distinguished from opinions, beliefs, impressions, ideas, interpretations, judgments, dogmas, doctrine and those guideposts of behavior which "everyone knows."

A Fact Is a Fact

A fact is incontrovertible. It either is or isn't. The cash balance is either $253,972.58 or it is not. . . . The question is a simple one: Did he or did he not sign the purchase order? . . . I cannot accept your estimate that we have had "many" calls for this type of service especially when you cannot recall the last time you had a request for it, so I suggest you keep a simple tab record in the future. . . . It is so easy to assume that you're away from your desk too often because the last two times I called you were unavailable; if I had bothered to get the facts, I would have found that these were exceptions.

A fact is not an impression of things. It is not established by mere belief or by inference. Even the reports of what people believe they have seen cannot be accepted handily as facts, for we have had too many cases of contradictory testimony of eye-witnesses.

There should be some safeguards against careless reporting — and there are. Experience with certain situations or things will enable you to develop check lists of common or recurring elements or characteristics. These assure at least a minimum adherence of the main points of coverage. The sequence of items will stimulate logical thought if they are laid out logically in the check list.

Admittedly, you cannot have a check list for everything. You must rely then on a general approach to descriptive analysis. Strange as it may seem, certain abstract properties of things or situations can be used as a basis for rendering them more concrete.

The Attributes of a Thing

For example, to describe a thing you must cover the following essential properties:

1. The physical properties of the thing — its density, substance, hardness or softness, condition, temperature, color, age, etc.

2. Dimension — shape, size and other attributes of physical displacement.

3. Quantity or number.

4. Structure and relationship — a part in relationship to a whole, actually or potentially; an assemblage of a number of parts in a manner that renders them a whole.

5. Function — a purpose or role or use.

Let us take a watch. Its physical properties include the ornamental and working metals of which it is made, the jewels in the movement and other conditions of craftsmanship. Its dimension tells you whether it is a watch or a clock. Its quantity tells you the number of such things with which you are dealing. The external structure of the watch tells you whether it is a pocket

watch, a lapel watch, a wristwatch or other special form as well
as whether the watch performs functions other than the telling
of time. The internal structure of the watch will enable the
expert to know whether, by standards of experience, it is a
better chronometer than others. It is a watch because all of its
parts, associated together as an interrelating system, perform a
known and recognizable function: it tells time.

The Attributes of an Action Process

For a description of an action or process, you must use an
entirely different framework. Here a famous bit of verse by
Rudyard Kipling seems appropriate:

> *I keep six honest serving-men*
> *(They taught me all I knew)*
> *Their names are What and Why and When*
> *and How and Where and Who.*

These are the famous questions used by the journalist in
gathering the facts for his story. He crams the answers into a
single lead paragraph. This analytical framework suggested in
the verse is sufficiently familiar as to require no example.

One additional attribute of an action is its relationship to
other actions taking place simultaneously or in sequence. As in
the case of the attributes of a thing, the action is either part of
a larger action, it may stand by itself or it may constitute a complex of subsidiary and unified actions taking place simultaneously or in a sequence.

One of the most common mistakes of management is to take
the facts of one situation and apply them to another, entirely
different. A careful analysis of environmental properties, then
and now, would disclose the differences that should give pause
to the proposed actions. An electric light bulb may seem to be
shining brightly and strongly at night, when it is the sole source
of illumination. In the context of day, however, its output
seems dim. In the still of the night you hear every creak and

every cricket while at the height of a day's activity you are totally oblivious of these otherwise shattering sounds.

To all of the foregoing we should add: *at a certain time!* The facts of yesterday may be the fiction of today or tomorrow. There are no constants other than change itself. Again, what differences are there between then and now?

The Attributes of a Term

In verbal exchanges people may take different meanings or understandings from identical words because of their different experiences as expressed by those words.

When figures are to be added together, multiplied, divided, subtracted, compared, etc., the things represented by the figures must be precisely defined. When we use the word "month," do we mean a fiscal month of four weeks or a normal calendar month of a variable number of days?

Obviously you cannot go around defining every term (although I can recall several who did their best to do so, to the dismay of their colleagues). To assist you in defining terms, here are a few rules:

1. Terms having common meanings need not be defined unless it is important to pin down time periods, dimensions, quantities, etc.

2. A definition must express the essence of the thing — neither more nor less — and it must distinguish it from all other things. The thing defined and its definition must be coextensive in meaning and, hence, must be interchangeable.

3. Unless not otherwise possible, the definition should be expressed positively. That is, don't define things in terms of what they are not.

4. You can, however, qualify the affirmative with the negative. Also, you can particularize the general by reference to the specific.

5. Of course, do not include the term itself as part of the definition.

HOW TO EVALUATE AN EXPERT

When facts are insufficient you may turn to authoritative opinions and judgments. This is not an unfamiliar problem. Fortunately there are some techniques for verifying the authoritative background of nonfactual expressions.

The Specific Fallibility of Experts

One of the classic incidents in publishing is the manuscript which, after having been rejected by seven or seventeen publishers, one day finds its way into print to become a best-seller to the great chagrin of all who previously had turned it down as a "turkey." A recent instance of one of these surprise endings was told by John Fischer, editor-in-chief of *Harper's Magazine,* in that publication.

"I hate to remember the time when James R. Newman first told me his scheme for a history of mathematics. . . . He wanted to gather all the basic documents of mathematical thought and arrange them into an anthology which would trace the development of this science in the words of the masters themselves. It would be a big book — perhaps 500 pages. What did I think of it?

"I told him it was impossible. Nobody would buy it; its subject was too specialized — in fact to most people (including me) downright repellent — and it would be far too costly to manufacture. Why didn't he turn his energies to something practical, such as a book on chess — a subject on which he was equally expert? Jim said he was bored with chess.

"A week or so later he said he had revised his plans. He now thought the book should be two volumes — a really comprehensive work. Did that make it sound more promising? I said no, it sounded worse. The next night I flew to North Africa.

"We didn't meet again until the war was over. Jim then told me that he had been plugging away at his anthology, in spite of

my advice; that it had grown to four volumes; and that Simon
& Schuster was going to publish it. I was dumfounded: S & S,
always known as a real shrewd outfit, must have lost their minds.

"The rest is almost too humiliating for me to repeat. As
everybody in the trade now knows, Newman's *The World of
Mathematics* became a phenomenon of publishing. Priced at
an impossible $25, it sold more than 120,000 sets — in addition
to distribution by two book clubs — and is still selling a steady
3,000 copies a year. It also shattered my confidence in my publishing judgment, probably for good."

The error in judgment in this case merely points out the
specific fallibility of the expert. It does not, in itself, diminish
the stature or credibility of the expert. He must be evaluated
in the light of the pattern of his judgments.

For practical guidance, then, you should evaluate the expert
on two levels of performance: (1) his general credibility and
(2) the likelihood that his background and judgment support
the conclusions reached in the case at hand, considering its
characteristics and conditions.

The General Qualifications of an Expert

We can learn about evaluating sources from the techniques
used by experienced intelligence agencies and investigative
bodies. When an intelligence agency evaluates publications, it
also evaluates the author, in each case. One method is to have
a panel of qualified readers go over the material and rate its
authenticity. Similarly, when an investigative agency uses a new
source of information, it usually obtains an evaluation of the
source. It is important to know whether the source is of known
reliability and whether it has any special interests or biases
which might predispose it one way or the other.

When conclusions are offered on the basis of research, it is
fair to ask for the method of research. You have a right to
ascertain whether the research method was a correct one. This

is not a matter of doubting one's integrity; rather, it is a challenge against possible error. It is common practice among scientists to examine the methods of others.

If an opinion, judgment or testimony is offered by someone who is reputed to be an authority or an expert, check the following points:

1. In the first place make sure of the identity of the authority. If a statement is made that "economists say . . ." ask which economists. Certainly you would never want to rely upon an authority so vaguely quoted as "they say . . ."

2. You must then ascertain the authority by which he himself may be adjudged an authority. Is he so regarded in the minds of people who are actually qualified to give him this recognition? Just because he is an expert in one field does not mean that he can hold forth in any other field. This includes baseball players, world-champion prizefighters and people who have lived a long time. Remember that the person who knows least about a subject may, in his very ignorance, feel fully qualified to make a judgment on the matter; after all, he doesn't even know enough about it to realize how little he knows.

3. The statements of the authority must be capable of verification. If the authority is no longer available or is dead, there will be a basis for doubt, for lack of verification.

4. The authority must not be known to have any bias or fixed notions. Nevertheless his judgment may still be acceptable, notwithstanding bias, if the consensus of those who properly can judge him is in accord with his testimony.

In a typical situation you may give an assignment to a staff member who is not an expert but who is regarded as having a dependable approach to fact-gathering and analysis. How may his findings and judgment be evaluated? How can you know when to call in the expert?

1. First, what has been the record of his performance in previous assignments covering the same ground, if pertinent, and also in other areas of subject matter? Has he consistently performed carefully and reliably? Have his factual findings been

found accurate? Has he been complete? Have his findings been well organized?

2. Having established his general credibility, are you now satisfied with the apparent fullness and logic of his presentation? Is the subject matter such that few actual facts are available, thereby forcing a reliance mainly upon opinions and judgments? The greater the degree of dependence upon the latter, the more important it is that you call in a fully authenticated expert.

CHALLENGING THE LOGIC OF INFORMATION

"Factual" presentations are not always what they seem on surface. Their falsity may stem from mere carelessness or from deliberate dishonesty. Sometimes the falsity may be a misguided effort to manipulate facts and figures in support of sincere conviction.

How can you be protected from falsity — whether inadvertent or deliberate? Fortunately there are a variety of tests you can easily apply. In fact, the list of challenges is so long I shall cover only some of the more important ones.

Factual consistency

If the story does not seem to be consistent with the situation as a whole or if it seems unreasonable, don't accept it without examining more deeply into the supporting facts.

If any "facts" seem mutually inconsistent, you may be sure of two possibilities:

1. There may be a missing element or meaning which, if discovered, would dispel any inconsistency.

2. There can be no actual inconsistency of facts. A fact is something which exists or "is." Things which are actual can be unrelated but they cannot be inconsistent. If "facts" are actually inconsistent, then part or all of them cannot be facts.

Verbal errors

Are you talking about the same things? If you have any doubts as to this, go back over the basic ground by doing the following:

1. Restate the problem or goal, using different words, to ascertain whether there is identity of understanding.

2. Define all key terms, to make sure all parties are in agreement as to what they're talking about.

3. Review all qualifying or descriptive terms, with a view to substituting more specific words in order to sharpen and limit meaning.

Observer errors

Most people are familiar with the classic experiments in which the same accident or incident is reported differently by each of a number of observers. We tend to see in situations what we want to find in them. What we don't recall we fit in by improvising or inventing. Because memory fades fast we do this often.

So here are some tests to apply against "facts" reported by observation:

1. Is this a first-hand observation or is it one made and verbally communicated by another party? The more there is of word-of-mouth transmission, the less dependence you can put on the report, *unless you find independent corroboration.*

2. Were the observations recorded immediately or was there a lapse of time between observing and recording or reporting? The greater the time lapse, the greater the risk in accepting the report.

3. Is the reporter one whose record for accuracy — or inaccuracy — is well established, for guidance either way?

4. Was the observer in a position to get the facts faithfully? Did he merely happen to observe the situation or did he deliberately intend doing so? If the latter, his report may have greater credence, if faithfully made.

Pseudoscientific techniques

Mumbo jumbo and abracadabra find wider acceptance than might be imagined. We are only too prone to accept any statement, explanation or evidence that seems scientific or authoritative. Consider, for example, this excerpt from an article on the making of effective presentations:

"... I am convinced that the fault usually lies not in the *manner* of presentation but in *what* is presented.

"The question then is: How do we arrive at the salable what? I suggest that we do it by resolving to management's advantage — and therefore our own — this equation:

$$S = \frac{MDP}{MFL}$$

"*Success of the proposal equals Management's Desire for Profit divided by Management's Fear of Loss.*"

Now, really, how does one divide fear into desire? If you could quantify these or assign values to them, you might subtract one from the other, but divide them — !? Even if you could how would this help you find the "salable what"?

The point, obviously, is that you must not accept, without question, any formula, diagram or technical display merely because it has scientific or learned overtones. If you don't understand the matter and it is of sufficient importance to a decision, get an expert to help you independently.

Authenticity

More subtle are techniques which tend to create an *impression* of authenticity: name-dropping and other false credentials, prestige associations, the confident manner and repeated affirmation.

All of these aim at creating a suggestive atmosphere or setting with the hope that it will rub off on the specific object or topic under discussion. Thus, if everyone else is doing it the implication is that you should, too, whereas dispassionate reason would tell you that it really is not for you, whatever it is.

There is a peculiar dynamics here which operates quantitatively. One really big authority — *the big-name approach* — can lend the clinching authenticity, especially if mentioned in a confiding sort of way. In the absence of a big name, many lesser ones may be used. If the idea salesman has no names to offer — or wants a supplemental clincher — he assumes a superconfident air, preferably low pressure. Over the long pull, repeated affirmation is like the technique of the big lie: say it often enough — confidently — and people will believe it.

In all these situations, throw off the mantle of implied authenticity and look at the facts themselves. Like the performing investigator, say: "Just give me the facts, ma'am."

Analogy

Probably the most common form of reasoning is by analogy. This is the comparison of two situations which seem to have attributes in common.

It is a powerful tool of visualizing and explaining, if correctly used. Some of the greatest scientific discoveries and inventions have evolved by using a model (which is a form of analogy) of one situation, in which cause and effect are known, as a basis for projecting conclusions into a similar situation. Newton's falling apple provided the analogy which led to his law of gravity. Franklin drew an analogy between sparks and lightning, leading to his electrical discoveries. But then governments have been compared to ships of state, with leaders at the wheel and on the bridge, etc. Political cartoonists use analogy freely. Thus a man restrained may be shown with a ball and chain or in ropes or in a balloon overladen with ballast.

The essence of analogy is resemblance. If situation A has the properties 1, 2, 3 . . . n and situation B has the properties 1, 2, and 3, it is then presumed it also has the property n. The fallacy, of course, is that the resemblance often does not carry that far. These are a few tests of the validity of conclusions drawn from analogy:

1. Are any of the *essential* properties of the two situations inconsistent? This includes both the object or activity and its environment. Wherein does the resemblance break down?

2. Does the general principle, drawn from the parallel situation, harmonize with the whole of the matter in hand?

3. Does the argument from analogy attribute to the given object or activity a property or quality which is inconsistent with another one it is definitely known to have?

4. Are the basic forces or problems essentially similar? Thus, are there similar problems, in one of which certain control mechanisms proved meritorious? Are there similarities in other essential elements of the problem setting?

The analogy is of value mainly in offering a starting point — a hypothesis — but it is then subject to proof. To the man who wants to put across an idea, it is too easy a means for convincing a receptive audience which does not have time to analyze and challenge as the argument moves quickly from point to point.

Completeness

In general argument, as well as in statistical presentations, a common error is to draw conclusions from incomplete information. A subordinate rushes in and announces, excitedly, "Did you hear that . . ?" Or another deliberately tries to provoke action by reporting the facts of a situation in part, or out of context.

Frequently such half truths are used when personality conflicts are involved or when the informant stands to gain from the action he hopes you'll take. Any evidence of personal interest should spur you to look further into the facts. Especially is it important to get all sides of the story.

One rarely gets the *complete* facts. It is necessary, however, to get the *essential* facts, a problem we'll consider further, below.

All or some

One of the most common errors is the effort to prove or disprove an argument or conclusion by a single case. To which one may usually say, "So what?" For one thing, the chances are that the facts of the single case do not apply. If they do it is risky, indeed, to draw a general conclusion from one instance, for it might not be indicative at all.

On the other hand, a single case may be the means of disproving a general statement that covers "all." Obviously "all minus one" might mean just that or "all minus some" or "all minus many," but not just plain "all."

Further down the road is the fallacy of *all or some*. "Some employees" may be shortened to just plain "employees." This implies all. Your test is to ask for a breakdown of numbers. How many altogether and how many of them are being reported? What of those not reported?

There are instances when "some" may stand for all, but then you must be sure of the sampling method.

As I mentioned above, the list of challenges just given covers only the most important ones. They overlap; answers to some of them will make it unnecessary to press forward with others. On the other hand the answers may provide clues to recognition of other kinds of statistical errors.

HOW TO RECOGNIZE STATISTICAL ERRORS

Challenging the Statistical Sample

One of the truly great contributions of the statistician has been the development of techniques for describing an entire universe of activity based on direct contact with a *representative sample* or "some" of that universe. The "universe" means the whole of the people, situations, or things being described. The advantages in time, effort and cost are quite obvious.

This is so very wonderful, *provided* the sample is truly representative and does not contain a bias which will slant the results — sometimes so badly that they topple over. The biased sample is one which is not truly a cross-section of its universe. As with all factual fallacies, bias may be deliberate or the result of error. I'm not quite sure where to place the unconscious bias which causes one to select the sample to assure that he gets the information he wants.

The two main types of samples are *random* and *stratified*. In the random sample you take every tenth, fifteenth or "steenth" person or object or else you select a certain number blindly from a well-mixed bowl which contains the entire universe. The stratified or quota sample sets up a proportionate cross-section of the universe. That is, it tries to cover, in a small group, the significant characteristics of the full population. Within its cross-section it, too, may employ random sampling.

Now there are many subtleties in this business of statistical sampling, so much so that a few paragraphs can only hint at the cautions we must exercise as business executives.

Let's take the random sample. Suppose you want a cross-section of the reaction of the general adult population. If you stop every tenth person you meet at noon at the corner of Fifth Avenue and Forty-second Street in New York, you may have a good sample, *but not of the general adult population.* You'll have a sample only of the kinds of people who are likely to be at that place at that time of day. It won't cover most women with children who are likely to stay at home. It will be different in content and results from samples taken in a residential section of Brooklyn, the Chinese quarter of lower Manhattan and the corner of Fourteenth and F Streets in downtown Washington, D.C.

So your first challenge should be to match the universe being described with the sample selected to represent that universe. If the sample does not cover the same ground, it must be rejected. Whatever it proves, it probably won't be what the author claims for it.

Challenging the stratified sample is more difficult, for you must go over the cross-section of the universe:

First, to verify that it *is* a cross-section and that nothing has been omitted.

Second, to ascertain whether the many parts of the cross-section are in proper proportion to each other.

Digging into the validity of a stratified sample requires almost as much professional insight as constructing the sample. The executive does have an advantage of a tangible product in which he can find flaws — provided he recognizes them. To some extent you may need to rely upon the reputation of the sample designer for professional competence and integrity.

Challenging Statistical Fictions

Facts can be analyzed and displayed so as to create almost any desired impression. In a strictly technical sense this can be done without lying, but, in terms of effect, one might as well come out with a blatant dishonesty. One of the neatest jobs done on this subject in recent times was by Darrel Huff in a book *How to Lie with Statistics* (New York, W. W. Norton & Company, Inc.). In it he explains how to detect biased samples, deceptive averages, incompleteness, slanted graphs and other statistical aberrations.

The use and misuse of statistics centers largely in the inferences we draw from them. Thus reports may be published showing the rise in the incidence of cancer and of other diseases. The rise can be shown against published figures of the past. On surface, this should be conclusive, but if you look more deeply you find that at least part of the rise is due to better diagnosis. Another part is due to longer life, because other diseases have been brought under control. This is a fallacy of not comparing the same things and conditions.

The best way to be alert to statistical fallacies is to become well versed in the subject. Next best is to have a professional statistician on your staff or on call *if* you can afford one. In any event, have a few rules of thumb in mind to which to refer when you want to check out a statistical argument:

1. Percentages cannot be averaged. They are not absolute values.

2. The *average* can be tricky. Thus the average of 2, 8, 29 and 33, when these are added and divided by 4, is 18, but this does not tell you anything about the actual numbers being averaged. To use another example, what good is it to know that houses in a certain neighborhood have 5.7 rooms on the average or that families there have 3.7 children? (What would .7 of a room or a child look like?) For a safer view of averages, ask additionally for (a) the size of the sample, (b) the range from lowest to highest, (c) the median — that number which lies in the middle when all the values are ranged from smallest to highest, and (d) the mode, which is the figure, number or value which occurs most frequently.

3. When a large number of occurrences is cited, ask for the period of time covered, *from the records*. Be wary of mere mental recall. For proper perspective, ask also for the dimensions of the activity as a whole.

4. When comparisons are made against a given year or base period, ask why the base was chosen. Ask for the characteristics of preceding and succeeding years. If two or more comparisons are made, for the same purpose, make sure they relate to the same base period.

5. Be sure the appropriate base is used for the expression of a percentage, as a measure of effect. Thus profit can be expressed as a percentage of sales or of investment. It can be shown as gross or net and as before or after taxes. It can be compared against a high base period or a low one. It all depends on what you want to show. You may need several bases of comparison to show a true picture.

6. If comparisons or trends are shown on charts, look out for distortions and incomplete pictures. Trends shown by a graph may be distorted by the proportions of the grid. A rise can be made to appear steep or gentle, rapid or slow — without really changing the actual facts. Without tampering with the grid proportions, bar and line graph presentations can be slanted by showing only part of the picture: by cutting off the

ends or by showing only the peak, the valley, the rise or the fall. Ask for the whole picture!

7. Growth projections cannot be expected to continue at the same rate indefinitely. For a true picture of the *rate* of growth, ask to have a projection drawn on *semilog* paper. Remember that most growth situations follow an S-curve pattern, with slow, rapid and tapering rises, in that order, unless special conditions are introduced. In spite of long-term trends you may have current drops — as in the stock market!

8. Watch out for dramatic correlations. The birth rate in Stockholm has been found to correlate closely with the number of storks' nests. The growth in the expenditure rate of the British Navy was once found to correspond directly with the growing consumption of bananas. These and other such correlation pairs can be charged off to coincidence; *for validity there must be some interdependence of the elements.*

CONCLUSION

There are figures and there are facts. Figures can be presented, in full sincerity, in many different ways, to meet the objectives of whoever prepared them. Even the person who works constantly with figures may not be able to perceive hidden fallacies or false mathematical or statistical logic. A healthy skepticism, without an opportunity to study the presentation, may not be sufficient to help you detect errors. A good safeguard is your insistence that you be given enough time to study the information before reaching your conclusions at another time.

Chapter XI

HOW TO UNRAVEL A PROBLEM

The present chapter may be one of last resort: what to do when you are stumped in your search for the critical element in reaching a decision — when solutions elude your grasp. More specifically this chapter covers:

1. Conditions for problem-solving which you should establish for best results.

2. Techniques for sharpening your creative approach.

3. A treasury of specific techniques for solving difficult problems, when ordinary analytical procedures won't work.

CONDITIONS FOR PROBLEM-SOLVING

Up to now we have covered some of the general conditions which precede problem-solving. We have also gone through the general techniques for fact-finding and evaluation of facts. Now we should devote some attention to two additional "threshold" aspects of problem-solving: (1) an open mind and (2) time for problem-solving.

The Open Door of the Mind

How often have you heard new ideas rejected flatly by the blunt assertion: "We don't do things that way here"?

We are creatures of habit. We are guided in most of the things we do by blind addiction to rules, habits and fixations.

For all ordinary purposes we could not exist every long if it were otherwise, because it would take too much time and energy to work out, anew, the courses of action in situations which repeat themselves.

If you drive home from work you do not need to work out the best route each time. If, however, new conditions arise, such as traffic congestion, detours or the building of new roads, you may have to face the problem all over again of finding a new best route. In doing so you might be surprised to find that many changes have taken place and that alternative routes should have been considered by you much earlier. It was a crisis of minor dimension that obliged you to think about the matter in the first place.

It is easy enough to say that you must have an open mind, but who among us would admit to having a closed mind? It is not a matter for admission or denial; rather, it is the need for an awareness on your part of a possibility that there may really be another solution.

Much can be learned, also, from failure. It is quite understandable that a failure is something one likes to bury and forget. Past failures produce a negative conditioning exemplified by those famous words of rejection: "We tried it and it didn't work." Charles M. Clark, author of the book *Brainstorming* (New York, Doubleday & Company, 1958) compiled a list of fifty-eight "killer phrases," indicative of the closed mind, of which the following are representative:

We haven't the time. . . . We haven't the manpower. . . . It's not in the budget. . . . We're not ready for it yet. . . . All right in theory but can you put it into practice? . . . Somebody would have suggested it before if it were any good. . . . Too modern. . . . Too old-fashioned. . . . You don't understand our problem. . . . We're too small for that. . . . We're too big for that. . . . We have too many projects now. . . . I just *know* it won't work. . . . Let's form a committee. . . . Let's think it over for a while and watch developments. . . . You'll never sell that to management. . . . Why something new now? Our sales are still going up. . . . The union will

scream. . . . Let's put it in writing. . . . Political dynamite.
. . . It'll mean more work. . . . It's not our responsibility. . . .
It will increase overhead. . . . It's too early. . . . It's too late.
. . . Our people won't accept it. . . .

These killer phrases represent two states of mind: first, a general resistance to change — a preference for the familiar and the existing and, second, a reflection of the cumulative hurts, unpleasantries and failures of the past — things we would like to avoid in the future. Additionally, of course, there is some amount of built-in resistance to anything which might call for the expenditure of any energy over and above the normal.

Much can be learned from failures if we approach them with an open mind, seeking from them the lessons of what not to do or what to do better, rather than to seek excuses or rationalizations from them. When you read that a new space rocket was fired, that it did not achieve its ultimate goal and that the launching was considered in other respects to be successful, the temptation might be to laugh it off, but as a matter of fact the scientists do indeed learn a great deal from these mishaps and possible errors.

Time for Problem-Solving

As a general principle, the less time available and the more urgent the matter, the fewer will be the number of significantly different alternatives. Many people say that they work better under pressure. I think that the biggest part of this is that you eliminate distractions and waste effort. This does not mean, however, that you can actually accelerate your mental processes. In fact, there is a danger that because of the urgency of decision-making you may seize incorrect alternatives or solutions and rationalize their acceptability.

Many decisions are made by default merely because adequate time for decision-making had not been scheduled. We tend to postpone actions because (1) there are other things we feel need to be done first or (2) we really do not want to face up to them. Accordingly, saying that you should allow enough time for working out solutions will not in itself be a remedy. It will not correct the two conditions just stated.

One reason for avoiding postponement is that problems may be deeper or bigger than you think, like the submerged part of an iceberg. The sooner you get on with them, the less the danger of time pressures at the end of the line.

If you feel you can (or must) postpone action on a problem, there are two safeguards you can take: (1) initiate any preliminary fact-finding, as indicated; (2) make some commitment to work on the problem, such as assigning contributory tasks to others or promising a solution by a given date.

One other aspect of time has to do with the selection of that point in your energy cycle when your mind works best. For example, if you work far into the night or at a sustained pace throughout the day, some distortion may work its way into your judgments. You may not realize it at the time but the next morning you may wonder if you are reading your own material. We shall cover this point later in the chapter, but here it is sufficient to note that the mind which has been rested cuts through problems with a sharper edge.

THE CREATIVE PROCESS

Writers on creativity are fairly well agreed that the stages of thinking through a problem fall into a pattern such as this:
1. Fact-finding
2. Analysis
3. Detachment from the problem
4. Production of ideas

The Fact-Finding Stage

The first suggestion is to write down and preserve all the information you accumulate during the fact-finding stages. What may seem of minor significance at the time it is noted may later be found to be the key to a final decision.

The second suggestion is to look for ideas and solutions from as many sources as possible. A parallel line of development in another field may provide you with a direct solution or one you can achieve by analogy.

Third, have as clear an idea as possible of what it is you are seeking. Forgetting the exceptions, the greatest luck is enjoyed by those who know what to seek. Louis Pasteur said, "In the field of observation chance favors only the prepared mind." Jerome S. Bruner, professor of psychology at Harvard University, told of pertinent experiences when working with the invention and design group of an engineering firm. His discussions with the group were recorded on a tape which was played back at the end of each session. Commenting upon this in *Printer's Ink,* he said, "What is striking is that after a good solution has been achieved, often a very original one, we find that upon going back over the tapes, the idea has come up three or four times before — seemingly unheard, surely uncelebrated and clearly ignored. . . . I do not think it is the matter of an open mind, nor a matter of some sort of principle of incubation. It takes a tuned organism, working with a certain kind of set, to recognize the appropriateness of an idea."

And, incidentally, did you note the value of his having kept faithful records of all the discussions?

Finally, one needs to be just plain curious. Nothing must be taken for granted. What if it did not work last year? Perhaps now is a better time. On what basis does everyone say that it cannot be done? I want to find out why and perhaps I will try myself because my intuition tells me that it should work.

Analysis (Up to a Point)

Let us assume that the problem is before you for the first time. If it is a piece of physical apparatus, you might pick it up, try to explain its workings and try to derive some general principles subject to further verification. If others are examining the matter, the interaction of minds will bring about further clarification. Thus, through coming to grips with the problem and "processing" what you know about it, your understanding of it assumes some format or structure.

G. Polya gives some excellent guidance for analyzing data in his book *How to Solve It* (Princeton University Press, 1945). Although his book deals with mathematical methods, his check list holds for a much wider range of problem-solving situations.

"*Have you see it before?* Or have you seen the same problem in a slightly different form?

"*Do you know a related problem?* Do you know a theorem that could be useful?

"*Look at the unknown!* And try to think of a familiar problem having the same or a similar unknown.

"*Here is a problem related to yours and solved before. Could you use it?* Could you use its result? Could you use its method? Should you introduce some auxiliary element in order to make its use possible? Could you restate the problem? Could you restate it still differently? Go back to definitions.

"If you cannot solve the proposed problem, try to solve first some related problem. Could you imagine a more accessible related problem? A more general problem? A more special problem? An analogous problem? Could you solve a part of the problem? Keep only a part of the condition, drop the other part; how far is the unknown then determined, how can it vary? Could you derive something useful from the data? Could you think of other data appropriate to determine the unknown? Could you change the unknown or the data, or both if necessary, so that the new unknown and the new data are nearer to each other?

"Did you use all the data? Did you use the whole condition? Have you taken into account all essential notions involved in the problem?"

As you make progress through the analytical stages, all ideas, no matter how likely or unlikely, should be recorded. As facts are examined and verified and as you draw conclusions or establish relationships, you should begin organizing, as early as possible, all of this material into some meaningful patterns, such as topical outlines, chronological sequences, logical divisions of activity, attribute lists, etc. Some of these will be discussed below under the heading of "How to Nudge the Elusive."

The deeper you dig into the problem, the greater is the risk of losing perspective. You may truly become lost in the trees of your forest of ideas. Accordingly, you should vary your approach: after a spell of intensive analysis detach yourself from minutiæ and attempt to get a broader view of what you have brought forth up to then. This will involve some generalizing and drawing of preliminary conclusions which you may then want to verify by moving back into the details. Continue this alternating approach throughout the period of problem-solving.

Problem-solving requires thought — hard thought. You must think and think and think just as hard as you can up to some point of frustration at which time it no longer will pay to think — consciously, that is. At the point of frustration you may then assign the problem to the subconscious.

Free-Play Analysis

The subconscious mind plays a most important role in the working out of problems. I am going to describe a procedure for assigning problems to it, but first I would like to present a concept of the intuitive process. Intuition has been defined as the "quick perception of truth without conscious attention or reasoning." In its commonly understood aspects it is the recognition of a situation accompanied by a rather prompt "hunch" analysis or conclusion as to the meaning or requirements of the situation.

Intuition, I believe, is a very high order of the reasoning process. In the first place, there must be a substantial body of experience stored in the mind where it is organized and classified without conscious effort and in ways undoubtedly unknown (or at least unproven) to us. When a new situation arises certain controlling facts are recognized and, by referral back to the memory bank of the mind, meanings for the present are established by analogy to the past. Under this assumption there is no such thing as being born with intuition; rather, one may have innate mental capacities and if he stores up bodies of experience within the mind, it will draw upon them for the analysis of present problems. Hence intuition will not work where there has been no prior experience.

Much is made of "woman's intuition." This may hold true only in certain limited areas, such as in social competition, man-getting and keeping, and other areas of feminine survival. The virtual exclusion of the woman from a major role in the business world has served to concentrate her attention on these other areas. It is natural that her inputs and her intuitive powers should be developed correspondingly. In entirely new and different areas of perception it may be questioned whether there would be any carry-over at all of her intuitive powers.

In its highest form intuitive reasoning operates on the most meager of evidence. The observer perceives only a few controlling facts and from these he is able to draw out his analytical hunches, often with surprisingly good results. It would seem that the fewer the facts from which to conclude, the greater is the need for prior input. As with electronic computers, you cannot draw from the mind any more than you feed into it.

A deliberate assignment of a problem for intuitive analysis is called "mulling over." Unlike an instantaneous intuitive reaction, the mulling-over stage comes into play when conscious reasoning has become frustrated. Prior to frustration, you have deliberately absorbed and analyzed all aspects of the situation as you perceive them. What seems to happen is that when you stop conscious deliberation a switch is thrown which brings out of reserve the intuitive circuitry of the mind. You know the rest: the great idea comes to you while dreaming, driving, shaving, reading or playing. Although generally the mind cannot manipulate concepts of number as well as the man-made electronic computers, it is able to do a superior job in the processing of experiences and ideas. With incalculable speed it is able to interrelate many variables both simultaneously and sequentially in a way not possible in any step-by-step system of conscious reasoning.

I mentioned occasions when ideas leap out of the subconscious. One of the earliest explanations for this came to me from my friend Dr. Raymond B. Allen, former Chancellor of the University of California at Los Angeles, who told me that there is something about an activity which interrelates mind and hand that stimulates the free play of the mind. This brought to recall experiences I had had in thinking problems through while doing manual work. I would find myself mulling over the problems of the day and often I would find fruitful lines of approach — if not solutions — to these problems. It may also have been a coincidence, but I observed that many of the creative types I have known also had more than an average interest in creative hobbies.

I noticed also that a change of activity might stimulate the production of ideas and solutions. For example, if I reached the saturation point on one matter and then switched to another, answers to some of the prior problems would come to the fore and I would note them down for further conscious attention.

The formula for assignment of a problem to the subconscious mind, then, appears to be: (1) consciously feed as much information as possible to the mind, (2) work this material over actively, seeking conscious solutions to the point of frustration, but not beyond, (3) engage in other kinds of activity, especially creative activity, and (4) keep a pad and pencil handy for those flash inspirations which come up at the strangest and most unexpected moments.

HOW TO NUDGE THE ELUSIVE

In a problem situation, even though you may have all the pertinent facts, the alternatives and the solutions may elude you. The solutions may lie in the discovery of new combinations of facts or in different ways of looking at them. It reminds one of the skilled portrait photographer who seeks combinations of lighting and camera angles which will bring out just the right mood and effect to show his subject to greatest advantage.

The standard dictum for the making of decisions calls for the listing of all alternatives and then selecting among them in accordance with predetermined criteria of choice and predetermined decision rules. This is fine, provided you have actually brought forth all the feasible alternatives. In the material which follows I am going to list about a dozen techniques for nudging the elusive. These are in addition to the various procedures and techniques described in other chapters.

Attribute Listing

Lists of attributes are merely extended descriptions of the object or situation in itself and in relation to its environment. Sometimes they turn into convenient check lists for analysis of a problem.

As a practical matter, we can't make up an over-all list of rules for drawing up a good set of attributes because these will vary with the object or situation being described. For example, the attributes desired for the best man for a certain job would be drawn for the particular position under then prevailing conditions. Later on you might devise a different set of ideal attributes for the same position.

A goal may be taken as a point of departure and a list of considerations drawn up for the satisfaction of that goal. In another situation you might list environmental attributes. For example, you might take a product and try to imagine every possible use for it. Somewhat related to this is the development of a list of attributes for a proposed alternative: how acceptable would the action be from the viewpoints of those affected or interested.

An interesting example of attributes of customer (or environmental) acceptability of a possible new product is found in a statement by Louis Marx, world's biggest and most successful

THE ART OF DECISION-MAKING

toy manufacturer, in an interview for *Life* magazine. Mr. Marx explained six factors which he takes into account in appraising a toy for possible manufacture.

"(1) *Familiarity:* 'The toy must reflect the life around the child. . . . Dolls should have hair. Trains and animals should be realistic in detail. Although an occasional fantasy toy will become popular, children usually want what they have actually experienced in some way. A toy can fail because it is too futuristic. Six years ago toy men began making space toys. They did not sell because children were not familiar with the space age. Today they are, and missiles and launching pads sell extremely well. Some months ago a toy television-telephone was put on the market. It failed. Children have not yet seen TV telephones.'

"(2) *Surprise:* 'This is a kind of bonus. . . . Toys should offer the child something he does not expect. For example, there is a toy mouse that takes its hat off twice. The first time the hat is raised, it reveals an egg on top of the mouse's head, but the next time the egg has become a chicken. A time element is involved, and this generates excitement. But whatever the surprise is, it should not be something that is ugly or frightening.'

"(3) *Skill:* 'A toy that requires a child to practice a little is good, because children like to develop skills and be able to display them. That is why the Hula-Hoop, the Yo-Yo and roller skates have been so popular, and why shooting and target games perennially sell well. So do simple gambling games such as dominoes and bagatelle.'

"(4) *Play Value:* 'This is what keeps the child occupied for hours in an entertaining or creative way. It is the great quality of dolls, tricycles, cowboy pistols and toy trains (of course, all toys must have play value to some degree).'

"(5) *Sturdiness:* 'It seems rather obvious to say that any product should be well made, but it is especially true of toys. Not only do they get rough treatment, but a child senses shoddiness. A toy should also be *safe:* there should be no sharp points or cutting edges.'

"(6) *Comprehensibility:* 'A child does not like toys that are too hard to understand. . . . A toy that forces a child to learn elaborate routines or intricate movements has little appeal. That is why most games are not successful. In spite of such successes as Monopoly and Authors, the vast majority of games with their own set of rules do not appeal to youngsters. Some years ago I brought out a game called Twelve-in-One which consisted of not one but 12 games, all of which could be played with the packaged equipment. It was a dismal failure, and I believe the reason was that the package *looked* too complicated, even though the games were individually simple.' "

Mr. Marx's attributes for a good toy were drawn out of practical experience. But even practical experience requires some safeguard analysis: conditions may have changed since you acquired your original experience; the present situation may not be covered by your past experiences.

Check lists

The check list is an analytical framework. The list of attributes may serve this purpose. The check list assures that you will take into account everything that should be considered before reaching a decision. Throughout this book I have used many check lists. You will find them widely used in textbooks and reference works. Trade associations and government agencies include them in their publications to their membership and to the interested public. You will find check lists published frequently in technical and professional journals and magazines.

If you make your own check list, circulate it among other people who have familiarity with the problem. If you are particularly close to it, you may have omitted some items, or the collective experience of the others may bring out things of which you may not have thought.

When you adapt check lists made by others, use them only as points of departure. No matter how good, they can rarely apply to your situation without some modification, whether by simplification, expansion, changing of items or changing of emphasis.

Let us take an example of a check list selected at random

from *Dun's Review & Modern Industry,* prepared with the assistance of K. F. Vasiliou, Director, Packaging Research Laboratory, Rockaway, New Jersey.

MANAGEMENT CHECK LIST ON REDESIGN OF AN INDUSTRIAL PACKAGE

Why redesign?
1. The product is getting banged up.
2. It's costing too much to pack the product, assemble the container and ship it.
3. The container needs to be integrated with others in the product line.

What are the major considerations?
1. Product manufacturer's needs:
   a. Adequate protection
   b. Easy assembly, packing, closure
   c. Low total cost
2. Customer's needs:
   a. Protection of product
   b. Easy handling
   c. Easy and secure stacking
   d. Easy opening

What are the tests of a good design?
1. Does it protect the product?
2. Does it stack easily?
3. Will it fit standard handling equipment?
4. Is it the right size for easy carloading?

This check list serves an excellent purpose: it provokes thought and it saves time by giving you a basis for analyzing your own situation. For example, under the heading "Why redesign?" three reasons are given. In your own case the need for redesign may be the result of opening new markets in another part of the world. You may need a new package because of shipping conditions or because of temperature and humidity conditions. It might be necessary under these conditions to redesign the package to make it safe against animal or insect pests. For another reason why, you might simply have to conform with government regulations on interstate shipments or with specifications in a government procurement contract. Then again, the redesign of the package may be necessary to permit it to go through the mails in accordance with the size and weight limitations of parcel post.

Classification and Division

It is said of Billy Rose, the famed song writer, that he spent many months in the New York Public Library studying the success attributes of song hits published in the thirty-year period from 1890 to 1920. He noted the characteristics of each popular song and then grouped all of the songs into categories in each of which the songs had similar attributes. With this information he could determine which were the most popular kinds of songs and which made the most money. In this way he hit upon the principle of the song which depends upon a succession of simple sounds, such as his popular "Barney Google with His Goo-Goo Googly Eyes."

Mr. Rose had used the analytical technique of classifying material according to like characteristics of the items. Classification and division are two opposing — and related — approaches to the organization and arrangement of subject matter for further analysis or use. They can save you time in the handling of material, they bring out the characteristics of the material on hand, and they also give you clues to information which you do not seem to have on hand. Instead of dealing with countless songs individually, Billy Rose was able to deal with a comparatively few categories.

Similarly, if I were to have one thousand separate cards on each of which some information was posted, I could work with them only with great difficulty, but if I found that the cards belonged in seven or eight main categories and I grouped them accordingly, I would simplify their further handling. I would also have my first analytical product: information about the contents of seven or eight categories. Also, I would identify missing information and I would discover relationships among the categories.

I would like to cite, as an example of the processes of division and classification, the technique I used in writing any of the chapters — or even part of a chapter — of this book. First, I would decide what I wanted to convey to the reader. Then from my files, references, conversations and personal recall I would jot down, at random, everything that would occur to me as being appropriate to that topic. I might at this stage put the material aside to gain perspective while devoting my attention to other matters.

Returning to my notes, I would pick out main thoughts or subtopics. This would constitute the first *act of division* of subject matter. Now would come the test of whether it is a correct division: I would go over my notes again and regroup them under the appropriate headings which I had just listed. This would constitute the first *act of classification* which is the grouping of items according to common characteristics and the exclusion of items which do not belong.

If there were leftover items, this might mean that they really were not pertinent or that I had to expand or modify my preliminary outline of subtopics.

Through juggling back and forth I would finally evolve a preliminary working outline. Working with it, I might find gaps or inadequacies in my assembly of ideas and materials. This would tell me that I had to make further explorations in the literature, in my files, among my acquaintances and in the recesses of my own mind.

Incidentally, I would keep subdividing until I had organized every last thought on paper. Thus, for this book, my working outline was about 125 pages.

For many people this seems to be a formidable task and a delaying one; their impulse is to start writing the first paragraph, following it with the second and so on. For me it is a great timesaver, apart from the other advantages. I find it much easier to work with outline notes than with the writing and rearrangement of the actual prose.

Variations and adaptations of these techniques may be applied to all kinds of business problems. The main idea is that you must have a sense of the whole activity or situation. You must strive to identify the major steps or phases in an operational *sequence* or each of the separate forces or elements which *simultaneously* are having their impact upon a situation. Then you test them, first by asking whether they cover the whole of the situation and, second, by verifying that each is separate from (although related to) the others. Your first outline need not be an elaborate one; it can consist merely of a list of main topics on a piece of paper.

With this approach you can attack a single aspect of a problem while being reminded of all the others. Your outline serves as a chart of interrelationships; it helps you determine sequences of attack on the separate phases and it also advises you as to those which should be brought into play simultaneously.

An important rule is to organize your ideas according to a single, consistent basis. Then you can more clearly check for completeness and interrelationship patterns.

Another important rule is to strive for some middle number of divisions or topical categories which will be neither too many nor too few. If too long, you tend to get too much fragmentation, the material becomes unwieldy and you have greater difficulty in recognizing differences and interrelationships. If too short, differences and relationships become obscured by the merger of topics. If your first listing of topics is a long one, you tend to have too few items under each topic; if initially it is too short, you tend to have too many items under each major heading.

Elaborating upon a Fact

". . . all life is a great chain," wrote Sir Arthur Conan Doyle, the Sherlock Holmes author, "the nature of which is known whenever we are shown a single link of it." In an earlier chapter I wrote on the nature of facts, pointing out that in the grand order of things all facts are interrelated, that no facts are inconsistent with each other and that if there seem to be any inconsistencies, these would be dispelled by the discovery of additional facts or the discovery that something claimed for a fact actually is not. It follows, then, that if all facts are interrelated, you can take so little as a single scrap or fragment of information and extend your knowledge from it alone to the broader structure of facts of which it is a part.

This was how the great detective Sherlock Holmes established the original ownership of a watch handed to him by Dr. Watson, who speaks in the first person:

. . . He balanced the watch in his hand, gazed at the dial, opened the back, and examined the works, first with his naked eyes and then with a powerful convex lens. . . .

"There are hardly any data," he remarked. "The watch has been recently cleaned, which robs me of my most suggestive facts."

Holmes then tells Watson that the watch belonged to his eldest brother. He deduces this from the age of the watch and the matching age of the initials "H. W." These must have been the initials of Watson's father and first-born son to whom the watch would pass as an inheritance.

"Right, so far," said I. "Anything else?"
"He was a man of untidy habits — very untidy and careless. He was left with good prospects, but he threw away his chances, lived for some time in poverty with occasional short intervals of prosperity, and finally, taking to drink, he died. That is all I can gather."

Watson is shocked. He charges Holmes with having made inquiries about his unfortunate brother and with now pretending to have read his character from his old watch. Holmes assures Watson that he never even knew he had an older brother.

"But it was not mere guesswork?"

"No, no: I never guess. It is a shocking habit — destructive to the logical faculty. What seems strange to you is only so because you do not follow my train of thought or observe the small facts upon which large inferences may depend. For example, I began by stating that your brother was careless. When you observe the lower part of that watch-case you notice that it is not only dented in two places but it is cut and marked all over from the habit of keeping other hard objects, such as coins or keys, in the same pocket. Surely it is no great feat to assume that a man who treats a fifty-guinea watch so cavalierly must be a careless man. Neither is it a very far-fetched inference that a man who inherits one article of such value is pretty well provided for in other respects."

Watson nodded to show that he followed this reasoning. Holmes continued:

"It is very customary for pawnbrokers in England, when they take a watch, to scratch the numbers of the ticket with a pin-point upon the inside of the case. It is more handy than a label as there is no risk of the number being lost or transposed. There are no less than four such numbers visible to my lens on the inside of this case. Inference — that your brother was often at low water. Secondary inference — that he had occasional bursts of prosperity, or he could not have redeemed the pledge. Finally, I ask you to look at the inner plate, which contains the keyhole. Look at the thousands of scratches all around the hole — marks where the key has slipped. What sober man's key could have scored those grooves? But you will never see a drunkard's watch without them. He winds it at night, and he leaves these traces of his unsteady hand. Where is the mystery in all this?"

Each fact, you will note, is given meaning within the context of its own little environment or sequence of happenings. That is, what would precede or follow the event signified by this one fact? The probable chain of events provides the investigator with a basis for further research and verification.

The isolated or unexplained fact cannot be allowed to remain so. Either it must be given meaning within the order of things understood or it must be established that it is unrelated and therefore must be excluded from consideration. Otherwise the unexplained fact remains to taunt you with the possibility that your analyses and conclusions may be faulty.

Isolating Strategic Factors

Let us now give to the key factor a more practical role within the realm of business affairs. Economy of time and effort is critically important in the entire analytical process. You cannot become mired in the profusion of relevant but unimportant details. One way out is to look for the critical or strategic factors which in themselves represent whole bodies of information or upon which other facts depend. Another way to look at it is to say that you should look for the exceptional factors with extended implications. Following are three approaches to this.

The first is the representative factor. The Internal Revenue Service looks for representative data in its pursuit of elusive tax dollars. How would *you* estimate the annual income of a waiter whose earnings are made up mainly of tips? Would you post investigators with long necks or spyglasses to make sample counts of tips received? This could be a very laborious and contemptible procedure. The Internal Revenue Service devised a short cut. It takes the gross receipts for food and drink and then takes 15 per cent of this figure as being the probable amount paid in tips to the servers. The estimated tip payments are then allocated among the servers in proportion to the amount of their base earnings or time worked. The one key factor, then, which sets off the whole chain of deduction, is the amount of gross receipts. The courts have upheld this method.

When estimating the income of a self-employed person, the

Internal Revenue Service uses another timesaving technique. Instead of trying laboriously to account for all possible income, the Revenue agent makes an estimate of net worth of the taxpayer. This becomes his representative factor; it tells how much income must have been earned to create that net worth. And this, too, has been upheld in the courts as a fair method of valuation.

I use the term "affinity factors" to describe those which go together in some logical or predetermined way. I learned this technique very early in life, if I may give a personal example. I had met a young lady at a social function. It was a classic "love at first sight" for me. Desiring to see her again, I made note of her home address but neglected to get her telephone number. When I got home I called the information operator and asked for the telephone number of 4938 Asquith Terrace, N.W. She reported no such street in Washington, D.C. My spirits sagged. What could I do?

Fortunately the city of Washington is laid out according to the unit block system: each block begins with a new hundred series. Thus the address 523 Buchanan St., N.W., would tell you that it is located between Fifth and Sixth Streets in the northwest sector. All numbered streets begin at the Capitol. Accordingly, I began to study the street map of Washington for a name similar to Asquith. First, I counted forty-nine blocks going north. Then I scrutinized each intersecting street name. This yielded nothing. Then I counted forty-nine blocks going west. Again I checked all the streets which intersected the 4900 line. There it was: Eskridge Terrace! Five and one-half weeks later, we were married.

The "fulcrum factor" is the term I use to describe a key element upon which a situation depends. Our first example, here, is from a Richmond, Virginia hatmaker, the M & B Headwear Company. As a large manufacturer of caps, M & B had been looking for ways to cut down on ever-increasing costs. The company president decided that one way of doing this would be to drop the more than forty jobbers who were adding on their costs of distribution and their profits. He would sell his caps by mail direct to the retailers. This, however, was a drastic departure from ordinary trade practices. What could be done to put this program across?

The company president decided that he needed to have something unique and dramatic to induce his retailers to change their buying habits. He found the answer in a cap with a stretch section in the back. He called it the Size-O-Matic. The elastic insert made it possible to manufacture only three sizes which would fit all the millions of boys in the country as well as men who ordinarily would wear sizes up through seven and a half. This was the answer! Manufacturing costs would be reduced and the retailer would need to order fewer sizes with less inventory risk. The elastic cap was the "fulcrum factor" upon which the new plan depended.

The next example is from my experience as executive director of the U. S. Salary Stabilization Board during the Korean War period. I had recommended to my board that we regulate the salaries of industrial executives, professionals and certain other salaried personnel with a minimum of paper work. Our main approach to this would be through self-administering regulations. We would set up standards and authorize business firms to make salary changes in accordance with them without having to send "petitions" to the Great White Father in Washington. This approach was heartily applauded by industry.

When it came to regulating promotions, however, we ran into trouble. Executive and professional positions were often evaluated mainly in terms of the man, rather than the position alone. We could set no detailed standards, yet we did not want to review individual promotion actions of companies throughout the length and breadth of the land. We could not substitute our bureaucratic judgments for those of the employers. We were appalled by the immensity of the task.

The solution: I recommended to our industry advisers and to the board that we require a corporate officer to certify to the legitimacy of each promotion in accordance with the criteria of the regulations. His certification was to be notarized. Later we were told that the self-administration achieved with this device was one of the outstanding successes of the control program. Our simple requirement was more potent than if we had made individual determinations enforced by a small army of investigators. Who would want to perjure himself for the benefit of others? Before affixing their signatures under oath, the officers asked for definite proof of the legitimacy of the promotions. An understanding of human behavior in this situation gave us a big and powerful enforcement army "for free."

The Work Simplification Approach

During World War II, when skilled workers and supervisors were scarce, the War Manpower Commission helped fill the gap through quick-training techniques — the so-called "J" courses: job instruction training, job methods training and job relations training. In job methods training we have a sequence of questions which have been used by efficiency experts and brainstormers alike to solve problems and come up with new ideas.

The technique uses Rudyard Kipling's "six honest servingmen" — the questions Why, What, Where, When, Who and How. Each of these questions is applied to every detail of the problem situation. By the time you will have finished your analysis, little will have been overlooked.

You are then ready to proceed to the four basic steps in methods improvement: eliminate, combine, rearrange and simplify. When you *eliminate* you drop anything that does not really earn its keep. The guiding questions are *Why* and *What*. You *combine* steps by having them done at the same time by the same person or machine. The guiding questions here are *Where, When* and *Who,* which are also the source of ideas for the rearrangement of details for a better sequence. Also, a search for similarities will help. You *rearrange* details to reduce handling and backtracking. Finally, when you *simplify* you ask *How*. This is a catchall, in case you overlooked anything. You might change proportions of effort and even add elements if the net effect is improvement.

Journey into the Real World

The imagination is stimulated by putting oneself into the real situation rather than working with ideas and words. To illustrate this I'd like to tell of an experience in writing my regular column, "Ultra-Miniature," which appears in *Modern Photography* magazine. I was explaining how to use the Minox camera to take pictures without being observed. Specifically, I explained the use of the reflex viewfinder. This attachment fits over the end of a camera, permitting it to be held at waist-level. With it you can take pictures with the fabulously small and precise Minox without your subject being aware of the fact. The instruction literature suggests one other use: to hold the camera over the head when you want to take pictures in crowds where neither waist-level nor eye-level photography will work.

Now if I were to write merely from the instruction literature available to me, these would be the two uses that I would cite. I have a general rule, however, that I must work physically with the equipment itself if I am to write about it. Hence, armed with a reflex viewfinder, I spent an afternoon taking pictures in a variety of situations. I discovered these additional ways to use the finder: (1) right-angle finder at waist-level, (2) right-angle finder at eye-level, held away from the eye, (3) rear-view finder at waist-level, with the camera held off to the side, pointing to the rear, (4) rear-view with camera held at eye-level off to the side, pointing to the rear and (5) rear-view while crouching, with camera held between the legs, pointing to the rear.

With the material of the situation physically in hand or visually before you, you are more likely to see relationships and solutions than if you try merely to think of them.

Input-Output Technique

In the input-output technique you start with the beginning and the end. Knowing that you must go from "here" to "there," you are at once guided and limited in the solution of the problem. The technique is to work out a plan which will show, step by step, what is necessary to be done in order to transform a present state into a future one.

The starting point is to take all of the known requirements, specifications and limitations. These are then related to prior experience, if any. From this point, creative ingenuity comes into play to develop the intermediate processes which must be performed simultaneously or in sequence. The natural inclination of many people, otherwise, is to be impatient to get underway with the matter at hand.

The value of the input-output technique is that you are constantly channeling your thoughts and efforts in accordance with end-product requirements you must satisfy.

Hypothesis

The hypothesis is an educated or informed guess. It is a hunch based upon understanding. Some of the greatest discoveries of all time, including Einstein's discovery of the theory of relativity, began with the making of theoretical assumptions. In point of fact, the world would be far less advanced than it is today if there were not many discoveries which started with an intelligent assumption.

You will note that I said "informed" guess. In the state of Israel and in the Arab lands great treasures have been unearthed in recent years: precious metals, oil, lost cities and Biblical artifacts. These came about initially through a knowledge of the Bible; assumptions as to the location of the hidden treasures were made by studying and interpreting obscure passages in the Bible.

The method of hypothesis starts with an idea: the nature of cause or effect or relationship. From this point on, the hypothesis requires verification through the application of facts. Here immense self-discipline may be required, for there is, too often, a predisposition to seek facts which will support what you wish to prove. You must be willing to discard ideas if repeated tests will not support them. On the other hand, if you are convinced that you are on the right track, you must not be dismayed by

temporary or even prolonged lack of reward. Paul Ehrlich did
not discover salvarsan, his magical cure for syphilis, until the
606th experiment!

The Problem Paper

A substitute for the method of dealing with the real situation — and sometimes a superior method — is the writing out
of a paper in which you state the problem, bring in the pertinent facts, analyze their significance and present a solution. It
has many advantages: (1) it forms a convenient means of finding and arraying facts; (2) it enables you to discover relationships among the elements of thought and fact which might not
otherwise be detected; (3) it identifies gaps in thought and
facts, and conflicts of ideas, thereby forcing you to think about
them, and (4) it serves as a most convenient means of recording
thought for later reference and re-evaluation.

One technique of preparation is first to get everything down
on paper without trying to put items in any particular order.
Then, as in the discussion of classification and division, the next
effort is to organize the material into some logical framework.
If a series of problem papers is to be written, covering different approaches to the same problem, it is best to have them
follow the same outline so that they may be compared more
readily.

Diagrams and Drawings

For a symbolic approach to the study of relationships as a
basis for solving problems, try drawing pictures using lines and
odd geometric shapes. Apart from the obvious advantages of
being able to spread ideas out in front of you, the act of drawing on paper seems to bring about the mind-and-hand interaction which stimulates the freer flow of ideas.

James T. McCay gives a number of hints for diagramming:

"1. *Index your diagram* — Put a date location in one corner. You may want to refer to the diagram at some future time, and it's often useful to know when you did it.

"2. *Use big bold strokes* — As soon as you let yourself niggle with a pencil or piece of chalk your thinking tends to get cramped.

"3. *Use a soft lead pencil, a broad marking ink pen, or chalk* — These are a guarantee against niggling too.

"4. *Use plenty of paper or chalk-board space* — A further way of keeping your thinking from getting narrow or static.

"5. *Keep your diagrams simple* — As soon as you get too much in a diagram it ceases to help you share your ideas.

"6. *Keep diagrams tidy, but not too precise* — Precision focuses too much attention on the method and takes it away from the development of the idea. Precision also tends to lead you into niggling.

"7. *Keep words to a minimum* — One of the values of a diagram is that it lets you escape to some degree from the projection effect of words. Manufacture your own symbols on the spot to act as the necessary labels for your diagram.

"8. *Stay away from regular geometric forms: circles, squares, triangles, rectangles* — They lead you into being too precise. Again the method tends to overshadow the ideas being diagrammed.

"9. *Use a range of colors* — Colors give added dimensions for your diagrams. They also keep interest higher than do black or white lines alone.

"10. *Don't correct your diagram; draw a fresh one* — Erasing takes your attention away from the development of the idea. Maybe the next sketch will suggest something else to you.

"11. *Don't try to make your diagram cover everything* — Remember that no one map can represent all of any territory. Use a separate diagram to feature one group of aspects at a time.

"12. *Don't take your diagrams too seriously* — Diagramming is a useful thinking and communicating tool, but remember that it is only a way of representing something. Tomorrow you'll probably think up a much better way if you're willing to let today's diagram go."*

The Varied-Approaches Technique

If you were to take a cross-section of a tree, cutting across the trunk, you would see all of its construction in the pattern of annular rings. If you were to take the same tree trunk and remove a section from it, vertically, you would see the same tree structured differently. In like manner, you should not content yourself with taking only one approach to the solution of a problem. Go at it from many standpoints: from that of the accountant, the lawyer, the personnel specialist, the industrial engineer and the economist, in addition to any other specialists who may seem to have their unique insights and approaches. Use more than one technique of analysis even within the same field of specialization.

You can analyze a machine's worth from the standpoint of employee productivity and employee safety. You can also analyze it from the standpoint of technological progress, competition and public relations. Then again, if the machine is in a line of work flow, it can be analyzed from that standpoint. And so on.

THE METHODS OF CRIMINAL INVESTIGATION

There seems to be a core of consistency in the methods of analysis used in many different fields of activity. On the assumption that one could learn much from the techniques of police investigators, I bought a bundle of magazines which carried histories of actual police cases. I made notes on police methods as disclosed by these magazine reports and then organized my observations in a format that I thought might have some transferability to the world of business. I do not know whether anyone else has ever used such a pattern, nor would

* James T. McCay, *The Management of Time*. Copyright 1959 by Prentice-Hall, Inc., Englewood Cliffs, N. J.

I suggest that this is an all-inclusive one. I offer it merely as a helpful one.

Intelligence Acquisition

In the first instance, the police must know that a crime has been committed. This may come to them through reports, but it may also come about through their surveillance and through their monitoring of unique sources of intelligence. They may rely upon informers and "stool pigeons." Unusual or unexplained circumstances may come to their attention and bring about an investigation. In a more active sense, having knowledge of a crime, the police may spread the story abroad of the information they are seeking, whether through the posting of notices or through newspapers or through the airwaves.

The police know that almost any act leaves some kind of imprint, if only it can be discovered. Most commonly known is the fingerprint, but incriminating evidence is also found in tire prints, the marks of a tool, the telltale rifling of a firearm or evidences of one's personal presence through microscopic examination. To assist them in their search for clues and evidences, the police use a wide range of measuring and laboratory examination devices.

Elaborate techniques must be used for the handling and processing of the mass of information that is collected, not only for the case at hand but for use in cases whose precise nature is not yet known. In working over the immediate case, the facts are inventoried and reinventoried. Only those facts which definitely are accounted for as being nonpertinent are set aside. Those who report the facts may be reexamined from time to time because a question put to them in a new light or with additional supporting facts may bring replies different from those obtained previously.

Situational Completion

The police take the facts of a situation and attempt to bring them together into a completed picture. Doing this, they can discern the gaps in a situation. One fact may suggest another. If they are investigating a series of crimes they look for the consistencies and the common patterns. Knowing these, they can also know what other things to associate with the known elements in order to complete the situation. On the other hand, when they are confronted with circumstantial evidence they test it by seeing how logically it fits into the completed picture.

The reconstruction of a crime is an effort by the police to gather evidence, to perceive the possible relationships of cause and effect, to identify additional facts which are needed, to identify *modus operandi,* etc. In trying to structure and complete the situation in this way, the police also make use of the technique of role-playing, although they might not identify it as such, through re-enacting their concepts of how the situation was at the time of the crime. Through injecting themselves into the nearest thing to the real situation, they are more likely to perceive aspects of it which otherwise might not occur to them from behind their desks or out pounding the streets.

Persistence Theory

The police operate on the theory, well substantiated through experience, that known criminals tend to operate in the same way. If a crime has been committed which leaves certain telltale marks of a particular method of operation, the police may then go to their *modus operandi* files to look for logical suspects. These may pertain to the use of certain tools or methods of entrance or the use of certain vehicles or certain kinds of accomplices or the previous commission of sex crimes, among others.

On the other hand, if they are concerned with a known individual, they may be able to predict his operating methods and his probable next moves on the basis of their knowledge of how he operated in the past. This accords with previous discussions in this book on the prediction of personal behavior.

Action-Vector Analysis

Any act may be presumed to have an antecedent cause as well as consequence. The technique used by police is to try to formulate the line of action which preceded the event, thereby disclosing *who* might have committed it or the *manner* in which it might have been committed. Similarly, they then try to project from it to try to learn what further acts may have been committed by the criminal. In this respect they try to build up what is often called a chain reaction. Sometimes, for purposes of entrapment, they may themselves create such a chain reaction.

When they look for motivations they reach back into time to try to identify the reasons for the crime. Assuming these, they may then be able to identify who might logically have been associated with such reasons.

Disequilibrium

There is a balance in the grand order of things. If someone disappears, that balance is disturbed and people take note of it. If a stranger appears upon a scene, he disturbs the previous equilibrium of the situation; he is a new element as yet unaccounted for and hence rather conspicuous. Thus the police look for their clues in any evidence of change or inconsistency. In their interrogations of suspects they seek to draw from them information which may point to lies or inconsistencies so that thereby they may open up new lines of inquiry. "There is no concealment; every element hangs out its flag." I do not know the origin of this expression, but it serves well to identify a source of lead for the investigators of wrongdoing. Any inconsistency with the presumed norm in some way makes itself known. It remains but for the skilled observer to identify it and to carry the play from there.

The police look for broken continuity in time: Where were you on the night of ————? A thing could have been either in one place or another. Does this seem obvious? If so, remember that criminals are caught in just this way.

CONCLUSION

Thus we see that, whether or not they are identified or recognized as such, the core techniques of problem-solving are employed quite widely. We would find them in fields of endeavor besides police work if we were to examine further.

So universal are the techniques that a great many people make their living as management consultants, solving problems in just about every line of endeavor. Since they cannot be experts in all the fields in which they operate, they offer instead an expertese in dealing with many different kinds of problems. Since World War II the new field of operations research (described in Chapter XIV) has emerged, justifying itself through the development of advanced techniques of scientific analysis in problem-solving.

On a more modest scale this suggests that experience in problem-solving in any field is transferrable — not the subject matter but the methods. Another conclusion to be drawn is that you can find talent for assignment to difficult problems by looking around in the organization for people who have already demonstrated their abilities in this regard, provided the assignment is not too technical.

Chapter XII

CRYSTAL-BALLING THE FUTURE

The ability to minimize risks and maximize gains depends largely on how clearly one can foresee the future. In this chapter we shall examine a variety of techniques for doing so.

1. The techniques of general forecasting are far from perfect, to say the least. Accordingly, guidelines are offered for using forecasts with safety in your own enterprise.

2. Much uncertainty could be minimized if you could predict individual and group behavior. In addition to suggesting techniques for doing so, we will review miscellaneous techniques for anticipating what is to come from around the corner.

3. This chapter describes how "models" may be used as tools of prediction. The model is a physical, verbal or symbolic replica of the real thing. You can use it to predict effects of changes in the real version itself or in the environment or in the relationship of the two. Practical suggestions are offered for building your own, without benefit of mathematics. Finally, we review techniques of trend projection.

PUTTING FORECASTS TO USE

The poet Thomas Campbell used poetic license when he wrote: "And coming events cast their shadows before." The shadows are the projections of the *past*. Forecasting takes the experience of the past and the present and converts it into a pattern or trend which can be projected as a probability.

While general forecasting techniques are improving constantly, they are far from that state of perfection which will permit their use as the main means of predicting conditions for individual enterprises. The present state of the art is indicated in the following comment by the American Management Association, summing up, in part, the results of a survey of economic forecasting for industry:

"Scientific economists themselves admit inability to relate basic economic forecasting to the affairs of a particular business at a given instant in time. They are often in disagreement, even on national trends. Debate continues on whether a slump is possible, likely, or inevitable; the significance of the latest unemployment figures in some segments of the economy; industry's plans for capital spending and their effect on future demands."

The economic forecast *does* have this absolute value: it leads you to a self-analysis of your present plans, commitments and resources which you otherwise might not do.

Applied Economic Forecasting

The businessman looks to economic forecasts to reveal portents of the future in the economy as a whole, his own industry and his own company. From the general marketplace he seeks answers to questions such as these:

Will money tighten and will interest rates go up?

Will the costs of materials rise or will they stabilize?

Will people operate on long or short inventories?

Will the labor market ease off or will it tighten?

What will be the mood of consumer spending and how will this be reflected in production and distribution of both industrial and consumer goods?

What will be the economic effect of a protracted strike outside your own business, affecting availability of materials or transport?

The answers provide general guides to specific action on decisions pertaining to one's cash position, raw-goods inventory, finished-goods inventory, investment in long-range and heavy-capital improvements, expansion, launching of new products, acquisitions and mergers and sales campaigns, to mention a few. Your objective, throughout, is to try to assure that your enterprise will at least maintain its equilibrium in relation to the economy as a whole, if not to do better.

With regard to your own industry, while some of the same questions may have pertinence, your two main concerns are the trend and drift of the industry as a whole and your relative position in it. Now you begin looking for more specific indicators:

What are the trends for the industry as a whole and how are these reflected in the actions of the leaders?

What distinguishes the successful firms from the poorer ones in your industry, as evidenced by their relative performance?

Are you maintaining your relative share of a growing market?

What are the prospects for invading foreign markets?

Are you likely to be affected by legislative and administrative actions of the Federal Government?

What are the prospects for competition in your own market, domestically, from foreign imports?

These questions will lead to a review of your position on products and services, sales promotion, sales engineering and legislative representation, to name a few. You may be thinking of diversification or of decisions to achieve a different balance in your operations.

Within your own company the forecasts you will seek will be obtained largely from operational data of the kinds discussed in Chapter III.

Where will you be on executive manpower five years from now, ten years, twenty years?

What will be your machine and plant requirements?

What goals must you set for the levels of professional, clerical, plant and outside employment?

How must you adjust the production goals to be in balance with corrected sales forecasts?

How must you adjust inventory planning to adjusted production goals?

Hazards of Forecasting

At best, forecasts are informed guesses. They are never completely free of uncertainties, in part due to absence of facts and in part due to method. Accordingly, it is well to know some of the hazards in forecasting and what may be done to offset them, through questions or actions, as suggested below.

1. Since a forecast is a thrust forward from some base of factual accumulation, how much confidence can you attach to the accuracy of the factual base and the situation which it purports to depict? Were the meanings properly drawn from these facts? Have there been any material changes in *how facts were accumulated* at successive stages? Have there been any material changes in *what the facts signified* at successive stages? If the definitions or relationships have changed without proper adjustment, your projections will be thrown off course.

2. Let's assume that the situation has been read correctly and that all of the representative facts have been properly structured, the best the forecast can do then is to say, *"Provided anticipated conditions actually exist at some time in the future."* Now there's the rub: nothing remains the same. Old relationships fail to hold, for the only constant is change itself. You are on reasonably safe ground if the essential attributes of the situation will remain the same. There is always the possibility of unanticipated acts or changes in conditions. Thus, if you predict the market for gasoline, you might use as indicators the anticipated increases in the number of automobiles, trucks and airplanes that use gasoline. Adjustments might be made for improvements in gasoline mileage due to more efficient combustion engines. Your predictions could then be thrown off

entirely by the successful introduction of a system for generating electric power from chemical energy sources.

3. Recognizing that there are many unforeseeables, the forecaster must hedge his predictions within some plus-or-minus range. One is reminded of the weight-guesser at the carnival who will peg your weight or your age within three pounds or three years either way. With a range of six, he could guess your age from forty-two to forty-eight and still be right. Plus-or-minus, then, gives you lots of elbowroom.

4. It is most difficult to project into the future when you have no past experience. Then you make assumptions or look to parallel experience, which is a form of prediction by analogy. Now you fall into the hazards of subjective comparison. You can be predisposed to find almost anything you seek. The greater the intangibilities or the unknowns, the greater are the hazards, as in such matters as producing a new book, a new play or a new product that may be years ahead of its time. Do you remember the Chrysler Airflow, a streamlined automobile of the late thirties, which did not meet with public acceptance because it was born too soon?

5. The more meaning there is to be extracted from the forecasts, the greater will be the need for more factual detail. This may lead to a new problem: as the volume of facts builds up, the greater must be your dependence on mathematical analysis which, in turn, makes you more dependent on the services of the expert. You will then be confronted with problems of bridging the communication gap between the forecaster and the decision-maker. The forecaster can help only if he is able to understand the real problems of the decision-maker. The latter needs to learn from the forecaster the meanings of his symbolisms, abstractions, generalizations and techniques of presentation.

6. Forecasts may be their own undoing. They may stimulate action to overcome or to take advantage of the condition which is forecast. If a peak market is forecast and everyone tries to sell to it, the usual tendency is for the laws of supply and demand to drive the prices down. Then, if the forecast is for a

low market, it can drive producers out which, in turn, lowers supply and pushes prices up. Conversely, a forecast may be for a recession. This may be a signal to the Federal Government to pour money into the economy through public works, accelerated defense expenditures and reduced taxes. A business action predicated on the expected recession would then no longer be valid.

7. The lag in data compilation which attends or besets most forecasting means that you are usually in the dark to some extent. When the missing facts are filled in, you will have again moved forward so that once more you have a factual lag. If the forecaster tries to narrow the gap, he finds himself incurring greater costs, which may be disproportionate to any greater certainty added.

Some Safeguards in Forecasting

Following are some additional suggestions for making forecasts more helpful and for minimizing risks in using them:

1. Use as many indicators or measures of future trends as possible in order to protect yourself against incorrect conclusions from single indicators. The most reliable indicators may be expected to go wrong because of new kinds of conditions. Thus forecasters will seek verification through using combinations of *leaders* (that precede coming events), *coinciders* (that accompany other indicators) and *laggers* (that are known to follow certain conditions and thereby may be used in confirmation of trends). Diffusion indicators should be used as a check against individual indicators; the diffusion indicator is one which reflects the market as a whole.

2. Divide the trend picture into three succeeding segments: the near-term trend, the midperiod trend and the long-term trend. The near-term trend is most easy to predict because you are closer to the facts and the visible situation. The duration of the near-term may be as long as you can foresee with reasonable certainty. The long-term trend is stated more generally and hence can be predicted with some safety if for no other

reason than that the very generalizations give you room in which to maneuver. It is the midterm trend which gives the most trouble: it is too fuzzy to warrant the specific prediction of the near-term and it does not provide clear outlines to justify long-term predictions.

3. Record in detail your forecasts as to future conditions, the assumptions and interpretations you draw from them, your action goals and your plan of action. Then, as you move ahead, you will have a clear basis for checking out and correcting both forecasts and plans. As you do so, use this more sophisticated understanding, gained through experience, to project forward again. Keep repeating this process. Maintain a broad perspective; don't adjust for minor fluctuations unless you are certain there have been changes in basic conditions.

4. Use long-term forecasts as a basis for making decisions of long-term effect. Short-term or spot fluctuations may well occur — as they do in the stock market — without really affecting the long term.

5. Take advice and counsel from all who might offer their services, but look critically on those who have any personal interests in the outcome of your actions. However sincere they may believe themselves to be, they have built-in biases which may warp their judgments.

6. Beware of forecasts which have generous allowances of a plus-or-minus nature. They provide too much leeway. You might as well do your own educated guessing.

HOW TO PREDICT BEHAVIOR

The prediction of human behavior is a form of persistence prediction. That is, it assumes that demonstrated behavior patterns will be repeated. This presents several unique challenges. Have you correctly read and understood the pattern of previous behavior? Are the conditions and stimuli such, in the new situation, that they will elicit a predictable response, such as generally occurred in the past under similar conditions?

Have there been personality changes of sufficient strength to require a corresponding change in the personality prediction?

You may want to reflect on these and similar questions as you try to apply any of the following guidelines to your analysis and prediction of individual or group behavior. All that I offer here is an approach — a way of looking at people in order to understand how they are apt to act under certain conditions. It is an approach, however, that many men of power and great position have mastered, whose success must be attributable in large part to their ability to understand the motives and reactions of their fellow man.

Prediction of Personal Behavior

The same Thomas Campbell who gave us the line on "coming events" gave us another which is of the essence in this chapter: "And learn the future by the past of man." Or, as inscribed on the National Archives Building in Washington: "The Past Is Prologue."

You will recall that in the first chapter we touched briefly on how individuals acquire patterns of behavior and response to new situations. We saw how everything that happens to the individual contributes to the shaping of a frame of reference to which his new experiences are referred for automatic guidance and response. If you can know the pattern of his past, the *chances are* that you can predict his behavior in new situations which contain important elements of past experience.

It is not unusual for people to go to great lengths to obtain "run-downs" on individuals with whom they expect to do business. Men in the field of international affairs do this as do also men of science.

Of course one of the difficulties is that the individual may actually have changed his pattern of behavior as the result of powerful motivations or experiences. He may have improved or debased his behavior patterns. Thus an exhaustive historical analysis would be required in order to see all aspects of the development of the individual. This, in turn, would require a disinterested professional interpretation. As a practical matter one could scarcely afford to arrange this except on rare occasions of momentous negotiation.

Accordingly, I suggest two approaches for obtaining an understanding of the probable pattern of behavior of your subject. One is to plot a current personal profile and the other is to assign him to a typical role category. These approaches, however, cannot substitute for direct contact, knowledge and understanding.

In plotting the current profile of the individual, you ask questions such as the following:

1. What can you tell about him from the kind of people with whom he has associated in the past as well as presently, both on and off the job? What clues to his behavior can you find in the personalities of others who most influence him? How does he respond toward his superiors? How does he behave toward his subordinates and toward people on his own level?

2. What are his ostensible business goals? Does he really have any goals? Is he supporting the goals set out by those in authority over him? Does he seem to pursue his goals actively?

3. What are his personal aims and ambitions, if any? Has he actively pursued any personal goals? What compromises may he have to make or whom may he have to please? Who are his apparent competitors and what issues stand between them?

4. What are his confidence areas — those aspects of his performance in which he feels most competent and regarding which he expresses himself most positively? What are his "showcase" interests — those aspects of his work which he chooses to use for display of his abilities and insights? What have been his "Waterloo" experiences — those instances or situations which have caused him embarrassment or which have revealed inadequacies — from which he may want to shy away now?

5. What is his action personality? Is he generally active or passive? Friendly or unfriendly? Does he go it alone or does he work as a team member? Is he a man of demonstrated integrity or will he take whatever position seems expedient at the moment? Does he express himself openly or does he hold himself out as a sort of enigma?

6. How secure is he personally? Has his independence of judgment been affected by financial insecurity? Is he financially independent, thereby being able to reach positions without fear of personal consequences? Does he feel reasonably sure of himself in his position so that he is not impelled to compromise his judgments in order to buy acceptance? What controlling considerations do influence his judgments?

7. Have you ever seen the man under stress? What would precipitate stress and how does it manifest itself? (It is under stress that many people reveal the more impulsive aspects of their personalities, thereby bringing out elements of their character which otherwise you might never discern.)

8. In the current situation what has your man at stake? What does he stand to gain or lose under each of the possible alternatives of action? What clues to his judgment can you find in the pattern of his associations with others involved in the decision? What has been the recent pattern of his judgments and actions in related matters? What related matters await decision and how are they likely to influence his current judgments?

We commonly predict individual behavior by typing people and then drawing inferences from behavior expected of people of that type. We say, "He's the quiet type" or, "He's the dominant type."

For our purposes there are a number of ready-made classifications of executive and managerial types. Before commenting on them, however, some warning is in order: the mere fact that a person is properly classified as a sales type, a production type or an engineering type does not mean that he necessarily will behave typically. All that can be said is that *most* people who fall within a certain classification are likely to behave according to a known pattern, but a minority will not. If you know nothing at all about the individual, you may say to yourself, "The chances are . . ." but if you have a chance to observe him or to obtain information about him from others, you should use the following guides only as points of departure.

Functional types. The consulting firm of Booz, Allen & Hamilton gave four widely used psychological tests to a group of functional executives in fields of finance and accounting, engineering, sales, manufacturing and general administration. Test results revealed characteristics of the group as shown in the following table:

DIVERGENCIES IN THE CHARACTERISTICS OF FUNCTIONAL EXECUTIVES AS REFLECTED IN TEST FINDINGS

CHARACTERISTICS IN
ORDER OF SIGNIFICANCE

	Strong	*Weak*
FINANCE AND ACCOUNTING	Computational Clerical Reflective	Mechanical Impulsive Scientific Vigorous
ENGINEERING	Scientific Mechanical Reflective	Persuasive Sociable Impulsive Clerical
SALES	Persuasive Impulsive Dominant Sociable Active	Computational Scientific Reflective Mechanical
MANUFACTURING	Mechanical Scientific	Intellectual Ability Sociable Dominant
GENERAL ADMINISTRATION	Reflective Sociable Dominant Persuasive Active	NONE

Now let's compare this with the results of another study. Four researchers — L. Huttner, S. Levy, E. Rosen and M. Stopol — reported their findings on functional types in an article in *Personnel,* entitled "Further Light on the Executive Personality." The types they reported are engineering and research and development executives, sales executives, administrative and accounting executives and production executives. These classifications are, then, sufficiently close for comparison.

Engineering and research and development executives evidence the following characteristics: great accuracy, both generally and specific; high powers of abstract reasoning; creative personalities; a tendency to be inept with verbal material; slow handling of simple routine computations as compared with their abilities for organizing abstract materials; unfamiliarity with business management; and a tendency to be poorly adjusted, to predispose toward subtle depression, and to keep apart from others.

Sales executives score high on verbal as against nonverbal factors. They tend to be other-oriented: sociable and extroverted while at the same time being highly dominant. They tend to be more open, more thick-skinned, more optimistic and more self-assured than other executive types. They show some evidence of self-centeredness and selfishness (which may not be at all incompatible with some of their outgoing attributes).

Administrative and accounting executives rate quite high on numerical ability. They tend toward the tangible rather than the abstract. They rate low in communication abilities, particularly in verbalizing. They tend to be less sociable and more withdrawn. They are the least optimistic group and tend more frequently toward open depression. They show the least originality or creativity.

Production executives rank higher than the engineering and research and development on abstract reasoning ability. They rank highest in numerical ability. They are oriented toward the concrete. They tend to make few errors. Although they tend to be optimistic, their moods tend to fluctuate.

As we see, there are some fundamental similarities in the results of the two studies. The differences are sufficient to enable you to take your pick or to blend the two together. Again, remember that these are quite general and must be made specifically pertinent to the particular individual. The fundamental differences serve as a reminder, too, that we have much to learn, yet, in our efforts to characterize personality.

Working-level types. Patterns of typical behavior can be discerned which correspond to the level at which one works. For purposes of presentation and simplicity I will describe three working levels: top management, middle management and the foreman/supervisor level. This, of course, is a simplification, for in actual practice the levels of management may range from two to six or more.

At the top level, management men deal mainly in broader goals, intangibles, value judgments and greater risks. The decisions they make have impact upon numbers of people as well as upon the fortunes of the enterprise itself. Removed as they are from direct contact with operations, their manipulation of goals and means makes heavy use of symbolism: operating statistics and the dollar sign. At times it might seem that this might be an end in itself, without considered regard for the human values. Social dexterity is a prerequisite to survival at this level because of the variety of contacts under diverse conditions and circumstances.

They may be blazing new trails or setting aside old precedents as they strive toward their ultimate decisions. The cautions they express reflect their awareness of the many factors in the more complex environments in which they operate.

For a description of *the man-in-the-middle* I'm going to quote from Lyman W. Porter and Edwin E. Ghiselli, who wrote a most interesting report in *Personnel Psychology,* entitled "The Self-Perceptions of Top and Middle Management Personnel." They said:

"Careful planning, thoughtful actions and well-controlled behavior characterize the self-perceptions of middle management as contrasted to those of top management. Middle management people see themselves as individuals who seldom take rash actions that are not well thought out beforehand. They consider proposed actions from all angles and aspects before they move ahead. They can be counted on not to make hasty or unfounded decisions. They seem to place more reliance on *operating within the rules and conditions of the system* rather than plunging ahead on their own ideas when these have not been previously tested. They do not appear as willing to take risks or to move ahead when the final outcome is uncertain, and they do not show the same sort of confidence in their own judgment as do members of top management. They seem more concerned about social traits that are especially important in the job situation rather than in general social situations. They indicate they want to avoid giving the appearance of being controversial personalities and of exhibiting self-centered behavior. They want to do nothing that might attract unfavorable comment about their behavior, and they avoid forcing their own ideas on others. In summary, they seem to describe themselves as stable and dependable individuals who try to avoid making mistakes on the job or elsewhere."

As one approaches *the first line of supervisory management* he becomes increasingly aware of a tightly structured environment for decision. The supervisor feels hemmed in by a prescribing and proscribing body of policies and procedures. He may stand in awe of the inscrutable judgments of those appointed over him. Consequently he is loathe to depart from "the system." He prefers to play it as a regular, that is, to "play it safe." On the other hand he has certain other advantages: he is able to see more tangibly the results of his decisions or actions (or of those above him) very soon after the actions are taken. The sequences of action with which he must cope stand out clearly, at least by comparison, for he is dealing usually with observed phenomena in a real world of action and consequence rather than with the manipulation of symbols. Consequently his decisions entail less risk for the enterprise, although the supervisor who makes them may not feel any the less relieved.

Collect-your-own types. If you are a keen observer you can collect data as to the behavior characteristics of people according to any classification you find convenient and helpful. You can do so by occupational type or personality type. Distinguished novelists have done this in their excellent characterizations which appeal to the readers because they identify self or others in them. Psychologists carry this a step further with their careful measurements of personality attributes.

At this juncture I must repeat a warning that clusters of personality attributes do not apply to all members of the class being described. The description, if valid, describes the class as a whole but you must make individual judgments as to specific members of the class who may vary considerably. I refer again to advice given me once by Judge Justin Miller, for whom I once worked, who said: "If you, as an administrator, want some positive, eager advice, choose a 'hot' lawyer; if you want to proceed cautiously or if you want to avoid decision, choose a 'cold' lawyer."

One keen reporter described his observations of "Business Men, Lawyers, and Economists" in an article by that title in the *Harvard Business Review*. The author, Melvin Anshen, said that *lawyers,* in the main, have intellectual personalities marked by the following dispositions:

To respect and be guided by antecedent thought and action, and hence to prefer conservation to innovation.

To practice precision and avoid discontinuities in thought, word and action.

To accept logic and reject emotion; to distrust impulse.

To value surface appearance above inner concept when they are in conflict.

To prefer qualitative to quantitative techniques.

To minimize technology as a social force.

To favor conciliation and compromise over authoritarian dissolution of differences.

For *economists,* with cautious exception, he suggests the following characteristic dispositions:

To be skeptical of all traditionally accepted theories.

To be willing to make bold experiments with new ideas, and

to be equally ready to withdraw from commitments if the results prove unfavorable.

To accept both logic and emotion as valid components in the process of understanding and predicting human and organizational behavior.

To value inner concept above surface appearance when they are in conflict.

To have confidence in the possibility of devising methods for bringing within the scope of quantitative techniques many phenomena hitherto handled only in qualitative terms.

To be interested in the process of manipulating people, and to believe that successful manipulation to achieve desired objectives is attainable in the foreseeable future.

To place a high value on technological development and innovation.

To welcome the resultant economic and social dynamics; to be unintimidated by change.

To suspect conciliation and compromise as potentially evasive in nature.

Anshen reports *the businessman* as one who regards himself as a man of practical affairs, who looks upon successful management as an art rather than a science. For the businessman he suggests the following predispositions:

To be pragmatic; to be skeptical of precedent and unafraid of, even eager for, change.

To be deeply conscious, in assaying change, that it rarely occurs quickly or by jumps, and that while it can be planned or guided it cannot be absolutely controlled.

To recognize that organizations are complex associations of people resistant to change and not easily enlisted in common tasks, with the result that the accomplishment of innovation is always slower than anticipated.

To prefer concrete to abstract reasoning, quantitative to qualitative calculation.

To regard professionals and technicians with a mixture of respect and contempt, as being the possessors of essential special knowledge which they often cannot put to use.

To consider the body of legislative and administrative law as being probably essential but frustrating and unreasonably arbitrary, and therefore as something to be outwitted, circumvented and, if necessary, evaded.

To approve technological innovation in principle, but often to deplore its speed in practice.

To acknowledge the necessity for long-range planning, while retaining an uneasy sensitivity and responsiveness to short-term fluctuations in economic indexes.

To profess a belief in the rationality of managerial decision-making, but to remain the servant of emotional judgments and hunches.

To respect and work for unanimity of staff opinion; to be disturbed by firm disagreement; and to accept group recommendations unmarked by dissent as evidence of thorough analysis and sound judgment.

Thus we see that the two main prediction tools of individual behavior are:

1. Making assumptions about the individual from an understanding of how people of his kind behave and

2. Verifying or modifying the initial general assumption by studying the past behavior patterns of the individual *under similar circumstances.*

Prediction of Group Behavior

The characteristic behavior of groups — a kind of group mold — is expressed in the behavior of its representatives. Thus, you may hear it said that "He's from purchasing [or legal or accounting] and you know how they are about . . ." By understanding the group, then, you can be better prepared to deal with its representatives and to anticipate the positions they will take. Once more, this is only another indicative approach, not necessarily conclusive. Groups have different behavior characteristics in much the same way as individuals, corresponding to their maturity level, as explained below. Also presented, as clues to future group behavior, are suggestions for analyzing group goals and attitudes, group leadership, environmental influences on the group and the dynamic posture of the group.

Growth stage. In Chapter I, I summarized the manner in which the group acquires maturity and homogeneity and how its operating characteristics undergo typical changes at successive stages of juvenescence, maturity and senescence. With that description as a reference base, analyze the group-flexibility pattern in the light of the following:

1. What is the maturity status of the group in the range from youth through maturity to old age? Does the group behave typically for its maturity status? Is the particular organizational component in which you are interested typical of the over-all or does it have its own independent maturity pattern?

2. Has the group done anything to arrest the normal tendency toward becoming rigidified? Are there any vitalizing forces from within which tend this way? Has the group taken on any challenging *new* programs which force new patterns of thought?

3. What is the organization's equilibrium status? Is it in a state of operating balance? Is there too much work or too little? Are key positions filled? Is the enterprise fully preoccupied with its current commitments or is it ready or eager for new activity? If the enterprise is in a state of disequilibrium, it tends to avoid decisions or commitments on new matters.

Indicators of goal and attitude. Out of the past may be drawn the indications of action positions to be taken in the future. Look for clues in the following, but remember that programs do change, especially in minor detail:

1. Program plans and targets

2. Publications and special reports

3. Operating and administrative manuals, circulars, memoranda and other instructional materials

4. Budget justifications and documents

5. Financial plans and reports

6. Reports filed with the Securities and Exchange Commission

7. Speeches and other public statements

In addition to the above, look for information relating to

previous successes and failures which may reveal both the likely and the unlikely modes of action based on experience.

Leadership impact. The leader and his group have an impact upon each other. Which will predominate is governed by strength of personality as well as by fortuitous circumstance. The actual leadership may be in someone other than the nominal head man. He may be dominated by one or more members of his group or by someone outside the immediate group. The focus of leadership must be determined and then the policies and views of that leadership must be analyzed so that the positions of any representatives of the group may be predicted.

1. Has the leader been in his position long enough to be in full command? Sometimes a new leader may strike out forcefully without challenge, but before long he usually must make his peace with the group.

2. Is there harmony between leader and group? If there is discord, action positions may not be dependable.

3. Is the leader amenable to change or does he hold to the groove? Does he initiate or is he passive?

4. Who controls or influences the leader's mind; what are his views? The leader may make up his own mind, but if someone else does so the latter is the *de facto* leader.

Environmental influences and constraints. No enterprise is a free agent entirely. Externally, it is influenced or constrained by government laws and regulations, financial elements, economic trends, customer and market reactions, competitors, suppliers, public opinion, technology, domestic and international politics and war. Internally, a segment of organization operates with regard to the outside world as well as within an over-all network of organization, procedures, goals, programs, schedules and personal relationships.

All of the external elements interact with each other and with the internal elements to guide the course of action of the enterprise. Men may consider themselves as masters of the situation but, in truth, they also are products of the environment and, inevitably, are subject to it.

Consider the following:

1. What meaning can you derive from the external elements, as just described?

2. Internally, what is expected of the group or activity by its superior management and other parts of the organization?

3. What is the larger operating and administrative system of which the activity is a part and what control does it impose? What freedom does it allow?

4. What is the over-all mood of the enterprise and how does it govern?

Dynamic Posture. Knowing all you can learn about the group or activity, within the framework of analysis thus far suggested, your picture will not be complete until you have assessed the elements of capability, mood and drive which add up to dynamic posture.

1. Estimate resources and capabilities in depth: availability of qualified personnel, fiscal and material resources and uncommitted time.

2. Evaluate power status relative to both outside world and internal alignment pattern; make estimate of ability to command situation — whether on the rise or decline.

3. Review pattern of past successes and failures to find clues as to capability and environmental interaction.

4. Assess the dynamic mood, will or determination of the group to achieve its objectives in spite of all obstacles or difficulties.

The prediction of group behavior is done more easily than with individuals. The group affords more opportunities for observation. It may be studied through its own behavior as well as through its role in its environment. It may also be understood through an analysis of its leadership. The group "stands still" much more than the individual and hence can be observed more easily.

Bringing the Future Closer

The assumptions you make about individual or group behavior should be verified through as many other indicators as possible. The techniques described above try to foretell through

CRYSTAL-BALLING THE FUTURE 309

studying the past and the present. The techniques now to be described aim to give you a clearer perception of reactions to specific acts or proposals. In each case the technique brings you closer in time to specific reactions.

Spot testing. A familiar technique in launching a new product is that of spot testing. Before a campaign is committed in full the product will be launched in a limited market. On the basis of results the approach may be confirmed or modified. Similarly, stage productions may be launched in smaller communities before being given their traditional New York openings.

The spot test or trial run is also used in production engineering, procedural installations and equipment installations, among others. The trial run may be used in prototypes of field organizations, personnel categories, work situations, distributorships, consumer samples, etc. The underlying principle is that you do not commit all your resources, yet you obtain most of the benefit of interaction with the actual environment of effect.

Testing action sequences. A variation of the trial run is the testing of successive blocks of an operation or action sequence before the activity as a whole is launched. Assume that you are laying out a procedure or work program consisting of steps A, B, C, D and E. You may plan the sequence as a whole from behind a desk, but then you may not be sure that the reaction to step A might not so change conditions as to require basic changes in step B and so on. Accordingly, each step is tested out in sequence and the lessons learned thereby are applied to planning of successive steps. This is one of the reasons for playing of war games by the military.

Outwitting time and space. An event may already have occurred but if there is no knowledge of it, the disclosure belongs to the future. Prediction, under these circumstances, is a matter of outwitting time and space. Thus, when the Rothschilds used carrier pigeons to carry news among the political and financial centers of Europe, they were able to learn more quickly of events that still belonged to the future, so far as others were concerned. This, of course, was before the telegraph and the telephone and all the later wonders of modern communication and transportation which compress the time factor in travel.

Similarly, earlier knowledge of the future may be obtained by better procedural arrangements. Anything which streamlines reporting, processing, transmission, review and other operational steps brings knowledge and action that much closer.

Intelligence procurement. A very old technique, probably as old as man, for finding out about coming events, is to go to the man who is in a privileged position to know. Some people make a living by doing this for a fee in an undercover sort of way. You'd be surprised how often you can get the information you want by building up good professional and reciprocal relations. Then there is the research approach. Nations learn much about each other by fitting together the publicly available bits and pieces printed in the general press and in the trade press. Careful industrial sleuthing can accomplish much the same.

MODELS OF THE FUTURE

A much more elaborate and "sophisticated" way of predicting behavior is through the "construction" of a model of the operating situation. The term "model" is encountered increasingly as one hears more of operations research, statistical decision-making, mathematical problem-solving and related techniques of scientific analysis. Actually, models have long been used in more familiar ways. A model is any representation of reality. Model airplanes are used as toys, of course, but they are also used as actual engineering configurations for purposes of research and development. Role-playing, as a technique of situational analysis, constitutes a form of model-building. A policy and procedure manual is a model of operating process. So is the accounting system. Also a blueprint.

The model is any integrating device which brings together in common relationship the essential elements of a situation, device, system or subsystem *as a whole.* It is used in place of the real thing as an object of study. This may be a matter of physical convenience or, when working in new areas, there may be no other choice.

Models are used in prediction because of:

1. Convenience in representing whole situations.
2. Ability to see the effects of varying any of the elements.
3. Assurance that the elements are in balance and are properly interrelated.
4. Identification of missing elements.

Here we will consider only such model-building techniques as do not require mathematics. In a later chapter we will cover briefly the use of models in more technical approaches to decision analysis.

The Probability Matrix

The probability matrix is a profile of experience which may be used as a basis for deciding probability in individual cases, as in personnel selection and insurance risks. In the case of executive profiles one technique is to analyze traits or attributes of a number of successful executives and then to convert the statistics into a weighted list of factors which may be called a profile of the typical successful executive. You can do the same for unsuccessful executives, as well as for successful writers, college presidents, golf pros, Presidents of the United States and career diplomats.

Such a profile — the successful executive, for example — is a wonderful tool for comparison of traits of a candidate you have in mind. If, however, you intend holding out for the man whose individual profile matches the model which is statistically derived, well, you might just wait and wait and wait. That profile is an average which may not necessarily represent any single being, living or dead.

For a sufficiently large number of selections, with the aid of a profile, the chances are that the results will be as predicted. Some won't turn out well, most will do very well and a few exceptionally well. There will also be some you'll reject who might turn out in the exceptional class. This is one of the prices paid for use of statistical tools: they deal in probabilities and therefore they let a few slip through. The lesson is that if, in spite of probability matrices or profiles, you have a feeling that you've picked a comer, you might just as well give it a try, unless there are strong negative conditions, such as might be revealed by a profile of unsuccessful executives.

A similar approach might be used as a basis for predicting successful behavior in different kinds of situations. Thus certain credit yardsticks are used in granting mortgage loan applications.

Again, situational predictors are fine for the generality of cases but they're not infallible. Moreover, if they involve situations in which the judge is emotionally involved, he may interpret them subjectively or ignore them entirely.

Psychological tests which produce numerical scores also have useful predictive value (providing the tests are valid and reliable from a psychometric standpoint). Here, too, the tests say only that a person who scores a certain grade ranks in a certain percentile grouping which corresponds to the distribution of results among those who constituted the original test group. In the long run a good test will produce the predicted results but not necessarily as to each person. As with the profile, some duds will get by and some good ones will be excluded by a poor but inconclusive test score.

Physical and Schematic Models

At the Ford Motor Co. they built a 6-inch test car, weighing 10.2 ounces, with a motor which developed .005 horsepower. It could fit into a glove compartment. It was designed for use on a circular test track in Ford's laboratory to see how changing an engine from front to rear — and back again — would affect stability. Also to see how other changes would affect performance.

The test car was not built to look like a real car. Of course, it had four wheels, a motor, a drive mechanism and other mechanical features. As a model, though, it reproduced engineering features only. It was built to 1/19th scale, reproducing weight distribution and moments of inertia (the car's ability to resist inadvertent turning or deviation from its path). By moving counterweights Ford engineers could simulate changes in weight distribution as though it were a real car. Thus, at much less cost and much earlier in the development cycle, the engineers could predict results. Eventually a real model would be tested on a regular track.

Aircraft development makes use of scale models, even with wind-tunnel tests. This does not eliminate full-scale tests later but does save expense and time in preliminary stages of development. Space planners and production-layout planners use scale drawings of building space, together with scale templates representing equipment and furniture. These are but a few of the many ways in which the shape of the real world-to-come may be anticipated.

Schematic models include the scale drawings with templates, in a sense. They also include engineering drawings and flow diagrams of all kinds. As with physical models, they bring all identifiable elements into mutual relationship and are likely to reveal things about the real world-to-come. They are not so good as the three-dimensional models, for they may accommodate omissions, inconsistencies, improbabilities, imbalances and incorrect relationships. They usually precede building of physical models.

Verbal models are the written programs and plans, policies and procedures and idea-concept drafts which assemble into one document an attempt to structure the future. While not so precise in structuring relationships as the physical or even the schematic models, they often supplement these, where pertinent, as a form of "verbal flesh." Used alone, they oblige the thinker to force his mind toward the future, utilizing the experiences of the past, with some effort toward integration and the production, thereby, of new approaches.

Experience Modules

The great philosopher John Stewart Mill gave us some principles of reasoning which have aided greatly in the pursuit of scientific inquiry. Among them were his method of agreement, method of difference and joint method of agreement and difference. Without going more deeply into their nature, suffice it to say that Mill was a great exponent of the study of cause and effect.

His methods have currency in techniques of engineering analysis. The engineer lists all his system inputs and their known qualities and effects in conjunction with other elements. He then proceeds to vary each element (or input), holding all the others constant, while noting the effects. In this way he builds up a body of known cause-and-effect sequences which can be used not only in the current problem, but also in the prediction of results in new problems embodying any of the same elements. (In some kinds of situations a good statistician will work with many variables simultaneously, thus getting more information for a smaller investment.)

When you look for a "man of experience" you seek one who has a reservoir of experience modules which he can apply to a host of situations, substantially unanticipated, without having to work or muddle his way through each new variation.

Budgeting practice makes extensive use of experience modules or blocks as a basis for predicting future costs, in conjunction with work-load forecasting.

The technique suggested is merely the systematic use of experience-building as applied by each of us in his daily combat with all the forces around him. It is a technique used alike by the successful master salesman, the confidence man and the disciple of Casanova for whom the conquest is an end in itself.

Here is a warning: in all of these techniques predictions may be good under the same operating or environmental conditions. If the latter should change, your experience modules may no longer be valid. At the very least they may need to be re-examined — perhaps modified — and in many cases they may need to be discarded. Accordingly, you should always start by examining the underlying conditions, taking your requirements from them before drawing upon your resources of experience.

Models of Action Sequences

It is a mild spring day and you are lazing by the side of a still pool with unbroken surface. Idly you pick up a pebble and flip it upward, then watch it fall "plip .. p ... pp!" into the water. You observe the little waves spreading out in ever-widening circles, finally dissipating into nothingness. There is no doubt, from having done this before, that the water will behave thus. Now you play another game: you toss one and then another pebble into the water; then a third.

Having engineered the action, you look for it to develop in that briefly unfolding slice of future. As the first waves approach those caused by the second pebble, they are overpowered by the latter, stronger because they are closer to their own center. You await the anticipated combat and the particular effect created in the overlapping of the circles. Even then a third zone of combat is building up, and you turn to watch the triple interaction.

In the real world of business (or of diplomatic or military gaming or combat) you set up a structure of general and specific aims which lie somewhere off in the future. Then, using your resource of pebbles, you seek to create desired action effects and interactions by the way in which you dispose them.

The model of the unfolding future which you build uses the forces of the past, continuing into the present and the future. Professor Harold D. Lasswell of the Yale Law School originated the term *developmental construct* in his writings on world politics, power and society. He described methods for taking selected cross-sections of the past and evolving them into a series of successively developing cross-sections of action situations that may finally be projected into predictable cross-sections of the future.

Here is a technique I have used for the programming of a specific business goal — perhaps the installation of a major change in operating method:

1. First, spell out the finally desired goal of action. Describe your operating state at that time as definitely as you can.

2. Then make an estimate of the obstacles, resistances, difficulties and competition you may encounter. Translate these into an estimate of the resources and effort required to achieve your goal by a certain time.

3. Look backward, now, for antecedents of the proposed action program. There may have been blocks of applicable experience whose effects may carry naturally into the future or which may be drawn into the situation. (When you hire a consultant or specialist to launch a program for you, are you not buying his known past, expecting its force to aid in carrying you toward certain ends?)

4. Lay out the nature and readily identifiable milestones of progress you should encounter. These are interim completion points. They may be strung out in a single sequence of action or in several subflows to be joined in varying ways into a final product of effort.

5. Anticipate the patterns of interaction at each stage: 1, 2, 3 . . . N. Each milestone effort is the synthesis of a cross-section of unfolding action. Use these cross-sections as guides to your own action requirements.

6. Carry forward the anticipated reactions, in the real world, to each stage of your master plan as it becomes evident. Incorporate these into your successive cross-sections (or evolving action models).

7. When you move from planning into activation you must note carefully the reactions and problems encountered as each step is taken. You are now in the real world: events may take shape in ways not previously anticipated. Estimates give way to actual observation and measurement. Take full benefit by looping back to the plans of the recent past, correcting them for the future and moving forward again with perhaps greater certainty.

Charts of the Future

As suggested in the discussion of forecasting, the statistics of the past may be projected into the future with some degree of assurance that the indicated trends will be continued. The simplest form of this is called persistence prediction; it assumes that whatever has been will repeat itself. This is behind the weather predictions of the *Farmer's Almanac*. In everyday life it is surprising how many behavior patterns are predictable on the basis of mere repetition. Thus a mail-order house, such as Sears, Roebuck & Co., is able to predict the day's volume of business and receipts, by department, by weighing the incoming mail and referring to past experience for such a weight on such a day. The danger in this predictive technique is that conditions and behavior do change, sooner or later.

A variation of persistence prediction operates on the assumption that rates of change remain stable. This is even more undependable, for at some point the curve of such activity must begin tapering off, if not turning down.

Cyclic projections operate on the principle that there are certain natural rhythms or time processes, obvious examples of which are the change from day to night, the swing of the seasons and the biological aging process. The famous researches by Raymond Pearl of Johns Hopkins University, published in *The Biology of Population Growth,* revealed certain growth patterns which have an amazing degree of applicability to the widest variety of situations, including population growth of fruit flies in a bottle, growth of yeast cells, growth in body weight of organisms, growth of city and national populations, growth of a business and many others.

The typical growth pattern takes the shape of an S-curve. Rate of growth starts slowly, then accelerates, reaches a peak and finally levels off or drops. On this basis practically every *business* enterprise is foredoomed to death, in spite of its transient prosperity, unless it takes steps to break the pattern. As a matter of fact, this is precisely the fate of most enterprises, as business mortality statistics do show. Two-thirds of the leading companies of fifty years ago do not exist today. Businessmen, accordingly, are constantly seeking to introduce new items to be made and sold, in order to keep themselves up to the demands of their markets. Retailers keep in touch with the rise and decline of neighborhoods, to plan relocations at proper times. Alert and far-seeing managements bring new points of view and new vigor into their organizations through the employment of key people at senior and intermediate levels, as well as of outside consultants.

The purpose in all this is to superimpose new S-curves, minor and major, over the old ones, in order to interrupt the inevitable trend toward decline. The time to do this is not at the point of decline, but before. Hence, when things seem to be going well, the time is at hand for preventive action.

The Pearl curve of growth has been found to be just as applicable to the growth patterns of individual business enterprises as to fruit flies and yeast cells. In plotting your own growth curve it is important to chart the *rate* of growth rather than merely the *level* of growth achieved. Thus, if you do $100,000 the first year, $150,000 the second, $200,000 the third and $250,000 the fourth, the growth seems quite encouraging. But is it? The rates of growth, for each year, are 50 per cent, 33⅓ per cent and 25 per cent. Thus, while the business is actually growing, its rate of growth is declining. Eventually, rate of growth may stop and then a leveling off and decline are likely to follow. Obviously a steady rate of growth cannot be maintained, but after a peak is reached it will take some doing just to stay there.

You can easily plot the rate of growth of your own business in order to predict its future and to plan any necessary action. Have your controller or statistician plot each year's volume, profit and any other significant data on *ratio paper,* also called *semilog paper.* This special charting paper accentuates rates of change. It will show when your curve of growth begins leveling off. (A constant rate of growth shows as a straight line on semilog paper.) If you have a variety of activities in your enterprise, you should chart each as a separate subenterprise.*

* For an interesting and helpful work on growth trends, cycles and rhythms, read Edward R. Dewey and Edwin F. Dakin, *Cycles* (New York, Henry Holt & Co.).

CONCLUSION

From time immemorial, man has tried to peer through the veil of the future with the assistance of magical talismans. He has sought guidance from astrology, moon phases, tea leaves, dream books, almanacs and crystal-ball gazers. Economic man need not rely upon such occult techniques today. The methods of science are at his disposal. Somehow, though, in the best of hands, the scientific method produces disappointments. Forecasts often have a way of being wrong. Some elusive element was not considered or too much weight was given to one factor, based on insufficient or inaccurate information.

The point is that the prediction serves only to narrow the uncertainty. It obliges you to think about the various possibilities of behavior in the future and how you must be prepared to meet them. The lesson is that you must not take action based upon predictions of reactions or behavior or economic conditions without some protective measures in mind. In other words, you must limit the risks of uncertainty. Apart from any specific techniques designed to accomplish this, you will want to keep in close touch with the effects of any actions you take. Confirmations of your expectations will enable you to press your action more firmly or in greater measure. Deviations which are detected early will give you a basis of taking prompt corrective action.

Chapter XIII

THE INTERNAL INFORMATION SYSTEM

Throughout this book we've dealt with facts from almost every conceivable standpoint. The one topic we haven't covered, until now, is how to assure that helpful information is *available* when you need it. That is, you cannot accumulate and analyze the raw facts for each and every decision-making problem when it arises. You must — and you do — accumulate data of all kinds which you believe may be helpful in future situations, both expected and unexpected.

Actually most organizations are oversupplied with facts, but abundance in itself is no virtue. What counts is whether the right facts — the helpful facts — are there and whether they are accessible when needed. What counts, also, is whether people who need to know are informed of new facts when they are fresh and important. Facts in a file case are of no value if no one knows of them or if they are not brought to people's attention when they are of timely value.

The subject of this chapter, then, is acquiring and making facts available for use: that is, the internal information system. It covers the reporting, circulation, storage and retrieval of data. It also covers the economics of fact-production, for this can become very, very costly. An oversupply of facts, also, will obscure the useful.

THE PATHOLOGY OF REPORTING

On several occasions I have delved deeply into the internal reporting systems of organizations in order to bring them under control. It is a common malady in business and government: internal reports grow and grow and grow in abundance to the satisfaction of scarcely anybody other than their authors. They cost a great deal of money to produce and too often they yield little in return. From my experiences with reporting systems I drew the following observations.

Symptoms of Poor Reporting

Have you thought about your reports lately? Have you wished you could do something about them — anything to make them brief, useful and timely? Have you wished you could put your finger on the trouble spots? If so, look over this list of symptoms of poor reporting. Some or all may fit your case.

1. Too much information is accumulated and reported, so that the data becomes unwieldy and cumbersome — too much for the management to digest. The sheer mass of material makes it difficult to select out of it.

2. In spite of its profusion the data somehow fails to include the very material which the management may need for current decision-making.

3. The data is often unrelated to current management targets and areas of interest, suggesting either the inflexibility of the reporting system or a failure to understand the requirements of management.

4. Much of the data may dangle. That is, the facts are unrelated to bases of comparison or management targets. This may suggest a lack of craftsmanship or the accumulation of data on a "nice-to-know" basis rather than on a need-to-know basis.

5. Data is often poorly displayed. Crowded sheets of financial or statistical information are not easily followed by executives who are situation-oriented rather than figure-oriented.

6. The reports may be submitted without adequate analysis and interpretation. This puts a burden on the executive who may not have the assumptions that went into the amassing of the data.

7. The separate, but related, reports, originating in different parts of the enterprise, are often unintegrated. They may use different reporting periods, different definitions, different bases of comparison, different data units, etc.

8. Whether by default, deliberate design or unconscious bias, reports are often designed to advance the most favorable impression and to suppress all that may not be favorable to the originators.

The Hidden Sources of Poor Reporting

There are certain hidden forces which bring about excessive reporting. I call them hidden because the supervisors and technicians who generate the reports may not be aware of the psychological compulsions which affect their production. I compiled the following list as a self-indicating guide to corrective action.

1. The law of inertia takes a heavy toll of effort: a report in being tends to remain in being long after its usefulness has been served or even its original purpose remembered. The antidote for this is recurring review of need against criteria of usefulness.

2. Reports are created in order to have them on hand "just in case" or because someone believes they are necessary "for the record." Usually no cost analysis of the reports themselves has been made to ascertain whether it would not be cheaper to obtain the information when actually needed, if ever.

3. The spot or emergency request by management for particular information may generate a new report which is prepared regularly even though it may never again be used.

4. Overlapping reports are prepared because of inadequate coordination and control. Sometimes new reports are created without anyone bothering to throw out the old, so the two ride side by side.

5. Frequency of reporting may be excessive. It stems from a

desire to keep management currently informed, to impose a psychological control over those whose work is being reported, and to keep electronic data-processing machines busy. There are reports which need to be made frequently — sometimes on a daily basis — but there are others which should be made monthly, quarterly or even annually and some even on a spot request basis.

6. While related to frequency, close timing — the effort to have current performance data on the desk of the manager as soon as possible after the close of the reporting period — is a problem in itself. This kind of expensive reporting should be reserved only for such matters as have a time sensitivity in relation to the operations being observed and reported.

7. Reports often fail to be useful because they have been designed and prepared by technicians without the benefits of the active participation of the operating managers who are supposed to use the information. Not having the perspective of the operating manager, the reports technician tends to present as much data as possible in various combinations which may show significant relationships.

8. The availability of electronic data-processing equipment encourages the invention of more reports and more elaborate ones. It is like a bookcase: if the one you have is completely filled you tend not to buy more books because you have no place to put them. As soon as you acquire more shelf space you tend to acquire more books. The fascinations of the modern electronic computers are such that there may even be a psychological predisposition to find uses which will justify their rental.

9. Nonselective distribution of reports swamps the users. Reports may be distributed on a "should-know" basis rather than on a "need-to-know" basis. The originating office may consider that it is more economical to distribute the entire massive report than to pull out sections for selective attention. I have even heard it said that wider distribution is desired in order to reduce the per-copy cost.

THE BASIS OF INFORMATIONAL NEED

Each enterprise must determine for itself the kinds of information needed for operation and decision-making. You can get ideas from other companies, such as suggested schedules of fact and outlines of analysis, but these can remain only suggestive. Your own management needs must be inventoried as a basis for engineering your informational needs. This covers the following:

1. The key areas of performance to which the management must currently be directing itself.

2. The kinds of information needed at each level of management, corresponding to the kinds of decisions to be made by each.

3. The varying needs for information at different stages in the operating or management cycle.

4. The distinctions in need on the basis of "action" or "information."

Key Performance Factors

Within the enterprise there are certain key areas of performance which seem to be common to most enterprises. Even here, of course, it would be necessary to vary the emphases according to the nature of the enterprise. For example, a foundation that gives grants of money for specific purposes would have an entirely different orientation from that of a department store or a factory. Most government agencies, as another example, are consumption organizations. That is, they spend money against certain targets of performance and then they obtain additional funds from the legislature. While the profit motive is largely absent, the emphasis instead is on units of service rendered and quality of service rendered.

To find guidance from the experience of others it is natural that one should look within his own industry. This may be helpful provided the parallels are drawn from companies with similar operating characteristics.

This was borne out in a study of British industry which indicated that it was more useful to draw from the experience of companies with comparable operating characteristics than to seek similarity of industry and size.

Following is a list of typical areas of informational coverage for use in management review of performance and for use in decision-making:

1. Return on investment
2. Quality of product or service
3. Relative market position
4. Productivity
5. Financial conditions
6. Technological position and vitality
7. Control of costs
8. Key personnel development
9. Employee morale and attitudes

Each of these would be subject to subdivision in accordance with your own needs. Thus "relative market position" would be broken down into specific product lines. It might be useful, also, to report geographically and by type of outlet. Financial factors are many, including cash flow, accounts receivable, accounts payable, overhead, etc.

Needs of Management Levels

Different levels of management need different kinds of information. The information must be generated and displayed so as to assist executives in making the kinds of decisions appropriate to their operating levels.

Thus, for the top management, information should focus on over-all planning and review of performance. The criteria of decision used at the top levels are necessarily generalized and frequently are expressed in dollar or statistical terms, such as return on investment, profit margins, cash positions, order backlogs, inventory turnover, etc. Top management is concerned with matters that relate to its function of planning and policy formulation. Information presented should enable the management to review the effectiveness of its formulations and to plan for the future.

The middle manager needs information which will enable him to control his assigned area. He also needs at least some of the information which his superiors receive so that he will know how best to serve them. Finally, he must be familiar with the informational requirements of his own subordinates if he is to supervise them effectively. In short, each has a primary personal need as well as a secondary need aimed one level above and one below. As he orients himself upward his needs veer toward dollars, statistics and ratios. As he deals with subordinate problems he is more concerned with performance criteria, operating conditions and work targets or deadlines.

At the working level the first line of management is concerned principally with information which reflects the most tangible and observable conditions. It is concerned with data on scrap and rejects, overtime worked, units produced, labor fraction of units produced, losses due to accidents, and sickness, etc.

Cycles of Informational Need

At least two kinds of cycles or sequential stages should vary the reporting requirements. On a grand scale, as the enterprise as a whole, or one of its programs, progresses through the various stages of development, problems that were of significance at one stage seem to lose their significance as new problems press forward.

Apart from this progressive shift in attention, certain kinds of activities are conducted on a recurring time cycle. This is particularly true in consumer-goods industries which operate on a style cycle. For example, in the women's ready-to-wear industry there is a period of designing followed by the manufacturing of samples, the marketing of the new-style goods, the planning of production based upon orders taken and market conditions, actual manufacturing and distribution, further selling, market analysis and production, etc. Much the same kind of cyclic operation takes place in the automotive industry, which has a longer lead time for the design and tooling of automobiles.

Within the enterprise individual project activities have their own planning and performance cycles. The budget, with associated reports, has a cyclic nature.

Action and Information Needs

A sharp distinction must be made between facts needed as a basis for taking action and facts needed merely to keep one generally informed. This distinction in need offers tremendous opportunities for limiting distribution and saving money. We'll go into this more deeply below.

The need for action identifies the hard core of document distribution. The "action" recipient must do something directly with it either because he has a decision matter now under consideration or because the item of intelligence will, in itself, precipitate the making of a decision. The subject matter invariably corresponds with an area of responsibility which has been delegated to the action recipient.

Copies of reports and other communications are also sent to "information" recipients. These people should be knowledgeable because their responsibilities are indirectly or secondarily affected.

One way to distinguish clearly between "action" and "information" is to ask who has the lead responsibility. It must be one point at any given moment. If the action is subdivided it will have *one* over-all leader, while the others will have action responsibility only for limited aspects. In the latter case the dissemination of information may be limited similarly.

How does this save effort and money? In the first place, it takes time to read, and — however obvious it may seem — this costs money. Secondly — but more important — the organization is much better off if its people become thoroughly informed on matters of their own direct responsibility.

If document distribution is not limited at the source, it is done through natural selection and rejection by the recipients. They simply must concentrate on the more important things. But here is a paradox: if you try to take their information copies away, they usually object. This may be due to a desire to have others conscious of their existence even in this way or it may be due to an informational insecurity — a fear that they may not be in the know on things that affect their interests.

Of course there is a middle ground; people do have to know how their functions or activities fit into the total picture. They have to interrelate what they do with what their colleagues do. Their awareness is achieved, in part, through informational dissemination of one kind or another. Nevertheless the bigger problem is to prevent the excessive distribution.

IMPORTANCE OF THE REPORTS STRUCTURE

As mentioned earlier, many reporting systems suffer by not being systems at all. That is, reports may overlap, deal with the same kinds of data from different standpoints and different control periods, grow out of balance with other phases of reporting, develop substantial gaps in coverage, etc. Obviously these variations must be rationalized if the reporting outputs are to be useful to management.

Integrated Reporting

Electronic data processing has drawn attention to the need for integrated reporting. This calls for thorough systems planning throughout the total enterprise in order that data outputs can be defined as to nature and scope and fed into a total framework. In such a system the information on every operating or fiscal document has its place in the total scheme of fiscal and operational processing. Essential by-product information is derived from these documents for use by management in controlling its operations.

In the integrated reporting system all of this data is successively synthesized and blended so that each higher level of management or each specialized function will have information pertinent to its needs.

Collaterally, the integrated reporting system must be built

around the organization structure, around centers of responsibility and action. For each such center there must be key indicators of performance covering each activity and program. One technique, related to the responsibility centers, is the building of reports around profit centers as against service centers.

The Variety of Reports

Accounting reports were originally the principal instruments of information for management. They still are highly important but they do not themselves tell the whole story. They do not tell the management how it got where it is and where it should be going in the future. The tendency more lately is to tie the financial reports in with operational reports.

The quantified internal reports, therefore, include accounting data, operating statistics and budget reports. The last is one of the most important tools for the decision-maker. It points up actual performance against targeted rates and levels of performance. Deviations stand out clearly as matters for management review and possible action.

Supplementing the recurring operational reports are a host of special data reports and narrative reports. They may bring special problems to the attention of management or they may be used to expand significant points in the recurring reports.

Narrative progress reports constitute one of the neglected areas of management. They contain nonquantative information, in the main, reporting progress toward some assigned goal or progress in correcting some situation. As the information is reported upward it undergoes a protective screening. It is a form of gentle conspiracy tacitly recognized in all organizations as a game between supervisor and supervised: the play is to keep back any information which might reveal deficiencies or give the supervisor a basis for distributing one's autonomy. Accordingly, the typical narrative progress report tells of positive actions and accomplishments. Rarely does it report deficiencies in one's own operations although it may point toward those of someone else. Lack of progress, if reported at all, is usually expressed in terms of "meetings," "studies to determine the desirability," "further review and consideration," etc. It reminds one of the oral reports of committee chairmen in a fraternal organization: each stands and reports progress even though there is none — including the treasurer, who may actually be in the red.

One technique for making these reports more incisive and more definite is to require reporting against specific targets and subtargets. The reporter can then either state definitely that the subtarget has been reached or that it has not. Then the reports analyst and editor, who must consolidate this information, can take the two or three pages of evasive verbiage and translate it into "no change" if that should actually be the status of accomplishment. The knowledge that the content will be monitored actually serves as a lever for getting things done.

The enterprise exists within a larger environment to which it must be attuned. It must know the general economic trends, the trends of the industry, domestic and international political trends, technological developments, export and import trends and one's own position in the market. There are public sources for all of this information available without cost as well as from specialized services at a price. This external intelligence should be correlated with the internal reports structure. Then you can compare your own performance with over-all conditions and trends. You can also sense new opportunities.

THE DYNAMICS OF GOOD REPORTING

Two important means for rendering reports serviceable are the exception principle and timeliness. In addition to covering these, the material following includes a check list of miscellaneous suggestions for improving reports.

The Exception Principle

In the face of the tendency of reporting systems to produce more than can be read and absorbed, an effective antidote is the exception principle. It is clear that *if* there are no changes in operating conditions, you have no need for reports to that effect — at least not in detail. *Since there always are changes,* the well-designed reporting system brings these to the fore while it subordinates or excludes the "no-change" content. That, briefly, is how the exception principle works.

The exceptions may include significant variations from specific operational goals or targets, significant deficiencies or excesses of expenditure under planned budgets, important or critical variations from operating standards and policies, predetermined exceptional incidents or occurrences which should be brought to the attention of management, and strategic checkpoints in key operational areas, among others.

A related principle here is "feedback." This requires that certain informational triggers be built into the operating systems and procedures to assure that when exceptions from plan occur, information about them will go to the appropriate officials. If management decisions are then made, information as to them is then communicated back to those who must carry them out. This completes one loop or cycle of management action. Subsequent reports may bring about further changes or refinements in the same way.

Timeliness

In some cases it is important that you have operational information reported to you with the smallest possible gap between the last day of the reporting period and the day when the information is reported. For example, the United Airlines daily receives flight-load statistics at its operating base at Denver, Colorado, from all components of its entire system. Each morning the key operating executives meet for a fifteen-minute briefing session at which they review all operating irregularities — and only these — for the preceding twenty-four-hour period. They also review a forecast of operating problems for the succeeding twenty-four-hour period. This is the common focus for all elements of operation, including passenger load, equipment availability, maintenance, operating personnel, weather forecasts, etc.

This kind of sensitivity is needed in very few enterprises. Nevertheless there are always some things on which you need more current information than on others. One determinant of this is flexibility of lead time. In the case of the airline its personnel, its aircraft and other resources must be redeployed on abrupt notice depending on conditions in any part of the operating system. Hence timeliness is most important. Putting the problem another way, the determinant of close timing is the effect of delay.

Another criterion for close-time reporting is the ability to respond quickly to the situation. The point is that it costs a great deal of money, in most cases, to generate information so that the management will have it with a minimum of delay after the closing of the reporting period. Accordingly, one should have criteria to determine the worthwhileness of accelerated reporting.

Timely reporting may be accomplished more readily if methods of approximation are used. For example, many reporting purposes would be served as well or better if the management were merely provided with close estimates of the important profit factors, to be revised later from the more exact bookkeeping data. In fact, the management would not even need to know the bookkeeping revisions unless the estimates were badly in error, sufficient to throw current planning in doubt. This technique makes it economically feasible to have time-sensitive reporting where immediately precise expressions are not needed.

Another technique is to identify the key points in a procedure or in the stream of action which forecast coming events. For example, orders are the customary source of production, inventory and labor forecasts. If you could anticipate the orders accurately, you would have even more time and flexibility for planning. Therefore, consumer-goods distributors anticipate distributor orders by touching the pulse of retail sales. One medium for this is the warranty card filed by the customer. It tells what he is buying currently and thus gives an indication of the reorder pattern of retailers and distributors.

Check List for Improving Reports

1. Plan the content and output in cooperation with the people who are to use it as well as with those who are to furnish the original data. In this way, assure that it will satisfy actual user needs and that the data will be available.

2. Present the report in language and format suited to the needs and understanding of the main recipients. If necessary, prepare different versions for different types of users.

3. Show information in reports by comparison with past activity, performance standards, performance of others, targets and forecasts, etc.

4. Ascertain that the information in the report fully covers the situation.

5. Verify the authenticity of the data source; verify the accuracy of the data.

6. Reduce the bulk of reporting by dropping supporting detail except when important findings should be elaborated.

7. Reduce reporting bulk even more by covering non-sensitive topics less frequently or on a spot basis.

8. Interpret a report with the assistance of the main user and any others best informed on the contents and their significance.

BUSINESS INTELLIGENCE SYSTEMS

Now we address ourselves to a problem of information processing which is at once more vexing and more challenging than that of controlling internal reports. This is the receipt, referral, storage, digesting and retrieval of the mass of miscellaneous bits of information which are grist for the mill of certain kinds of organizations and activities. The great promise for the automatic processing of this information lies in the twin technologies of photography and electronic computers.

This is an area of concern for many business organizations engaged in research, economic analysis, publishing and world-wide marketing, among others, apart from government departments covering many fields — particularly military and foreign affairs matters. New solutions are now near.

In enlarging upon this topic I shall discuss:
1. The problems of intelligence processing
2. Trends in business intelligence systems
3. Things being done today

Problems of Intelligence Processing

In certain organizations the working material consists of a variety of informational inputs; their product is also information. In others information is collected from many sources in order to produce more tangible products or services. These organizations are beset with problems of effectively managing a massive flow of individual items of information, each of which may need to be referred for action or information, digested, stored and retrieved, as called for. This has come to be known as intelligence processing.

The information may come in from many different sources in many different forms. Individual items may call for specific action or they may be ground into the intelligence mill to be studied along with related items of information. Copies of internally generated documents are referred to members of the organization who have an information interest in them.

Speed is of the essence. When a communication center receives action documents, it must get them to the action points quickly, whether or not information in them may be of use to others. The sensitivity of the communication center to speed requirements will be conditioned, over-all, by the general operating characteristics of the enterprise. If it has a high action output, speed is of the essence. If this output is research reports, pressure on timing will be less severe.

The action recipient may need to know to whom else the document has been sent. These are people with whom he may need to coordinate, from whom he may need information or to whom copies of his action should go for their further information.

The selection of the prime recipient of the action document may influence the final outcome of action. The prime recipient should be the one responsible for the subject matter, as defined in manuals of organization and official directories. There cannot be more than one *action* recipient. Obviously the communication centers need to be kept informed currently as to the who's and the what's of communication interest. This applies to nonaction materials as well.

Identifying the action- and information-recipients is complicated when more than one subject is covered in the original document. Then there may be more than one prime recipient, but each will be prime only as to his slice of the whole, as specifically identified.

Having enough copies for distribution is another problem. Internally generated documents can be prepared directly on reproduction masters or stencils. Not so with the array of dissimilar incoming documents. Either these must be copied photographically or they must be retyped, which is much more expensive.

As an optional tie-in, follow-ups may be worked into the system, to remind action-recipients of action not taken.

I have not gone into the additional complications imposed on military and foreign affairs organizations as security precautions. These may require cryptographic procedures as well as assignment of security classifications and special handling in transit and in storage.

Business Intelligence Systems

The day is not far off when you will be able to call for any stored information from your desk and moments later read it on a built-in screen. Not many more moments later you could have paper copies, if you desire, merely by pressing a button or by asking for what you have seen.

Conceivably your own retrieval system could be linked to outside private and public depositories from which you could obtain publicly available information either on the screen or on paper. Apart from your own private accumulations of company information, you would not need to acquire materials for which you had only occasional use.

Such systems have been forecast for some time. Now they are within reach. The technologies have already been developed successfully. They call for (1) extreme reduction of the original image by photography, and (2) indexing of the image content so that through computer search or optical or electronic scanning the image can be found and "read out."

One such system is Kodak's Minicard. On a piece of film measuring 16 by 32 millimeters (or ⅝″ by 1¼″), 12 legal-size images can be recorded. This is a reduction of 60:1 or 1/3600th of the original area. Any kind of documentary information can be reproduced — written or printed pages, charts, maps, drawings and photographs.

A machine-readable abstract of the reproduced material is code-printed in a pattern of black-and-white dots. Thus the desired record can be located readily by searching for predetermined index codes. A system of multiple entries permits the localizing of searches and the completion of a detailed search of a single file section in a few minutes.

Dissemination for "current awareness" is made by matching against standing request lists. Specific requests for stored data are also serviced through the intermediate step of preparing a punched tape which is then fed to a retrieval device. Recipients are provided with duplicate film records which may also be furnished mounted in 3″ x 5″ aperture cards for personal filing. They may also be enlarged as full-sized paper prints.

Some controversy exists as to whether the greater flexibility in sorting the tiny film chips is not offset by the more elaborate machine handling as compared to a system using film reels. Theoretically, the mechanical simplification of the latter is offset by the inconvenience of not being able to collate related frames when they are separated. Actually, a slight loss of time, in this regard, is inconsequential when you consider the time required beforehand to decide what to ask the machine and the time spent afterward in processing and digesting the information.

An example of a storage and retrieval machine which uses reels of 35-millimeter film is the FMA FileSearch. Images are not as small as on Minicard chips but this offsets other technical hazards such as dust and pinholes. The FMA film reels are edge-coded for search of individual frames. Information can be viewed on a screen or printed out on other film or on paper.

The operation of a proposed business intelligence system has been described by H. P. Luhn, who is in charge of information retrieval research at the Yorktown Heights laboratories of the International Business Machines Corporation.*

His proposed system embraces the following main elements:
1. Microfilm or other photographic copies of documents
2. Auto-abstracting of documents
3. Auto-encoding of documents
4. Automatic creation and updating of *action-point* profiles

After the original document has been reproduced on micro-film or other photographic medium, its contents are transferred to a magnetic tape which is, in turn, fed into an auto-abstract-ing and encoding device. Automatically, then, key sentences are selected out to produce an auto-abstract which is printed in code on the microcopy storage medium. The next step is to reduce the information, further, through auto-encoding which provides the necessary index entries.

The action-point profiles which are fed into the system are lists of activities and informational needs of the various action points. It is then possible to refer a new item, by mechanical matching, to all action points which have listed a need for the information. The item referral at this stage consists of a brief identification. When received at a monitor station a request can be made, if desired, for the auto-abstract. This is done by dial-

* H. P. Luhn, "A Business Intelligence System," in *IBM Journal of Research and Development*, October, 1958.

ing the serial number on a telephone instrument. The abstract can then be sent by messenger or by Telefax or TV display. If the full document is now desired it can also be obtained by dialing.

The system keeps its action-profiles current by automatic adjustment, in accordance with the pattern of informational requests and acceptances. It will, upon request, provide lists of all those interested in a given subject. It will search for related documents when given a particular subject entry.

Features of such a system, using conventional IBM punched-card equipment, are already in use at the Advanced Systems Development Division. It is called the Selective Dissemination of Information System.

Recipients are selected by comparison of "key words in context," selected from the original document, with interest profiles of all potential recipients. When automatically selected recipients read the abstract on their notification cards, they indicate response by treatment of a detachable stub. Usefulness of the information is indicated by mere return of the stub; request for the document is made with a check mark on the stub; referral to another person is requested by writing his name on the stub; inapplicability is reported by failure to return the stub. As in the ultimate system described above, the computers then take over to bring the interest profiles current.

The next report is of a device that serves a more common need: the Dynasort Automatic Message Center, in operation at the editorial offices of *Time* and *Life* magazines. This equipment correlates incoming news messages with the information needs of appropriate editors in accordance with the contents of a given cabled message. It is a product of the USI Robodyne Division of U.S. Industries, Inc.

When the message is received, a duplicating master copy is made immediately. An operator, who needs no special training, determines the categories of informational content and pushes corresponding buttons. An electronic memory bank and logic control instantly produces a complete list of people who should receive the news. The operator depresses a "count" button which automatically obtains the exact number of copies needed for distribution. Finally, actual distribution is further simplified through pressing buttons which cause slots in a sorting device to light up. Each lighted slot corresponds with one of the recipients.

These technological advances are merely indicative of the progress yet to come. It is clear that science must produce means of organizing and disseminating the bodies of information being generated in increasingly greater quantities.

Meanwhile there are simple expedients which would help bring about improved dissemination in any enterprise, without use of electronic devices. When these do come, various of the suggestions which follow would be requirements.

Simple Improvements in Dissemination

Listed below are a number of things than can be done to improve dissemination of internal information without having to go to more advanced technologies. These improvements, however, are also things you must do when you go to a mechanized system. They will be discussed under the following headings:

1. Standardization of message formats
2. Clarification of need to know
3. Development and support of communication centers
4. Follow-up

Standardization. Materials received from outside sources are least subject to standardization so we will pass them by. Internally generated materials *can* and should be standardized. This includes materials received from field or branch office establishments or from other "house" correspondents.

1. Standardize stationery forms and sizes.
2. Prescribe basic identification elements to go on different types of documents and standardize their placement on the documents.
3. Limit topical content to one subject per document.
4. Restrict paragraph content to one basic thought.
5. Encourage writing in a direct and active voice.

6. Require paragraphs to be self-indexing through use of topical sentences.

7. Standardize office duplicating equipment and materials for mutual compatibility in light of ultimate needs of a business intelligence system.

Need to know. Development and use of need-to-know principles involve all participants in the action/information system. Apart from achieving improvements in the information system, clarification of need to know also serves to sharpen awareness of action responsibilities.

1. Build a need-to-know foundation through specific delineations of prime and secondary responsibilities in the organization manual.

2. Have action and research points list their primary and secondary interests and see that these are consistent with the organization manual and individual duties descriptions.

3. Distinguish between action and information designations on routing lists.

Communication centers. The old-time concept of the mail room has changed. More and more it is becoming an intelligence center.

1. Staff the communication center with some people, at least, who are able to make discriminating judgments as to significance of subject matter and responsibility for it.

2. Keep the communication center informed as to the developing areas of subject-matter interest together with identification of key responsibilities.

3. Assure that communication center is properly staffed and performs adequately, so that informational transmission is not delayed.

4. Provide organization manuals, interest profiles and other who-needs-what information.

Follow-up. With automatic assignment of incoming materials it becomes essential that there also be an automatic follow-up on *action* assignments. Accordingly, all action documents should, *at least,* have rule-of-thumb deadlines which should be subject to monitoring.

CONCLUSION

The internal information system is a part of every organization, whether it is specifically planned as such or not. It is the means of identifying problems that are emerging; it routinely provides the facts upon which most decision-making must depend; and it enables the enterprise members to participate intelligently in decision-making discussions. It does these things well if the system is properly engineered and currently maintained.

Unfortunately internal information systems, especially internal reports, tend to become ends in themselves, refusing to subordinate themselves to current and changing requirements of management. To assure that the systems are brought up to date and operate economically requires a constant vigil, a need which seems to be recognized by few managements. In the long run it is cheaper to spend the effort and money for current inventory and updating than to produce information that becomes increasingly nonuseful and degrades the quality of decision-making by its deficiencies.

Chapter XIV

SCIENCE AND ELECTRONICS IN DECISION-MAKING

The role of science in decision-making is to provide a method for the solution of problems in which there are many variable elements or in which it is important to minimize uncertainties. The tools of the scientific approach are the conceptual model, the mathematical model and, usually, the computer.

We encountered the model in Chapter XII. The models to be described below serve the same purposes. They are different, however, in that they reduce the elements of a situation to numerical values which can be manipulated mathematically. This is where the computer makes a contribution. Problems that might ordinarily take very long to solve — sometimes years — might be solved in minutes or hours on computers now in use.

The computer, in itself, has been the means for improving the factual bases of decision-making. When it has been used indiscriminately or nonselectively, however, it has hampered the decision-maker with a profusion of data.

A variety of management-science techniques have developed, largely since World War II. Collectively they are called "operations research" or, for short, "opsearch" and "OR." For the executive in many enterprises they present a challenge: he needs to understand when and how to use them. He needs means for bridging the communication gap between himself as a nonscientific generalist and the operations researchers and computer programmers.

342

Accordingly, this chapter is one of orientation. It contains "how to" guidance also: when to use management-science and electronic computers in your decision-making and how to have the most effective relationship with the people who bring these facilities to bear on your problems.

THE METHODS OF OPERATIONS RESEARCH

The beginnings of *scientific management* go back to men such as Taylor, Gilbreth, Emerson, Gantt and others of their society — men preoccupied mainly with problems of factory efficiency. These men put aside the methods of tradition, custom and "common sense" in favor of methodical observation, collection and classification of data, analysis, experiment, formulation of laws and principles and refinement of results by application, follow-up and more observation.

The beginnings of *management science* — and there is a difference — are attributed to World War II, when teams of physicists, chemists, engineers, biologists, social scientists, lawyers, mathematicians and others trained in methods of research attacked the combat and logistical problems of the military. The methods of the latter group met with singular success, at least in some areas. After the war the military continued to use the opsearchers. This support enabled them to multiply and to look for new areas of application. It was only natural that they should be attracted to the economic and managerial problems of big enterprise.

One of the advantages claimed for operations research is that it brings men of diverse scientific backgrounds together into a team effort; they are able to bring different perspectives to bear on a common problem. There is much to this but it is not the only road to Mecca. I shall explore this as well as the methodology of management science in the following sequence:

1. The heart of *management science* — the approach which distinguishes it from traditional *scientific management*.

2. The artist and his model — the characteristics of the conceptual model and how it is used by its designer.

3. Optimizing and suboptimizing — what these terms mean.

4. The varieties of opsearch — examples of different kinds of problem-solving approaches.

5. The practice of management science — who may carry it out.

The Heart of Management Science

As you trace through the methodology of operations research — or its applied cousin, management science — you may get that feeling of familiar terrain, of having been along this path before, although the signposts may be different. You may never have been exposed to operations research before and still get that feeling. I'll explain why shortly.

Typically an operations analysis may cover the following steps:

1. Definition of real problem, in context of its environment and in relation to a goal.

2. Observation and examination of the problem situation, collection of pertinent data, and classification and analysis of data — successively performed at progressive stages of problem-solving.

3. Identification of the knowns, unknowns and apparent irrelevancies, thus further clarifying informational needs.

4. Identification of key elements in the situation and in its environment.

5. Identification of interrelationships among the elements and of patterns of behavior in the situation as a whole.

6. Development of a logically ordered description of the entire situation, in verbal, diagrammatic or symbolic form.

7. Conversion of the description into a mathematical model of the situation.

8. Experimentation with possible courses of action through manipulation of the elements in the model or in its environment.

9. Identification of feasible alternatives for action and estimate of outcomes for each.

The only new steps in the foregoing — the ones which are

basic to operations research — are the formation and manipulation of the mathematical model. Mathematics is used as the tool through which all measurements are brought into common interrelationship. A familiar parallel is the accounting system: it converts values to dollars and manipulates them through formulas (or models), thus bringing out useful information for management.

The operations-research methodology thus has the following advantages:

1. Embraces and interrelates more elements in a situation than could otherwise be manipulated by the mind alone.

2. Integrates a variety of approaches and phenomena through the common medium of mathematics.

3. Provides greater precision in problem-solving by replacing subjective judgment with measurement and mathematical manipulation.

4. Saves time and effort in problem-solving through working with symbols which stand for the real situation.

5. Avoids the errors which are otherwise likely to be made when dealing with parts of problems.

6. Identifies more precisely the uncertainties, alternatives of action and loss-and-gain probabilities.

The mathematical model and its manipulation are what differentiate management science from the varied methodological techniques previously grouped loosely under the title of scientific management. This is not to suggest, however, that the mathematical approach has taken over the areas of personnel management, organization planning, command and control, market analysis and planning, procedures analysis and procedures writing, among others. Far from it: management science is scarcely more than in its infancy. There may always be great areas of management activity which will be more suited to conventional approaches. Of this I shall have more to say.

The Artist and His Model

Not all models used in operations research are purely mathematical. Much use is made of schematic models, especially in the study of complex procedural sequences. Flow diagrams and block diagrams have been used extensively by engineers as well as by traffic analysts, methods and procedures analysts and others (without realizing that they were engaging in operations analysis!).

Regardless of its format, whether schematic or mathematical, however, the design of the model depends upon the imagination of people. It is, therefore, a subjective creation. It must also follow, then, that it is fallible: the model represents the real world only as seen by its designer. As a matter of fact, the model can never simulate fully the real world. One could not, feasibly, work into the model *all* the factors in the situation and its environment. Moreover, as a tool for analysis, experimentation and prediction, it cannot be so complex and cumbersome that it gets in its own way.

Accordingly, some artistry — call it perceptiveness, experience and ingenuity — enters into the development of the model. Hence the caption of this part of the chapter, for particular emphasis.

The fact that the model may be challenged, no matter how smart its designer, does not detract from its usefulness, as already described. On the other hand, even if it can be challenged *successfully,* the existence of the model provides a basis for challenge. The model-builder renders a service, at least, in that regard.

Going further, the model-builder can provide the executive with a basis for contributing his own real-world experience and insight. Depending on its format and communicability to a non-mathematical executive, the model can be used by the latter in the following ways:

1. He can grasp the entire presentation comprehensively, quickly and precisely, because of the elimination or minimizing of verbal content.

2. He can perceive interrelationships and cause-and-effect sequences not always apparent in verbalized presentations.

3. He can select key factors and ask questions about them, while seeing them within the context of the whole.

4. He can perceive the effects on the total situation of manipulating individual elements in the situation or its environment.

Thus, even though the model may not faithfully simulate the real world to the satisfaction of the executive, its use by him enables him to clarify his own thinking — as well as that of the opsearchers.

Optimizing and Suboptimizing

A selling point of the opsearcher is that he deals with problems as a whole; he avoids solutions which may be in conflict with the interests of the larger situation. The bringing into balance of all pertinent factors or opposing forces is called optimizing. Dealing with subdivisions of the whole is called suboptimizing.

Theoretically and actually you should not deal with parts of the whole unless you have first optimized the arrangement of everything that goes up to make the whole. Practically, there are several things in the way of this:

1. You can never pin down *all* factors; at least some may not be apparent.

2. The practicalities of keeping a business going require that decisions be made of the moment; in comparatively few cases does this permit analyzing the whole in order to see the part.

3. The scientist's urge for truth may prevent him from ever bringing a problem to a head; it may be difficult to know where to stop laying out and defining the over-all situation.

The business executive deals daily with problems of suboptimization. The manufacturing superintendent wants a new machine tool, supporting his request with data on current production economies. The purchasing manager wants the parts made outside because of the high rate of obsolescence on this kind of machinery. Each sees the situation from his own standpoint. The marketing manager wants a heavier inventory to support his anticipated sales; he is supported by the production manager who wants his lines kept busy. The controller asks for a firm market forecast, supported by an actual order rate; he wants inventories of raw and finished goods kept to a minimum, to protect the cash position.

In these and countless other examples someone must decide the over-all goals, policies and programs. They permit making decisions in specific instances consistent with each other and with the whole.

Of course what is optimizing for one may be suboptimizing for another who may have a broader perspective at a higher level. It's all in the point of view.

Probably the most common instances of optimizing are resource allocations. In our personal lives we are constantly reallocating the money we have and expect to have to satisfy many competing demands. Our individual expenditure decisions are determined for us in general by levels and standards of living partly by current satisfaction demands.

Since the possibilities for expenditure generally exceed availabilities, we are forced to make value judgments which lead to allocations for savings, investment, housing, clothing, food, transportation, recreation, entertainment, personal services, etc. If you were to analyze your own expenditures you would find they represent a vast complex of goals, needs and value judgments. When you commit yourself to new expenditures without considering their impact on your financial capabilities, you may find yourself in trouble. Then you must either change your expenditure plan or you must obtain debt financing.

The resource allocation problems of a business enterprise are, naturally, much more complicated for they bring into play additional factors of depreciation, return on investment, cash requirements, debt ratios and make-or-buy determinations, among others.

Another common problem in optimizing is that of determining the distribution of the marketing dollar: how much for general advertising, how much for direct sales promotion and how much for special promotions. Also, each product line — perhaps each product — demands its share. Assuming a national or regional marketing plan, the advertising budget may take into account territorial differences in markets. Then there are sales trends and forecasts and new-product releases — all of which may require management decisions. To complicate matters, there are competitive strategies, varying profit margins on items, etc. There is also some minimum effort required for commensurate return and there is some point of no return.

Obviously there is too much here for the unaided mind to balance out. It is a task for the mathematical model, which can simultaneously interrelate all the elements. The opsearcher advises management as to the anticipated outcomes for various combinations under anticipated conditions. The latter, of course, must coincide with management's own views.

The contribution of the operations researcher is to identify and bring all of the key elements into mutual relation so that you can see the effects of changing any of them. The actual judgments must be made by the management, item by item, in ways that satisfy current goals and criteria of value.

Hence the executive plays an important role in optimizing. The researcher sets up a pattern of relationship and makes recommendations. The executive raises new questions and makes tentative decisions; the researcher points out the consequences as he sees them.

The Varieties of Opsearch

In operational activities certain typical problem situations are encountered which lend themselves to application of operations research techniques.

One such technique is the application of "waiting line" or queueing theory to such familiar matters as tollgates, supermarket checkouts, cafeteria lines, airport runways, production lines and service devices, as well as to innumerable component processes in electronic or mechanical devices. In each situation there is a gate or channel through which people or things must move. In a simple application the problem is to know how many gates need to be manned or opened for the volume expected at different times. In some complex situations one must move through a series of gates, each requiring a different time in process. The problem then is to optimize the gate capacities in order to achieve smooth flow without back-up. The classically simple example of this is the mess-kit line: the soldiers lined up behind two GI cans to wash their kits and then moved behind two sterilizing rinse cans. Since it took three times as long to wash as to rinse, the ratios were changed to three wash cans and one rinse can. This evened out the live movement.

Somehow the theory does not always work out in practice. Thus, at toll booths, the exact-change line may often be longer than the others at which change is made by attendants. The difficulty may be in the computer or in a failure to anticipate the number of people who may not have the exact change or who may miss the coin chute.

Applications of game theory are used to analyze competitive situations. Game theory is a lineal descendant of chess, having progressed through war games using physical or symbolic replicas of the real thing on down through modern computer-aided exercises. Apart from its obvious military applications, it has been found useful in such commercial applications as market planning and bidding. The opsearcher devises a business-strategy model which can be used to study the effects of different actions or approaches by one's own side as against what the competitor might do. The executive must make the final action judgment in accordance with his choice of values.

Inventory models play an important role in integrating the main industrial functions of marketing, purchasing, production and distribution. In order to buy as closely as possible, you must not exceed production requirements. Since these must be anticipated to permit advance procurement, some reliance must be placed on sales forecasts. These, however, are often inaccurate, so the forecasts must be corrected by the actual pattern of orders received. Production estimates and schedules, as well as inventory reorders, must be corrected from the same intelligence which, also, is used for fiscal documentation. Thus, without going further into the intricate interplay of elements, it can be seen that a model of this interplay would show the effects of varying the inputs.

These are brief samplings of operations research applied to

certain problem situations. Researchers are striving toward a "theory of the firm" which would more fully integrate all key ingredients of operation, including product planning, finance, investment, production scheduling, inventory policy, pricing, marketing and distribution. Central to such a theory is the supply and internal allocation of funds. How practical this will be remains to be seen, for the model must be simplified if it is not to be too cumbersome.

Others are working on theories of organization and models of man. Again, the practicability of these in specific applications may be questioned. While models of organization or of man may be of use in dealing with the mass of situations, one must inevitably return to the particular situation and its unique characteristics which must be uniquely determined.

The Practice of Management Science

In much of the literature and promotional material of operations research the use of teams of scientists with diverse backgrounds — physicists, electrical engineers, chemists, social scientists, etc. — is held out to be the essence of the scientific method applied to operations analysis. This should be challenged.

When problems are big enough or require technical specialists, teams may be needed. Sometimes the specialists can be called in as consultants. Often one man can solve the problem.

Operations researchers may claim that they provide the scientific, impersonal, detached view as against the predisposed views of functional proponents. They may claim, correctly, that they replace custom and tradition with the dispassionate methods of science. Still, it does not follow that operations research must be practiced by men trained only in the physical, biological or quantitative sciences.

Since we are concerned here with the management applications of operations research, I shall dwell on qualifications to engage in those applications. The separate skills which may be needed are:

1. Perception of the total situation at successive stages of

problem definition, analysis and identification of alternatives and outcomes.

2. Collection and analysis of facts.

3. Design and manipulation of conceptual and mathematical models.

4. Presentation of recommendations to decision-makers: the management.

The foregoing may be used as a guide by the executive to ascertain what he is getting for his money and whether the analysis project is properly staffed. Sometimes, but rarely, these abilities are found in the same practitioner. Also, not every situation requires full use of all these abilities. Finally, even if most or all of them are required in separate people, they may not need to spend full time on the project throughout its life.

While a fresh outlook, without the possible prejudice of prior experience, is always desirable, this does not mean that you must have people who have never worked out solutions to similar problems. In fact, related situational experiences should be a first-order requirement. A second should be the demonstration of open-mindedness: a desire to find the differences in the new situation which require solutions not encountered previously.

The point is made quite often among operations researchers that good communication is needed between them and management. This is essential at the inception, at intermediate conferences and when making final recommendations. It is a two-way street. The operations researchers should be anxious to obtain good executive briefings, but they should not be so antiseptic in their efforts to remain scientifically objective as to tend to disqualify executive guidance. Moreover, while they claim only to make recommendations, they should avoid becoming so enamored of their conclusions that they become persuasive to the point of losing their own objectivity.

Of the four capabilities listed above, the first and last provide the best linkages with the management point of view. In fact, if the practitioner is a man of experience and maturity he will already have a feel for the management side. Thus he must have the dual orientation of management and researcher.

For the second item — fact-finding — experience in the scientific method is desirable. This is usually acquired by people trained in methods of scholarship in the physical, biological, social and quantitative sciences. Others may also learn the techniques of fact-finding. A good part of this book is devoted to them. One does not have to be a scientist unless the subject of inquiry is in itself scientific.

Finally, there is the analytical skill — the third item listed above. The high order of intelligence and creativity needed here must be highly disciplined. Accordingly, suitable training in management science is usually desired, although scientists with the necessary aptitudes may be drawn from other specialties. Competence in mathematics is important; it is, of course, an accompaniment of scientific training. Advanced model-building and problem-solving may require advanced mathematical training.

PERSPECTIVE ON OPERATIONS RESEARCH

In the preceding pages you may have noted some discounting of the claims of operations-research practitioners. This should not be interpreted as disparaging the fundamental values of the operations-research approach. There is no doubt that this approach is here to stay and grow and make ever greater contributions.

As in any new professional approach, some practitioners may make extravagant claims — the products of enthusiasm and inexperience. In time there will be a shaking down and a maturing as operations research itself acquires the objectivity that it imputes to its work on the problems of others.

To put the subject in perspective I shall draw from the critiques of others. Again I must emphasize that these criticisms are recited only for purposes of delimiting the field of operations research rather than with the aim of eliminating it.

Accordingly, this will be followed by a recital of the circumstances under which operations research may be employed profitably.

A Critique of Operations Research

Briefly the main criticisms are these:

1. The new breed of opsearchers, searching eagerly for areas of application, overlook the simpler approaches that would do as well or better. Opsearchers are accused of a messianic complex.

2. For their own part opsearchers tend to cope with complexity by oversimplifying, with attendant dangers.

3. Mathematical techniques are largely inapplicable to situations involving people.

4. The conceptual model can be no better than the perceptions and objectivity of its designer, who cannot be completely subjective.

5. The subjectivity of opsearchers is impaired by their economic need to find applications for their techniques.

While we're at it we might as well consider two other criticisms which are not limitations upon the use of operations research. One is philosophical and the other is an admonition to opsearchers:

6. The preoccupation with minimizing risk through science, as applied to business matters, is destructive of the spirit of enterprise.

7. Opsearchers have been ineffective in selling their own wares.

The messianic complex. Because operations research is new and because it has committed the error of demeaning the accomplishments of more conventional practitioners, it is understandable that it has evoked resentment. I'm reminded of the executive who labored for almost two years to accomplish certain organizational and procedural improvements. He made a great deal of progress in a situation that had been very, very bad — but there was still a long way to go. One of his accomplishments was to bring in some new-blood executives. Coming afresh upon the scene, they saw that things were pretty bad but they did not bother to find out how much they had been improved. So they fired the man who had been responsible for their being hired!

This, in short, is behind much of the criticism of operations research. Dr. George S. Odiorne, whose distinguished versatility covers fields of personnel management, production management, statistical quality control, economics, operations research and the teaching of management science, said, "Like the Darwinists of the natural sciences or the Freudians in the psychoanalytic field, the OR men since the end of World War II have mounted an ideological and theoretical assault upon management theory which still rages. Representing a thin line of brothers who hold hands across the land, the movement has the excitement — bordering on fanaticism — which has characterized many earlier fights against obsolete ideas."*

In my own experience in management over a period of more than two decades I used techniques — which I did not regard as *avant garde* — which operations researchers have discovered anew for themselves. I never heard of "suboptimizing" but I waged a constant war against fragmentary decision-making.

To put operations research in critical perspective, Frank W. Mansfield, Director of Marketing Research for Sylvania Electric Products, Inc., said: "In a nutshell . . . the mistakes that have been made by the practitioners of orthodox OR have been as follows: To assume that it could solve all problems . . . that it is the only valid tool for use in scientific decision-making . . . that its techniques are a panacea . . . that the validity of conclusions can be greater than the validity of the premises and assumptions which made up the model . . . [and] that experimentation lends itself to all business processes."†

He goes on to acknowledge the contribution of operations research with this admonition: "If I have, therefore, any quarrel

* "Some Limitations on Operations Research," *Michigan Business Review,* January, 1959.

† " 'Orthodox' and 'Basic' OR: A Critical Distinction," *Operations Research Reconsidered,* AMA Management Report No. 10, American Management Association, 1958.

at all — and I am not sure that I do — with the concepts under which these tools have been peddled to the business world, it revolves around the intent, either implied or expressed, to prove that we have now found the magic formula. This attitude can perhaps be best described as the 'messiah complex.' "

Oversimplification. The analytical models and solutions of operations research tend to become oversimplified — and there's not too much that can be done about this. The major reason is that we must reduce problems to their key essentials, else they will become too unwieldy. In so doing we may omit, combine or oversimplify elements that did not originally seem too important. They may also be ignored, in some cases, for lack of perception. Another trap is reliance upon one's own simplified analogues to other situations or phenomena. The greater the number of situations you try to cover by one formula, the more it tends to be simplified. The necessity for communicating problems and solutions to nonmathematical executives also engenders a built-in pressure for simplified solutions.

Dehumanizing people. The greatest outcry has been against using mathematics for the prediction of behavior where people have an influence upon the outcome. Thus the more orthodox marketing man may resist at least some kinds of OR applications, such as in localized management situations, because of the human factor. The case against use of the mathematical techniques of OR in many areas of personnel management is expressed by George Odiorne:

". . . it is always possible to theoretically reduce Bill, Harry, Joe, and Mike to the number '4.' It might not always be possible to recoup them from this state. Yet, in fact, Bill and all of them possess a certain quality which nothing else in creation possesses, even if it is nothing more than the property of being Bill or Harry or Joe or Mike. Somebody. Bill is never really Number 1; he is forever 'Bill.' "

Fallacies of the individual model. Earlier I pointed out some of the limitations of the conceptual model. They need not be stressed again here other than to reaffirm that the model can be no better than the objectivity, creativity, perception and adequacy of fact-finding of the model-builder. Some of the fallibilities of the individual model are suggested in these illustrative questions: Are all significant elements included? Have extraneous ones been included? Have correct weights and relationships been established for the elements? Has the correct form of model been chosen? Have proper values been established as guides for choice of outcomes?

Technique orientation. Operations researchers need economic support, like all other people. That is, they must sell their services; they sell the techniques they have learned. Often (but not always, in fairness) this tends to conform the problem to the technique, instead of the reverse. The case against OR, on this count, was stated by Peter Drucker:

"Every other discipline of man began with a crude attempt to define what its subject was. Then people set to work fashioning concepts and tools for its study. But management science began with the applications of concepts and tools developed within a host of other disciplines for their own particular purposes. It may have started with the heady discovery that certain mathematical techniques, hitherto applied to the study of the physical universe, could also be applied to the study of business operations.

"As a result, the focus of much of the work in management science has *not* been on such questions as: What is the business enterprise? What is managing? What do the two do, and what do the two need? Rather, the focus has been on: Where can I apply my beautiful gimmick? The emphasis has been on the hammer rather than on driving in the nail, let alone on building the house...." ‡

The riskless society. Benjamin Franklin had some advice on how to be a good parlor conversationalist. It was simply to listen; then the talker, appreciative of the audience, would desire its company again. What a silent failure the party would be, however, if all followed the same advice on listening! All

‡ "Thinking Ahead," in *Harvard Business Review,* January-February, 1959.

of which is to say: what a peculiar business world it would be if all important enterpreneurs and competitors neutralized their relationships by eliminating risks! Yet the "minimization" or "elimination" of risk seems to be a central objective of operations research.

"To try to eliminate risk in business enterprise is futile," said Drucker. "Risk is inherent in the commitment of present resources to future expectations. Indeed, economic progress can be defined as the ability to take greater risks. The attempt to eliminate risks, even the attempt to minimize them, can only make them irrational and unbearable. It can only result in that greatest risk of all: rigidity.

"The main goal of a management science must be to enable business to take the right risk. Indeed, it must be to enable business to take *greater* risks — by providing knowledge and understanding of alternative risks and alternative expectations; by identifying the resources and efforts needed for desired results and by mobilizing energies for the greatest contribution; and by measuring results against expectations, thereby providing means for early correction of wrong or inadequate decisions."

The selling factor. Some years ago I appeared at a police desk to post a fine for improper parking. When asked my occupation I said "management consultant." The desk officer looked at the form which allowed less than one inch for this insert, then looked up at me quizzically and then, with the tiniest shrug, wrote "salesman."

Practitioners in the field of management science must be salesmen every inch of the way. This holds not merely for their persuasive tactics but for their own operational tactics as well. Thus, if a simple task is made overly complex, this is not good salesmanship. Nor is it good to solve some problem other than that which the executive thinks he's having solved. It is not good, either, to seem to be the Olympian spirit descending momentarily to mingle disdainfully with the less-than-erudite laity who happen to be in control.

The proper posture of the opsearcher or OR man was well

stated by Thomas M. Ware, president of the International Minerals & Chemical Corporation, speaking before the Operations Research Society of America:

". . . The good OR man is neither pure scientist nor pure executive, but something in between. He must function, if you will, as an extension of the mind and personality of the executive who pays his fees, but he must be careful to remind himself that the executive has decision-making responsibility and authority while he does not. The problems to be solved are an executive's decision problems, not the problems that happen to be capable of neat mathematical formulation, manipulation, and solution. The solutions must be put in terms relevant to the decisions to be made, and all of the important aspects of the work must be communicated at least to the executive and usually to many of his subordinates as well. The good OR man recognizes, too, that his problems are problems faced by people; that much of his information or misinformation will come from people; and that the personalities, capabilities, and ambitions of corporate personnel constitute data that cannot be ignored if successful OR work is to be carried out."§

The Proper Use of Operations Research

In offering criteria for use of operations research techniques, I do not want to commit the error of oversimplifying. A problem might seem to qualify under all of these criteria, yet the executive might properly decide that it is not a matter for operations research. Conversely, in spite of these criteria, the executive's judgment might properly be to call in the OR men. The list is intended only to provoke the separate analysis each situation requires.

These criteria are mainly applicable to use of mathematical techniques. Assuming that you have a real problem on which you require assistance, you may find it quite satisfactory to use available talents of lesser sophistication. Your staff assistant, an accountant or an orthodox methods analyst or consultant might do just as well or better — for the problem at hand.

§ "An Executive's Viewpoint," in *Operations Research,* January–February, 1959.

1. *An actual problem,* pressing for solution, rather than a technique or solution searching for a usage. Admittedly, this is conservative but is intended to offset pressures to find applications for techniques. There may be occasions for periodic study, solely for the purpose of structuring one's current posture in the changing environment.

2. *A complex problem* embracing a large number of elements or variables or one in which there is a highly sensitive interplay among the elements. Change one element and the others change (the wheels-within-wheels concept). Actions precipitate many reactions, interactions and counteractions.

3. *Few uncontrolled elements* or variables, especially in the environment of the situation or where there are too many human variables. That is, the solution must not depend on too many unpredictables.

4. *Statistical magnitude* or many things happening many times in order to wash out individual differences or have them in sufficiently measurable and controllable subgroups.

5. *Measurable elements* for which adequate data are available. The validity of using operations research is questionable when assumptions, assertions, estimates or guesses are made in the absence of data. Be careful of situations in which there are many critical intangibilities; there may always be *some.*

6. *A defined and self-contained problem.* Beware of open-ended assignments. They may be as costly as the instruction to the auto service manager to "do whatever is necessary"!

7. *A cost of service commensurate with expected returns.* Put in a slippage factor for underestimating and unforeseeables. Then set the budget as an outside limit. Even so, if the problem needs to be redefined (as often happens) you may need to find more money for it or lose the whole investment.

It would seem that operations research is practicable mainly for large organizations. This is not quite true. It is the character and dimension of the problem which governs, not the size of the enterprise as a whole.

ELECTRONIC COMPUTERS IN DECISION-MAKING

Earlier in this chapter I said that the computer is one of the tools of the scientific approach to decision-making. It is an important tool for the operations researcher because of its ability to solve complex mathematical problems. The computers used for problem-solving are not necessarily the same computers that are used for routine data-processing, although some computers serve either purpose. Both types, however, perform supporting functions in decision-making.

These functions will be discussed now under the following topics:

1. What the computers can do
2. The control of the computer
3. Computers of the future

What the Computers Can Do

The most important thing to keep in mind about the computer is that it can produce information derived in some way from other information previously given to it. It cannot imagine things on its own. It depends on inputs from its human users.

The computers covered below are digital types (as distinguished from analogue computers, whose use is not really pertinent here). Conventionally, clerks must convert original source information so that it can be fed to the machine as a series of impulses. This may be through direct keyboard, punched card, punched tape or magnetic tape. For certain purposes "reading" devices have been developed which automatically convert standardized forms of information into a form acceptable to the computer. Information fed to the computer may be for immediate processing or for future use.

The computer can combine (add-subtract), calculate (multiply-divide) and organize (rearrange). Its output may be in the same form as its input — card or tape — or it may be printed out alphabetically and numerically for direct use.

The machine receives information both for storage and for

inquiry. The storage may be of new or substitute information (calling for internal changes in storage patterns). As an inquiry, information is given to the machine for comparison with its stored information, in accordance with its programmed instructions. In making the comparison the machine thereby makes a decision mechanically or gives you the results for a clerical or executive decision in accordance with your own criteria.

The computer stores tremendous quantities of information which can be retrieved upon demand, in the form desired, without loss of memory. A high-speed computer can perform millions of calculations in an hour. It thereby collapses time and brings management closer, in current awareness, to its own operations and their significance.

Computers perform these "business" functions for the enterprise:

1. They "process" masses of clerical paper incident to invoicing, inventory adjustment, payrolling, cost accounting, etc.

2. They make simple decisions — yes-or-no choices — selecting from among preprogrammed alternatives against which inputs are compared.

3. They display operating intelligence which may be used as a basis for management control and decision-making. They do this by arithmetic conversion of the mass of individual informational inputs.

4. They solve problems by rearrangement, arithmetic conversion and comparison with preprogrammed criteria.

5. They store and retrieve business intelligence.

I have not covered the various special purpose computers, including those involved in automation processes.

As mentioned earlier, you can only get out of the machine what you put into it. The computer can't think . . . can't use intuitive judgment . . . can't make value judgments . . . and can't improve on its own instructions (unless given specific criteria for doing so).

To illustrate the many uses of an integrated data system which has been programmed properly, I shall cite from an actual system installed by the General Services Administration for the Federal Supply Service, using a medium-scale computer.

The first stage in the integrated system is the processing of customer orders. Automatically the computer:

1. Checks stock availability and orders bin replenishment when necessary.

2. Creates and releases back orders and provides for control of future orders by blocking stock at the appropriate time.

3. Produces item selection tickets for specific locations.

4. Prepares bills of lading and consignee address stencils.

5. Maintains a perpetual inventory control by location and condition.

6. Establishes operational controls and audit trials.

Thus the computer has already performed a mass of integrated clerical operations and has also made a number of minor clerical decisions. As a next step the computer will convert its day's operations into a production schedule for the next day, including:

1. Optimum work load for warehouse capability.

2. Proper distribution of orders between bin and bulk selection.

3. Division of orders in lots as a basis for controlling work flow through selection, packing and assembly and shipping.

4. Consolidation of orders by shipping route.

5. Number of packages and their weight and cube.

The next stage of the system, beyond current order-handling, is the management of inventories. This, also, is accomplished by adjustment from current inventory inputs and actions taken, as a result. The system tells when, where and how to buy. It maintains a bidder's list and selects appropriate bidders. It prints, automatically, a complete purchase order. Deliveries are expedited or delayed, based on current conditions.

Unusual demands are recognized and "kicked out" for exception review by management. The system will automatically tell when stock-turn ratio for each item is too low or too high; when an individual buyer is overloaded or delinquent in work;

when a physical inventory should be taken for certain items; and when an employee should be rewarded for performance in excess of standard.

I think this is sufficiently illustrative, although many other services and minor decisions are made through the one integrated system.

Management of the Computer

Many companies have been disappointed in the payout from their expensive computer installations. The reasons are many: original savings expectations were too optimistic . . . programming was poor . . . excessive capacity was installed . . . reports were proliferated rather than reduced . . . clerical staffs were not reduced . . . and so on.

The conclusion that many have reached is that for most companies, the processing of payrolls and other paper work on a computer is not economical. The exceptions are those whose main operation is paper, such as insurance companies, banks and book clubs, among others.

More attention is now given to use of the computer as a system tool, as in the GSA example given above. Clerical uses are now receiving secondary consideration. Instead of trying to realize direct savings from computers, the main interest seems now to have shifted to how they can help improve operations and provide data for control and decision-making.

A friend of mine, Irving Zitmore, chief of the Automatic Data Processing Branch of the General Services Administration, remarked recently on the importance of carefully planning and programming a computer installation before you actually go "on the air."

"After a business system has been on a computer for about a year and management comes to evaluate results, they are usually disappointed. . . . They find they are getting business data faster but not usually better. . . . They find that instead of one totally integrated system, as originally envisioned, they have a series of related *but unintegrated* systems. . . . The fault, usually, is that the necessary time was not allotted before installation to making a thorough systems analysis. . . . One of the biggest advantages to be gained from a computer systems program comes out of the preliminary work of re-evaluating needs for records and reports and re-engineering procedures.

"We must not be trapped into putting on our electronic computers a rehash of manual and semimechanical systems as forced by expediency and compromise. . . . The operating people must assign to study teams their very best people. As a practical matter, I realize the operating people must 'keep the store open,' but they must make the extra effort if they want the integrated data system to yield desired payoffs.

"The time to design an optimum integrated system for an electronic computer is long before it is delivered . . ."

If you're contemplating leasing or buying a computer you might consider using the services, *ad interim,* of a computer service firm. There are now quite a few of these in major cities. Some computer manufacturers, such as International Business Machines, Radio Corporation of America and National Cash Register, have their own service bureaus for customers who cannot afford or have no need for computers full time, have occasional overflow or need "in training" help pending delivery of a computer. Then there are independent services, a notable example being C-E-I-R, Inc., which provide analytical as well as programming and machine service. II

I asked Dr. Herbert W. Robinson, president of C-E-I-R, Inc., a research and computer service company, for advice on how to get the most out of a computer service which provides analytical aid. He said:

"There are three things that will assure the best relationship between the service and the customer:

"1. Have a single point of liaison for any given project, regardless of distance. Otherwise there are bound to be communication slippages.

"2. If you have a new problem, not clearly defined or worked

II For a helpful leaflet on use of outside computer services, write to the Small Business Administration, Washington 25, D.C., and ask for Leaflet No. 109, "Using Computer Services in Small Business," by I. J. Seligsohn of C-E-I-R.

out, the cheapest thing might be a study contract. It will save its cost many times over on the main task.

"3. Become familiar with the facilities of the computer service. Learn how long it takes to provide service. Then adjust your own schedules accordingly. Everyone will be happier; you'll get a better job at least cost.

"When you use a professional service, you should be utterly candid about your problems. Regard the relationship as a confidential and cooperative one."

Computers of the Future

Computers are getting bigger and more versatile. I mean bigger in capacity, for technological advances in such areas as solid-state physics and molecular electronics may actually make them smaller in real size.

More important than capacity may be the development of computers that can do their own programming. That is, proceeding from relatively simple, logical instructions, the machines will give themselves more detailed instructions. Self-programming is already a reality. It will reduce tremendously the time between problem-formulation or systems design and machine output. The executive will almost be able to say, "Tell the machine that I want to know . . ."

Even more exciting developments lie in computers, now being designed and developed, which are capable of learning from experience. They may actually be able to think! Progress along these lines has been evidenced in recent scientific congresses and demonstrations.

Thus, in 1958, an international conference on "The Mechanization of Thought Processes" was sponsored by the National Physics Laboratory in Great Britain. Fantastic? Well, we already have computers that can compose music.

In 1959 Robert Kalaba and Richard Bellman of the Rand Corporation presented a paper on "Adaptive Control Processes" at the national convention of the Institute of Radio Engineers in New York. They contemplated machines that would make decisions under conditions of uncertainty in the absence of adequate information with which to conceive and construct mathematical models. There may not even be enough information to enable one to know what the situation requires, what the cause-and-effect relationships are and what the elements of control need to be. As the machine has information fed to it, it will begin to structure the problem in its environment, derive from it a sense of purpose and use this as the basis for defining and solving the problem itself.

Actual progress in the development of a thinking machine or automaton has been achieved by Dr. Frank Rosenblatt, a psychologist employed at the Cornell Aeronautical Laboratory. His device is called the Perceptron. He has demonstrated simulated models and he has also built operating segments of the ultimately complete system. What it and other thinking machines will do, which distinguishes them from conventional computers, is to draw meaning from the environment itself.

In an ultimate sense the goals of an enterprise are really the expressions of its posture with respect to the environment. In the final analysis, unless we serve some useful purpose as agents of the environment, we cease to exist. Assuming the validity of this, it can be seen that if a machine can properly interpret the environment, it is but another step toward deriving the goals for the enterprise in relation to the environment.

The implications of such self-teaching machines are so tremendous as to require no further comment. The seriousness with which scientists regard these developments is further evident by the activity going on in at least a half-dozen American universities as well as in our own National Bureau of Standards.

Somewhere in this onrushing complex, Man must find his place.

When these things become part of our way of life our present concepts of decision-making will undoubtedly have undergone radical revision.

Synthesis

Chapter XV

ORGANIZING FOR DECISION-MAKING

A system for decision-making can flourish only within a framework of good organization. The elements most important for decision-making are:

1. A system of responsibility assignment to assure that action is taken by the proper parties with appropriate participation by others.

2. A framework of objectives, policies, plans and procedures, which provides guidance and assures consistency of action.

3. A system of intelligence which identifies problems and brings facts to bear on their solution.

4. A climate for initiative.

This can be an elaborate structure and, indeed, for very large enterprises it must be. Nevertheless the elements would be found even in the smallest organization. Some of the material which follows will be familiar, for, in part, this chapter serves also to recapitulate a number of points covered in preceding chapters.

STRUCTURE OF RESPONSIBILITY

The structure of responsibility is the total plan for division of work. It is the network of assignments of responsibility according to the nature of work performed and the extent of responsibility for it. The organizational network establishes centers of accountability as well as centers of initiative. Thereby it serves as the means through which to assure that responsible persons participate in the making of decisions affecting their spheres of responsibility.

Focus of Responsibility

There are various ways of distributing responsibility within the enterprise such as by major purpose, nature of the things sold or worked upon, serial flow of work, specialized work techniques, etc. For our purposes that is not important (so long as it suits the needs of management). It is important that responsibilities be focused sharply to avoid confusion as to who shall initiate decisions or be consulted in their making. Here are some suggestions:

1. The same area of responsibility should not be shared or divided between two or more people. The prime responsibility should be given to only one, although related responsibilities may be assigned to others.

2. Related matters should be assigned in clusters — or homogeneously — to the same person. This consolidates responsibility for decision-making, and it also makes it easier to know clearly who is responsible for what.

3. The assignments of responsibility should be set forth clearly in writing and communicated to all within the organization who need to know. The very act of committing these statements to writing and having them reviewed brings about a sharpening of the statements.

The "Bouncing Ball" of Action

Primary responsibility for a matter must be limited as to the phase of action that is involved.

The decision to market a new product may involve all elements of an organization, but responsibility will be lodged in different executives at different stages of activity. For example, until the time that a decision is made actually to undertake the marketing of a new product, responsibility for developing the facts, the proposals and the pros and cons may rest with the new-products manager. He will bring others into the act, including the marketing manager, the engineering manager, the production manager, the legal department and any others to whom a cognizant degree of responsibility is assigned.

Once a decision to go ahead is made, responsibility will then move, presumably, to the engineering department. The decisions that must be made here are more technical in nature, but before the design and styling of the product is frozen, the engineering manager will need to bring the others in for review and advice. By the time responsibility passes to the production department, the matters of technical decision-making or of production quantities will require entirely different patterns of decision participation.

Hence interrelated responsibilities must be defined precisely. Words like "cooperates" or "participates" or "is responsible for [a given area]" do not provide the clear distinctions which are needed. Transitive or active verbs must be used which precisely delineate the different action, advisory or coordinating responsibilities.

As another example of the need for precise definition, there is the infamous duties description which reads "handles correspondence." It says so very much that it says nothing, for the office boy handles correspondence as he stuffs it and seals it within envelopes to which he affixes postage, the secretary transcribes it, a drafting officer composes it, others will review it and someone stationed above them will sign it. In each case you need the precise words to describe the precise responsibility.

Levels of Responsibility

This brings us to the *scalar* principle of organization. The first-level supervisor ordinarily does not have much discretionary responsibility although this is not necessarily the case in a very small organization or in a staff unit. Above him, however, are other supervisors and executives who have cognizance over his slice of responsibility in increasingly broader degree. A parallel may be found in any large organization whether it be an industrial organization, the Army, a government department or the hierarchy of a church. You can find it in the societies of the social insects, such as bees and ants!

Accordingly, the functional statements should define the levels of responsibility for decision and action. We commonly think of this in the context of delegation.

The effort should be to delegate down the line as close as possible to the point of effect, consistent with knowledge of governing factors and with need for control by higher authority.

At the very least, responsibilities should be delegated for the routine or recurring decisions which consume substantial amounts of time but do not individually affect policy control, major financial commitments or the achievement of important goals on which higher cognizance is desired. The economics of this should be self-evident, for it enables the superior executive to devote his energies to the things that count most.

Decisions that are made close to the point of intimate knowledge of conditions can usually be made faster. They are apt to be more realistic and more responsible. The person who decides has no one to whom to "pass the buck" and therefore considers the personal consequences, if something important should go wrong. A by-product of operating under delegation is the experience acquired in making decisions.

Any rules of delegation must be tempered by actual conditions. The patterns of delegation within the enterprise will vary with the ability of superior officers to relinquish authority and the ability of subordinate officers to assume it. Usually the very large organizations cannot alter delegations, significantly, to accommodate variations in personality and capability. Rather, the incumbents tend to be selected for their abilities to perform in defined positions. They hold office to the extent that they perform as required. Smaller organizations have much more flexibility, unless the head man tries to decide all. Sometimes delegations are made on the record but there are implicit understandings that notwithstanding such delegations, the executive will consult up the line.

Specialists and Generalists

A disadvantage of specialization is the tendency for the specialist to see problems colored by the tint of the functional glasses he wears. To some extent organizations relieve this disability by rotating their executives through a succession of different positions. The problem yet remains, however, to assure the wholeness and balance of decision-making.

Staff officers and specialists can help by balancing the more expedient views of line operating officials with their own long-range and broad-policy points of view. It need not be stressed that they must be restrained from exercising line responsibility where they have none.

Another means of assuring that the enterprise operates as an integrated whole is to create centers of coordination. At their very simplest these are typified by the individual with the title "assistant to." Relieved of all operating responsibilities, his task is to make his superior officer more effective. He keeps abreast of all that is going on, identifies and monitors potential trouble spots, follows up on action, reviews staff papers for completed staff work and in other ways expands the reach of his superior. This, too, can be a position of great help to the organization as a whole, or it can be a source of great irritation if the incumbent carelessly identifies himself with the authority of the man whom he assists. He operates more safely when his authority is in behalf of his superior and is therefore more implicit than explicit. He should do nothing in his own name as regards any action in behalf of his superior.

Aside from such individual positions, organizations of sufficient size to afford them may establish staff units whose sole responsibility is to plan for the future. Then there may be activities which coordinate the development of policy and procedure and provide for the dissemination of those which are officially established. Staff units such as these take their points of view from the over-all objectives and standards of the total organization. They may review proposed policies, procedures and programs for over-all consistency and for adequacy of staff work, among other things.

The Span of Control

The concept of the span of control was popularized by Major Lyndall F. Urwick, who attributes its origin to the late General Sir Ian Hamilton. The idea, briefly, is that no supervisor should direct the work of more than five or six subordinates whose work interlocks. The burden of supervision is caused not so much by the number of people being supervised as by the added burden of managing the relationships among them. The more closely interwoven are their duties, the greater will be the number of occasions for — and the deeper will be — his involvement.

There is an optimum number of people who can be supervised: too few and the supervisor will not be adequately occupied or challenged; too many and he will be spread so thin that he will not be able to give adequate attention to his responsibilities. The importance for decision-making is to assure that no one is so overloaded that he cannot get into new problems that require reflection, analysis and judgment.

The number of subordinates to be supervised must be determined uniquely in each case. You must consider the demands upon the executive from those above him, from his colleagues on the same operating level, from outside clientele or business relationships and from subordinates. These are in addition to the nature of the work supervised: whether or not it proceeds along well-established lines or requires much original determination. And then there are other factors to be determined in each case, including the general pace of activity, the form in which the work is received, the review required before it must go out, the standards imposed by recipients, etc.

FRAME OF GUIDANCE

The framework of guidance of an organization helps assure that each new decision may be made with due regard to all other activities in being as well as those contemplated for the future. When you formulate goals, plans, policies, procedures and methods, you are making decisions in advance as to how future matters will be handled.

Goals and Plans

Both goals and plans serve as rallying points through which to coordinate common endeavor. The goals define both the long-range and short-range targets. For goals to be realistic there must be a fair estimate of the effect required to advance from the present to the desired future. Obstacles must be identified clearly, and the means and effort required to overcome them must be understood by all concerned.

Goals are made tangible by subdividing them and assigning responsibilities for the carrying out of specific tasks. The assignments must be made consistent with the framework of organizational responsibilities, as described above. When this cannot be done it may suggest the desirability of realigning the official pattern of functional responsibilities.

The tasks assigned to each of the elements of organization must be subdivided into specific action targets to be achieved over a period of time. These targets and the criteria for their achievement must be carefully defined as must be the requirements for progressive coordination and review.

Each change from the original or subsequently revised master plan becomes an occasion for decision. Many things will arise which had not been anticipated at all. The availability of the master blueprint enables you to fit the new problem into the known pattern of activity.

Guidelines

Policies, procedures and standards tell how to handle conditions that may arise in the future. Thus there may be a policy that public statements may be made only by the president and certain other officers. This advises all concerned that should any questions be raised by a member of the press, they must be referred up the line. Specific policies governing make or buy will guide the engineering and manufacturing departments as well as the purchasing department.

In many organizations policies are evolved on a precedent basis. They are the cumulative expression of the stream of experience and decisions. This is a passive approach which may not provide adequately for future conditions and situations. Specific policy formulation is the more active technique for bridging the past and the future.

Policies *in themselves* can be very broad or very narrow, but the briefer the policy statement, the broader is its *coverage*. On the other hand, each additional qualification, specification or limitation worked into a policy statement narrows its coverage and applicability. Policies may be framed to govern the conduct of the enterprise as a whole, of its major components of activity and of individual tasks.

The systems, procedures and methods of the enterprise may be likened to road maps. We have main arterial highways, secondary roads and purely local roads. The systems of an enterprise weave together the policies, procedures, methods and standards for given activity areas. These may or may not cut across departmental lines. The term "system" suggests that all interrelated activities or tasks are brought into common control; any component action may have an impact on the rest of the system.

The same may be said in lesser degree of procedures. These usually suggest the sequence of specific, repetitive acts; they spell out the documentation that is required, the information that is to be procured or furnished, the reviews which are to be obtained, etc.

The methods are the most specific prescriptions in the hierarchy of working guidances. These are usually the step-by-step instructions for the performance of specific tasks. While they, too, are objects of decision, their formulation and their revision usually engage the attention of lower levels of management.

Standards are yardsticks or measures of activity. In a sense they are interwoven throughout the entire structure of guidance but more generally they are applied as to repetitive, production situations. Thus there are work standards, quality standards, productivity standards, cost standards, time standards, etc. These, too, are usually the concern of lower and middle levels of management as well as of methods departments. They may, however, be used as measures of larger performance, examples being rate of return, operating ratios, etc.

All of the guidelines are estimates, at best, based upon past experience with an eye to the future. They are not a fixity. Changes in the environment and in the conditions and characteristics of the objects or materials worked upon, among other things, may require changes in the guidance.

This expresses the logic of it, but the tendency is to avoid suggesting basic changes, so as not to "rock the boat." In practice there tends to be a lag period during which specific exceptions are made, supported by justifications. If there is any frequency to these exceptions, this should impel a recommendation for new guidance. Major exceptions may call for fundamental re-examination of the goals, plans, and other guidelines and constraints, in appropriate degree.

COMMUNICATION SYSTEM

Information is the material of decision-making. It must be procured and sensed. It must be conveyed to those known to have need for it. An efficient mechanics for this requires established intelligence centers, channels of communication and media of communication.

In all organizations the preoccupation with getting today's work out today tends to take priority over the development of information for use in control, planning and decision-making. If the organization can afford it — and the larger organizations really have no other choice — independent centers of intelligence research should be created to study the raw intelligence and draw from it the comparisons and trends which may have implications for the enterprise. They do not take action on the basis of this intelligence but they refer it to people who should.

Staff and functional specialists may serve this purpose. They may, however, derive their own inputs from separate intelligence procurement units. The arrangement must depend upon the nature of the organization, its size and the pace of operation, among others.

The outside intelligence usually bears upon marketing, customer relations, technological developments, economic indicators, labor markets, political conditions, foreign developments, etc.

From within the organization raw data is derived as a by-product of ordinary work process, to portray operating and financial conditions.

These intelligence centers — as well as the responsible action executives themselves — should perform an additional function which is too often handled quite carelessly: the observation of the effects of an action. Individual executives should perform this function on matters within their specific areas of responsibility, but staff centers should monitor the effects of action as they have meaning for future planning or for operation of the organization as a whole.

The appraisal of enterprise capabilities is also within the scope of intelligence research. It is important to have this intelligence before decisions are made which commit resources. On the physical side there are obvious sources of information on inventories, capital goods and financial resources, to name a few. Statistical reports on human resources are usually forthcoming without much difficulty, but appraisals of individuals are more difficult of procurement; you may need to supplement supervisory estimates with research performed by the personnel department.

The appraisal of individual components of organization is also done through the channels of command, but here, too, it may be desirable to use the services of organization planning units or outside consultants, when warranted. They can make their independent appraisals and then they can leave, taking away with them such animosities as are invariably generated.

Channels of Communication

Centers of responsibility serve as centers of communication. When we talk of operating through channels we mean that

people communicate with those next above them in line of
authority or next below them and that they do not bypass such
intervening steps. Communication through channels assures
that those people who have appropriate responsibility will have
full knowledge of any communications pertaining to them.
Communication up and down the supervisory line is called
vertical communication. These channels are invariably followed on matters of policy and major commitment and often
on matters of personal judgment.

If the vertical channels were *always* followed it would be for-
biddingly difficult — and expensive — to communicate even the
most routine of operating intelligence to persons having a
counterpart interest in another part of the organization — in a
different vertical channel. Communication across channels is
called horizontal communication. Executives usually have a
fair degree of latitude in communication with others on their
same general level for purposes of keeping mutually informed
and for purposes of coordination.

These formal channels of communication, when used alone,
do not promote the fullest exchange of information because
they tend to put one "on the record." Accordingly, organizations may have, by actual design or natural development, informal media and channels of communication. These may be
the executive dining room, informal acquaintanceship groups,
social functions and even car pools and commuter trains. They
promote mutual understanding and they dissolve many of the
barriers of communication. Sometimes they have side effects,
such as the creation of cliques, but this is another subject.

Media of Communication

The enterprise must achieve common workways, thereby
knitting all together into one. This is achieved through the
dissemination of information in manuals, handbooks, standard-
practice instructions and miscellaneous information or bulletins. These must be kept current or they will fall quickly into
disrepair and disuse, losing their authenticity. They must be

written with selectively defined readership in mind, for if they try to cover too broad a clientele, of different levels of responsibility and interest, they will fall of their own weight. Thus major statements of policy should not be intertwined with detailed instructions for clerical processing of work documents.

Unless the organization operates under a high degree of discipline, these instructional devices tend to be ignored — perhaps because it is more comfortable to continue with the accustomed ways of doing things. Accordingly, there must be training sessions, seminars, executive conferences and staff meetings, follow-ups in written memoranda and actual management audits to assure that people understand and comply with official instructions.

Current operating intelligence is distributed by the producers on a selective basis through original communications or through courtesy copies of memoranda and reports. More formalized media of communication are regular and special reports, digests, house organs and special briefings. The means of communication available are many. They must be monitored in the over-all, for otherwise they may get out of hand.

CLIMATE FOR INITIATIVE

One of the greatest obstacles to deciding is fear of the consequences of a wrong decision. This can be overcome only in a climate of tolerance which recognizes the fallibility of people. The management must instill within decision-makers a feeling that their personal security and advancement do not depend upon the outcome of each decision. Executives should have the feeling that they will be judged mainly by the pattern of results rather than by how individual decisions turn out.

A climate for initiative encourages the free expression of opinions, even though they may not seem to accord with those of others in authority. The executive should feel free to argue, in good taste, until the decision has been made, when he should do all in his power to effectuate it, although it may not be what he preferred. This implies, also, that there be techniques for resolving differences of opinion without loss of face or without a feeling of defeat upon the part of any of the participants.

The people of the organization should feel that their superiors are actually trying to help them make decisions. They should feel a sense of identification with organizational goals so that thereby they will generate within themselves the enthusiasm which is a prerequisite to virile decision-making. As a corollary, they should feel that there are rewards for such initiative.

As reported in *Nation's Business,* one company which was celebrating its fiftieth anniversary looked back upon this long experience to see if it could find some pattern of elements that attended the making of decisions at critical stages. These five points were listed:

1. Enough time.

2. Enlistment of the positive talent of many people in the decision-making process.

3. An atmosphere of freedom to maintain a critical position.

4. Absence of pressure from top management for false unanimity among those participating in or contributing to the decisions.

5. Genuine participation in the decision-making process by those who would have to carry out the decision.

In short, this company successfully fostered a climate for initiative and action.

Chapter XVI

FINAL ADVICE AND COMMENT

Whatever other message I have succeeded in conveying throughout the pages of this book, I hope that one has made the deepest and most lasting impression. It is:

Nothing is as simple as it seems.

As you explore problems of enterprise you find that the smallest of problems tie in with other small problems and other big problems. To reach a policy decision on A, it may require first that you bring to a head decisions which have been pending on B and C. Almost any problem has wheels within wheels and all must be integrated within one smoothly working complex.

Enterprise decisions are made within a highly competitive environment. I refer here not merely to the ordinary business competition with which we are all familiar but to the striving within organizations for personal advantage. The positions that people take are colored by considerations of personal ambition which may or may not coincide with the best interests of the organization. What is so dangerous about this is that the people involved may not be aware, themselves, of the extent to which they color their judgments.

The Organizational Base

The organization must create for itself a posture for decision-making which enables it to respond to situations as they arise and to deal with them promptly and effectively. Some of the key points in achieving this posture are:

1. The organizational structure itself must be so designed that key responsible people know what is expected of them. Responsibilities for decision-making should be delegated as close as possible to the point of effect, but then adequate mechanisms of review and coordination are needed to assure that individual decisions are made consistent with the over-all complex.

2. A procedural base must be created which routinely takes care of small matters or those of lesser importance in order that prime attention may be given to matters of magnitude or priority.

3. An internal information system must be designed to assure that emerging problems are recognized on a timely basis, that information is made available for current decision-making and that those asked to participate in decision-making are adequately informed.

4. An action system should be installed which assures that the right participants are brought into decision-making at appropriate times, that procedures are available for coordinating the viewpoints and that decisions will be brought to a head on a timely basis. The action system must provide for effective follow-up, appraisal and modification.

5. The enterprise should make full use of experts from inside and outside the organization, as appropriate, but in the final analysis decisions must be made by qualified executives. All of the finest procedures will not replace the finest executives and supporting aides.

6. The leadership must provide an environment within which its people will want to make the best decisions for the enterprise. They must want to feel that their best interests are coincident with those of the organization. There is no better way to infuse this desirable dynamic quality into the decision-making process as a whole.

An Action Posture

The organizational base for decision-making, as just summarized, provides a vehicle for decision-makers. To carry this analogy just a bit further, the driver needs to have a way of operating his vehicle which gets him where he wants to go quickly, efficiently and safely, within all of the restraints and limitations imposed by society. In the conduct of enterprise the following key points stand out as suggestions to be summarized:

1. Move in on the problem in its early stages. Don't make the decision before you get the facts but don't wait for all the facts. You will never obtain "all" of the facts so you will always have at least some element of calculated risk.

2. Bring decisions to a head as quickly as possible. Then watch the effects so that you can appraise them and modify the original action if necessary.

3. Protect yourself on decisions of major import, especially those where substantial resources are being committed. Have alternative actions prepared in advance so that you can move quickly if original assumptions do not prove correct.

The Posture of the Individual

The actions of the enterprise are taken by people. In fact, while we may talk of something having been done by an organization, if we examine more deeply we find that inevitably the decisions were made by people. However obvious this may seem, in our ordinary parlance we continue to attribute actions to impersonal organizations. It just isn't so. The final decisions of organizations represent the consolidated contributions of people representing many different knowledges and viewpoints. The following suggestions, then, are made for improving individual decision-making from the standpoint of the organization as a whole as well as individual members:

1. Become a good team member. Learn to work as a good participant in meetings. Learn also to interact constructively with your colleagues in your day-to-day relationships.

2. Observe what goes on about you with particular attention to the forces that influence decisions. Observe both cause and effect so that if you perceive one, you may assume the other.

3. Study the behavior of those with whom you maintain a continuing relationship with particular attention to typical patterns which may be expected to govern future behavior. Learn to anticipate responses of individuals to specific kinds of proposed actions.

4. Observe all that goes on within the organization, within your sphere of cognizance, and compare, reflect and generalize on all your observations. Develop, in this way, a framework for personal analysis and evaluation. Keep it current.

5. Develop a constructive skepticism. Take nothing for granted. Look for inconsistencies, for, if present, they may identify the real points at issue and they may also provide a basis for challenging incorrect proposals.

On Using this Book

This book is intended to serve two purposes. First, it aims to provide a point of view — an enterprise philosophy and an individual philosophy which should govern decision-making. Second, it is a compendium of techniques for approaching a variety of decision-making situations. At least as to the latter, it is not the kind of book one reads and, having absorbed its message, puts aside. Neither is it the kind of book which you would open up at the conference table in order to find a solution to a knotty problem right then and there.

Many of the chapters of the book might conveniently be used as check lists for analysis of how the organization is conducting its affairs. They may also be used for individual self-inventory. It could be a long-range project just to employ the book in this manner. Another suggestion is that from time to time, when you perceive a pattern of need, you might find certain of the chapters to be helpful in providing guidelines for finding a new approach or remedying a deficiency.

Finally, there is an old saying which comes to mind: "Nothing succeeds like success." When you try to change the operating personality of an organization, no less than that of an individual, you encounter deep-seated resistances. We are creatures of habit. We do not like to have our accustomed modes of operation changed around. We would all be happy to have most things continue as they are, preferring minor discomforts to the greater inconvenience and uncertainty of change. While there are times for sweeping change, these cannot come too often or too close together. In the main we must build upon small victories. Each one will pave the way for the next. Together they will create a momentum of success which, in itself, will help put across future improvements.